The Hadj

❖ ❖ ❖ ❖ ❖

The Hadj

❖❖❖❖❖❖❖❖❖❖❖❖❖❖❖❖❖❖

An American's

Pilgrimage

to Mecca

❖❖❖❖❖❖❖❖❖❖❖❖❖❖❖❖❖❖

Michael

Wolfe

THE ATLANTIC MONTHLY PRESS
NEW YORK

Lines from "The Reader" are from Thomas Merton, *The Collected Poems of Thomas Merton.* Copyright © 1949 by "Our Lady of Gethsemani." Reprinted by permission of New Directions Publishing Corporation.

Lines from "Neither out Far Nor in Deep" and "The Secret Sits" are from *The Poetry of Robert Frost,* edited by Edward Connery Lathem. Copyright © 1969 by Henry Holt & Company, Inc. Copyright © 1964, 1970 by Lesley Frost Ballantine. Copyright © 1936, 1942 by Robert Frost. Reprinted by permission of Henry Holt & Company, Inc.

Lines from "Asides on the Oboe" are from *Collected Poems* by Wallace Stevens. Copyright © 1942 by Wallace Stevens. Reprinted by permission of Alfred A. Knopf.

Published simultaneously in Canada
Printed in the United States of America

Library of Congress Cataloging-in-Publication Data

Wolfe, Michael, 1945–
    The hadj: an American's pilgrimage to Mecca / Michael Wolfe.
    Includes bibliographical references.
    ISBN 0-87113-518-3
    1. Muslim pilgrims and pilgrimages—Saudi Arabia—Mecca.
  2. Wolfe, Michael, 1945– —Journeys—Saudi Arabia—Mecca.
  I. Title.
  BP187.3.W65 1993   297'.55—dc20   93-21782

Design by Laura Hough

The Atlantic Monthly Press
841 Broadway
New York, NY 10003

FIRST PRINTING

This book is dedicated to

Cathy Summa Ford

Khalil al-Khalil

Mohamad Mardini

Abou el-Mahassine Mostopha

ACKNOWLEDGMENTS

*M*any people and several institutions have helped me in the seven years that led up to this book. For financial support at two critical junctures I want to thank the Marin County Arts Council (Scott Brynd, r.i.p., and Yankee Johnson) and the California State Arts Council. For a different form of generosity I owe real gratitude to Prince Muhammad ben Faisal and to Sheikh Khalil al-Khalil of the Department of Islamic Affairs at the Royal Embassy of Saudi Arabia in Washington, D.C. My experience of the pilgrimage would have been very different without them.

In California, the congregation of the Islamic Center of San Jose, its imam, Dr. Khalid Saddiqi; Abed Imam, who showed me in; Imam Bilal ibn Muhammad; Yusef Salem; Munir and Karima Sperling; Javed Mohammed; and Hesham Zeitoun all welcomed me warmly and showed understanding. The American poet Abd al-Hayye Daniel Moore deserves special thanks for his early and energetic encouragement. Alan Ritch of the library at the University of California at Santa Cruz provided invaluable help in tracking down rare texts that informed my writing; Professor Edmund Burke lent some much-needed direction to my reading; Gwen Markham encouraged and supported; Professor Linda Lomperis shared her interest in Ibn Battutah and the early travelers of Islam; Professor Abd al-Haqq Alan Godlas supplied humor and insight throughout; Driss Britel of the Moroccan Tourist Bureau in Los Angeles wrote me useful letters of introduction.

Tekla and Harry Grace, Daniel and Jennifer Wolfe, Peter and Hazel Weiser, Vicki Hiatt Khan, Joseph Koppal, Dr. Ronald Garren, and Professors Murray Baumgarten and Eugenia Matute-Bianchi gave crucial support and encouragement along the way. I owe thanks to the Men's Group of Carmel. Thanks also to Richard Wilbur for his loyalty and postcards over these years. And to Brian McGarry for his reading suggestions. I am grateful to Barry Gifford for sage advice and for the epigraph that opens chapter 1, from his *Museum of Opinions*.

In the manuscript stages Abd al-Haqq Alan and Silvie Godlas; Ed, Camille, and Matthew Helminski; Ken and Melissa Florence; Tekla Grace; and Sheikh Majid al-Gheshyan all helped focus my words and correct my views with their candid comments and marginal notes. For help with the book's publication, I want to thank Tom Dyja, who kept a clear head in the early stages; Ned Leavitt, who knew what to do; and Michael Carlisle, Michelle Tessler, and Matthew Bialeri, who saw things through. Finally, thanks to Anton Mueller and to my publisher, Morgan Entrekin, who took a chance and showed both style and patience.

In Morocco, Rene Doe, Paul Bowles, Mohammed Mrabet, Abd al-Wahed, Yusef Menari, Claude Thomas, Ira and Raphael Cohen, Rodrigo Rey Rosa, Buffie Johnson, Hamza and Sa'ida Kropf each made my stay more pleasant and meaningful. In Marrakesh, I owe everything to Abou el Mahassine Mostopha, his family and friends.

In Mecca, in addition to those mentioned in the text, I want to thank the following men at the offices of the World Muslim League for their generous assistance, time, and books: Dr. Abdullah Omar Nasseef, Sayyid Ameen Attas, Adil Jamadar, Mohamad Abedan, and Mohammed Sindi. My gratitude goes to Ziad and his family, for their friendship. Thanks also for guidance through the city and the rites of hadj to Sheikhs

Nasser al Sayeed, Abd ar-Rahman, and Ibrahim Qulaibi. Thanks to David Paulson, for car information, and to Faraj Mansour al-Asmara, for the sandals. Finally, to my great, good friend Jo Menell, this work owes more than I can tell.

AUTHOR'S NOTE

*T*his book is the personal account of one traveler's pilgrimage to Mecca. I have tried to convey the current flavor of that journey and, without writing autobiography, to give some sense of what moved me to undertake it. It has not been my aim to provide a handbook on Islam or a pilgrim's guide. I have tried to address non-Muslims as well as Muslims, recording the essentials of Islam as a modern Western writer might perceive them, without proselytizing. In taking this approach, I have attempted to shed a more objective light on the least understood of the world's great religions.

Anyone writing about the hadj without access to the vast, untranslated literature in Arabic could be said to be working in the dark. As a non-Arabic reader, I have accepted this judgment. My pages owe a great deal to the handful of works that I could read in French and English translations. In addition, I have gleaned many facts about Mecca and the hadj from primary texts by Western travelers—John Lewis (Johann Ludwig) Burckhardt

(1814), Sir Richard Burton (1853), Eldon Rutter (1925), Harry St. John Philby (1931), Mohammed Asad (1954), Malcolm X (1964), and Saida Miller Khalifa (1977). For vital geographical and cultural information, I am also indebted to guides and companions who enlightened me with facts, insights, and dates. Some of these I undoubtedly have garbled.

Without exception every Muslim quoted here, when mentioning the name of the Prophet Muhammad, followed it with the traditional epithet, *sala Allah alayhi wa salaam* ("God's blessings and peace be upon him"). In a similar way, the Arabic word for God, Allah, is followed by a classic Arabic equivalent of our "Glory be upon him," *subanna wata Allah*. For the purpose of narrative flow in my native language these and similar attributives have been omitted in this edition. Muslims are free to add them as they read.

In deference to Western readers historical dates in this edition are given in the common era. As for the English spelling of Arabic words, I have applied the system of the Library of Congress in most places, reserving a more phonetic approach for people's names.

Many ways of life passed away before your time.

Then, go about the earth and behold what happened.

Qur'an 3:137

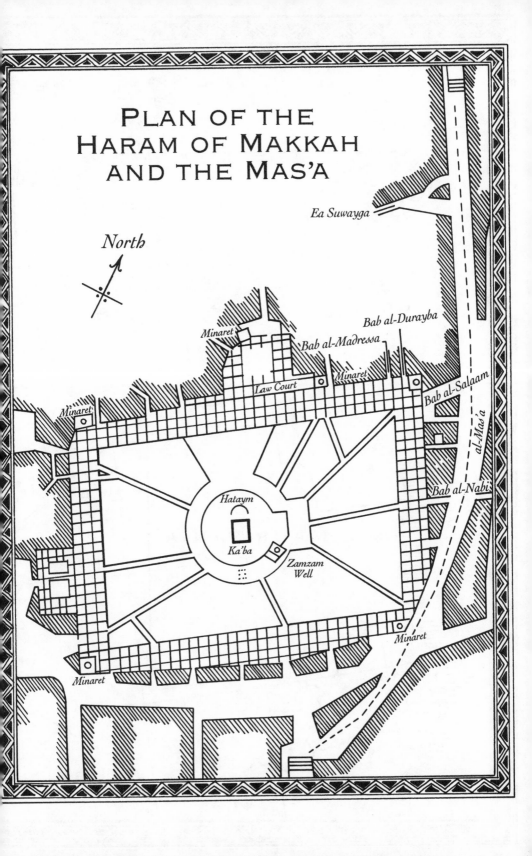

PLAN OF THE
HARAM OF MAKKAH
AND THE MAS'A

Ea Suwayga

North

Minaret

Bab al-Durayba

Bab al-Madressa

Minaret

Law Court

Bab al-Salaam

Minaret

al-Mas'a

Bab al-Nabi

Hataym

Ka'ba

Zamzam Well

Minaret

Minaret

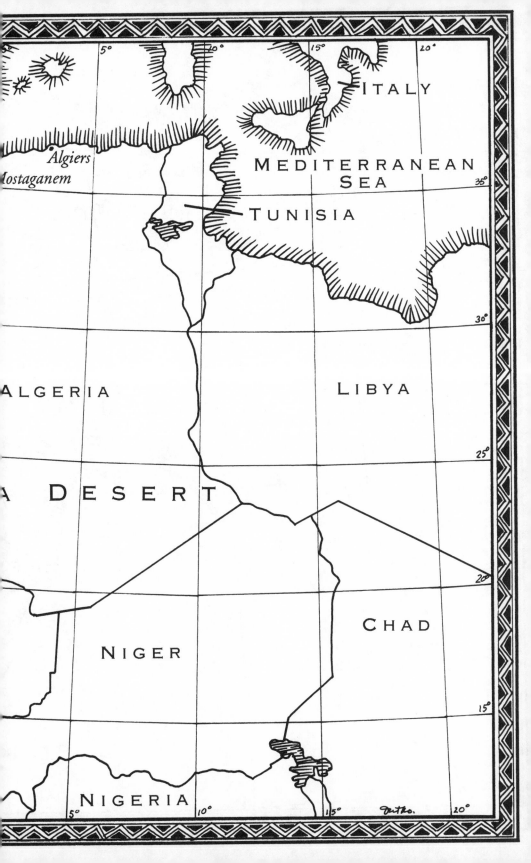

Part One

❖❖❖❖❖❖❖❖❖

CHAPTER ONE

A Taste of Fasting

A man alone is the epitome of conflict.

*E*arly one night in April in the month of Ramadan, I found myself at New York's Kennedy Airport, booked aboard a night flight bound for Brussels, on the first leg of a long trip to Tangier. I had no itinerary beyond Morocco, only an interest in learning about Islam and an appointment in July in Saudi Arabia, several thousand miles to the east.

The mental excitement at the start of a long journey, the heightened fascination with new scenes, was working overtime in me that evening. Even standing in a ticket line, I stared hard at the travelers around me, searching their faces. The most exotic of them, a group of Moroccans in traditional djellabas, were not surprising; I was heading for their homeland, after all. It was the Jewish contingent that surprised me. As we flocked to the first gate, I made a head count. Half the group were Orthodox Hasidim.

Many more men than women made up their party, and several dozen children, mostly girls. The men in their Old World black frock coats looked novel and remote against a Sabena Airlines backdrop. Hints of old-time

Lublin marked their clothes and curly earlocks. They paced the floor with hands clasped at their backs or leaned in twos and threes against partitions. A smile, a nod, did nothing to soften these faces. They glared back at me the way they glared at the airport, as if its modern lines were a reproach.

The women, on the other hand, looked like prosperous U.S. house-wives. A trio sat within earshot on a stainless steel couch, laughing, gossiping, fashionably dressed, wearing cosmetics. They neither stared nor averted their eyes like their husbands. They seemed to have slipped free of the old conventions. At one point a young mother casually opened her dress to nurse an infant. They all spoke Yiddish.

The announcement that our flight would be delayed established my first bond with these private people. Disappointment pierced their defenses, opening a patch of common ground. At last I was able to put the usual questions to an elderly couple in line with me buying a soft drink.

The man appeared to have stepped out of pre-Bismarckian Europe. His wife wore a blousy print from Bloomingdale's. Were they going to the Holy Land? I asked her. The husband answered. They were going to celebrate Passover with a branch of his mother's family back in Belgium.

I felt increasing fascination with these people. Among the older ones certainly were some whose relations had not escaped the pogroms. The man and wife fit this category. What, I wondered, had made his Belgian relatives trustful enough to settle in Western Europe? What had driven others across the sea to the Bronx and Queens? I asked these questions of myself, for private reasons.

My father's father had come to America from Byelorussia, an 1890s refugee from Skidel with sufficient cause to cross the sea (via Sweden), then cross into Ohio from New York. Like a lot of his peripatetic generation, he had not come to the States to preserve a faith. He had come to succeed, to escape a depression, in flight from economic ruin and probable conscription by the czar.

His second son, my father, a cocky product of the Roaring Twenties, turned away from Jewish orthodoxy, took a Christian wife, and settled across the state in Cincinnati. These choices had enormous consequences.

The city, for instance, brought him to the capital of Isaac Mayer Wise's radical reforms.

Wise was the first great organizer of Reform Jewish institutions in the country. He came to the city in 1854. As a novice rabbi, Wise installed family pews inside the synagogue, breaking down the division of the sexes. Later he anglicized and standardized his prayer book. He established the first rabbinical college in the States. In adapting Judaism to modern life, Wise emphasized its universal mission. He firmly opposed the establishment of a Jewish state in Palestine, viewing it as a meaningless distraction. He died in 1900.

My father arrived in Cincinnati in 1930. By the time I was born, he had joined a Reform congregation more liberal that even Wise imagined. He remained observant of the Jewish holidays but raised his family in a secular setting. Yiddish culture and kosher cooking fell by the wayside. He neither kept an Orthodox household nor regretted its absence. We celebrated Hanukkah; we had Christmas trees, to boot. Ours was a pattern, repeated many times over, that pitted modern American life against the Talmud. Arthur Hertzberg describes it well in an essay called "What Future for the Jews?": "American society no longer forces people to assimilate into a dominant culture. It is possible for people to allow their Jewishness to fade without making a decision to be anything else. The drift of life in contemporary America is toward free association."

I grew up in the gentile suburbs of a largely Germanic city where Jews and Christians mostly got along. I attended a public school during the week; I went to a Jewish "Sunday school" on Sundays. I had two sets of friends, one at each end of the city. In the leafy, postwar village where we lived, Catholic, Protestant, Episcopal, and Baptist churches were all around, while the nearest synagogue lay twenty miles away, in a district that increasingly was black. I caught on early to the richly disjunctive business of belonging to a minority in America. I learned to read passable Hebrew at the synagogue while singing in my high school Christmas choir. I was "confirmed" at fifteen (the Reformers' bar mitzvah) while dating an Episcopal minister's daughter. I thought nothing of these apparent contradictions. By the time I was twenty, however, I had grown out of both religions and left Ohio. In me, and in many others, life's drift won.

* * *

The Hasidim queued up at JFK were almost as far from my own past as from Poland's. Their regulation three-piece black wool suits, matching knee-length overcoats, starched shirts, and hard fedoras clearly marked them as a breed apart. No wonder space-age airports made them nervous. Like Shakers, they inhabited a sartorial time warp dating from their European exile. Yet dress was not what really unified them. Their clothes were a veil, a surface, a layer of armor, protecting a tradition much more ancient.

A young man seated near me, with auburn ringlets and a beatific face, began to fidget. I watched him search his suitcase, then lean back on the couch, roll up a sleeve, and tie onto his arm the identical leather phylacteries used by King David. This was the tradition that most mattered. Despite their outer garments, he and his people predated Europe. Their real roots went back three thousand years.

Like their opposite number, the twentieth-century Muslims, these were people of a sacred book. They knew their book and lived by it and so received a faith that unified them as a Chosen People. Their way was lighted by a revelation fixed in writing while the rest of the world ran out like candle wax. Later the man could not quite look at me. Careful not to bump our baggage carts, his eyes swept the tips of my shoes as we passed in a doorway.

On board I learned that his group comprised a block-booked package tour of thirty people on a two-week tour of Jerusalem. Others, like the couple I had met, would stop in Brussels. I was embarked on a different pilgrimage, one that would end four months from now, in Mecca. Setting out alone tonight, I felt a complex kinship with these strangers, a tenuous relationship—as history is tenuous, a connection less of blood than irony. I had never been much of a Jew by any standard. By theirs I did not even qualify. Yet even now, as a recent Muslim convert with proof on a piece of paper in my wallet, I understood the world the Hasidim recalled.

❖   ❖   ❖   ❖

I hadn't gone shopping for a new religion. After twenty-five years as a writer in America, I wanted something to soften my cynicism. I was searching for new terms by which to see. The way one is raised establishes certain needs in this department. From a pluralist background, I naturally placed great stress on the matters of racism and freedom. Then, in my early twenties, I had gone to live in Africa for three years. During this time, which was formative for me, I'd rubbed shoulders with blacks of many different tribes, with Arabs, Berbers, and even Europeans, who were Muslim. By and large these people did not share the Western obsession with race as a social category. In our encounters being oddly colored rarely mattered. I was welcomed first and judged on merit later. By contrast, Europeans and Americans, including many who are free of racist notions, automatically class people racially. Muslims classified people by their faith and their actions. I found this transcendent and refreshing. Malcolm X saw his nation's salvation in it. "America needs to understand Islam," he wrote, "because this is the one religion that erases from its society the race problem."

I was looking for an escape route, too, from the isolating terms of a materialistic culture. I wanted access to a spiritual dimension, but the conventional paths I had known as a boy were closed. My father had been a Jew; my mother Christian. Because of my mongrel background, I had a foot in two religious camps. Both faiths were undoubtedly profound. Yet the one that emphasizes a Chosen People I found insupportable; while the other, based in a mystery, repelled me. A century before, my maternal great-great-grandmother's name had been set in stained glass at the High Street Church of Christ in Hamilton, Ohio. By the time I was twenty, this meant nothing to me.

These were the terms my early life provided. The more I thought about it now, the more I returned to my experiences in Muslim Africa. After two return trips to Morocco, in 1981 and 1985, I came to feel that Africa, the continent, had little to do with the balanced life I found there. It was not, that is, a continent I was after, nor an institution, either. I was looking for a framework I could live with, a vocabulary of spiritual concepts applicable to the life I was living now. I did not want to "trade in" my culture. I wanted access to new meanings.

* * *

After a mid-Atlantic dinner I went to wash up in the bathroom. During my absence a quorum of Hasidim lined up to pray outside the door. By the time I'd finished, they were too immersed to notice me. Emerging from the bathroom, I could barely work the handle. Stepping into the aisle was out of the question.

I could only stand with my head thrust into the hallway, staring at the congregation's backs. Holding palm-size prayer books, they cut an impressive figure, tapping the texts on their breastbones as they davened. Little by little the movements grew erratic, like a mild, bobbing form of rock and roll. I watched from the bathroom door until they were finished, then slipped back down the aisle to my seat.

We landed together later that night in Brussels. Reboarding, I found a discarded Yiddish newspaper on a food tray. When the plane took off for Morocco, they were gone.

I don't mean to imply here that my life during this period conformed to any grand design. In the beginning, around 1981, I was driven by curiosity and an appetite for travel. My favorite place to go, when I had the money, was Morocco. When I could not travel, there were books. This fascination brought me into contact with a handful of writers driven to the exotic, authors capable of sentences like this, by Freya Stark:

> The perpetual charm of Arabia is that the traveller finds his level there simply as a human being; the people's directness, deadly to the sentimental or the pedantic, likes the less complicated virtues; and the pleasantness of being liked for oneself might, I think, be added to the five reasons for travel given me by Sayyid Abdulla, the watchmaker: "to leave one's troubles behind one; to earn a living; to acquire learning; to practice good manners; and to meet honorable men."

I could not have drawn up a list of demands, but I had a fair idea of what I was after. The religion I wanted should be to metaphysics as metaphysics is to science. It would not be confined by a narrow rationalism or traffic in mystery to please its priests. There would be no priests, no separation between nature and things sacred. There would be no war with the flesh, if I could help it. Sex would be natural, not the seat of a curse upon the species. Finally, I'd want a ritual component, a daily routine to sharpen the senses and discipline my mind. Above all, I wanted clarity and freedom. I did not want to trade away reason simply to be saddled with a dogma.

The more I learned about Islam, the more it appeared to conform to what I was after.

✧   ✧   ✧   ✧

*M*ost of the educated Westerners I knew around this time regarded any strong religious climate with suspicion. They classified religion as political manipulation, or they dismissed it as a medieval concept, projecting upon it notions from their European past.

It was not hard to find a source for their opinions. A thousand years of Western history had left us plenty of fine reasons to regret a path that led through so much ignorance and slaughter. From the Children's Crusade and the Inquisition to the transmogrified faiths of nazism and communism during our century, whole countries have been exhausted by belief. Nietzsche's fear, that the modern nation-state would become a substitute religion, had proved tragically accurate. Our century, it seemed to me, was ending in an age *beyond* belief, which believers inhabited as much as agnostics.

Regardless of church affiliation, secular humanism is the air westerners breathe, the lens we gaze through. Like any world view, this outlook is pervasive and transparent. It forms the basis of our broad identification with democracy and with the pursuit of freedom in all its countless and beguiling forms. Immersed in our shared preoccupations, one may easily forget that other ways of life exist on the same planet.

At the time of my trip, for instance, 650 million Muslims with a majority representation in forty-four countries adhered to the formal teachings of Islam. In addition, about 400 million more were living as minorities in Europe, Asia, and the Americas. Assisted by postcolonial economics, Islam has become in a matter of thirty years a major faith in Western

Europe. Of the world's great religions, Islam alone was adding to its fold.

My politicized friends were dismayed by my new interest. They all but universally confused Islam with the machinations of half a dozen Middle Eastern tyrants. The books they read, the news broadcasts they viewed depicted the faith as a set of political functions. Almost nothing was said of its spiritual practice. I liked to quote Mae West to them: "Anytime you take religion for a joke, the laugh's on you."

Historically a Muslim sees Islam as the final, matured expression of an original religion reaching back to Adam. It is as resolutely monotheistic as Judaism, whose major prophets Islam reveres as links in a progressive chain, culminating in Jesus and Muhammad. Essentially a message of renewal, Islam has done its part on the world stage to return the forgotten taste of life's lost sweetness to millions of people. Its book, the Qur'an, caused Goethe to remark, "You see, this teaching never fails; with all our systems, we cannot go, and generally speaking no man can go, further."

Traditional Islam is expressed through the practice of five pillars. Declaring one's faith, prayer, charity, and fasting are activities pursued repeatedly throughout one's life. Conditions permitting, each Muslim is additionally charged with undertaking a pilgrimage to Mecca once in a lifetime. The Arabic term for this fifth rite is *hadj*. Scholars relate the word to the concept of *kasd*, "aspiration," and to the notion of men and women as travelers on earth. In Western religions pilgrimage is a vestigial tradition, a quaint, folkloric concept commonly reduced to metaphor. Among Muslims, on the other hand, the hadj embodies a vital experience for millions of new pilgrims every year. In spite of the modern content of their lives, it remains an act of obedience, a profession of belief, and the visible expression of a spiritual community. For a majority of Muslims the hadj is an ultimate goal, the trip of a lifetime.

As a convert I felt obliged to go to Mecca. As an addict to travel I couldn't imagine a more compelling goal.

The annual, month-long fast of Ramadan precedes the hadj by about one hundred days. These two rites form a period of intensified awareness in Muslim society. I wanted to put this period to use. I had read about

Islam; I had joined a mosque near my home in California; I had started to practice. Now I hoped to deepen what I was learning by submerging myself in a region where Islam infuses every aspect of existence.

I planned to begin in Morocco, because I knew that country well and because it followed traditional Islam and was fairly stable. The last place I wanted to start was in a backwater full of uproarious sectarians. I wanted to paddle the mainstream, the broad, calm water.

❖   ❖   ❖   ❖

Before leaving home, I had spent a month condensing two years of reading into a set of photocopied binders. One file contained a grab bag of scholarly highlights: the long, pertinent chapters on historical Islam from Edward Gibbon, followed by Maxime Rodinson and Martin Lings on the Prophet Muhammad, Ernest Gellner's view of the Atlas Berbers, Vincent Crapanzano on psychotherapeutic dance, and Ibn al-'Arabi's book *The Sufi Saints.* Classical Arab authors (Ibn Battutah, the Marco Polo of Islam; Ibn Khaldun, the father of modern sociology; the syncretic philosopher al-Ghazali) were represented. So were modern authors like Jalal al-e Ahmad, an Iranian journalist, and Muhammad Iqbal, the Punjabi poet.

I planned to spend my spring in North Africa. Other binders reflected this decision. Besides Gellner and Crapanzano, I had boiled down useful essays on the region from a mass of academic social studies. These included articles and books by gifted scholars like Roger Joseph, Donna Lee Bowen, Paul Rabinow, Edmund Burke, and Elizabeth Fernea. One file held nothing but excerpts about Morocco by Western writers: Isabelle Eberhardt, Edith Wharton, Wyndham Lewis, Jorge Luis Borges, Elias Canetti, Peter Mayne, Paul Bowles, and others together with translations from the works of local authors like Larbi Layachi, Fatima Mernissi, Mohammed Mrabet, and Mohamed Choukri.

If Morocco was my starting point, the holy city of Mecca was my goal. It lies on the other side of the continent, across the Red Sea, in Saudi Arabia. This would be my first trip to Arabia. I had read most of the firsthand accounts in English, including books by John Lewis Burckhardt, Sir Richard Burton, Charles M. Doughty, T. E. Lawrence, Eldon Rutter, Muhammad

Asad, Wilfred Thesiger, Malcolm X, and Saida Miller Khalifa. I carried excerpts of their writings, too.

These files were not academic exercises. I felt determined, before going home, to formulate a clear view of Islam, and I believed the best way to do this was by reading and personal encounter. There was plenty I would need to know.

My files, in rubber cases to keep out the sand, weighed twenty pounds. I had a dozen hardbacks with me, too. Too much paper, too many books, friends told me. But libraries were scarce where I was going, and guidebooks difficult to find.

Reading matter filled my largest suitcase. Equipment of various sorts took up the rest: a 135-millimeter camera, a shortwave radio, a tiny tape recorder, a feather-weight word processor, and some information disks. Tucked in among these battery-powered items were a big Swiss-army knife, a water-purifying kit, a compass, and basic medicines.

I had packed with a view to informing myself and to recording what I found. This approach left me almost no room for clothing: a few shirts and pairs of trousers, windbreaker, footgear, sunglasses, a zippered money belt, no formal wear at all, no dinner jacket. With warm weather coming, I wouldn't need a jacket. I had been to Morocco many times. Where I was going, people would not fault my dress.

At Tangier's Boukhalef Airport, I found travelers in the crowd with twice my load.

One marcelled woman in her sixties had exercised a passion for the hat shops around Brussels and now needed two porters to deplane. Her dozen cylindrical boxes looked innocent enough. Approaching customs, I set my bags by hers on the conveyor belt.

The gear passed a couple of guards without inspection. I had begun to feel relieved when an officer at the head of the line laid a cane across the belt, dividing my luggage from the woman's. God knows why a customs line instills such instant guilt in the single traveler. The man leaned over expertly, plucking a six-pound Gibb and Kramers's *Shorter Encyclopaedia of Islam* from my T-shirts. He hefted the book. I smiled at the binding.

"Are you a journalist, monsieur?"

"No, no."

"What is your profession, monsieur?"

"Schoolteacher."

I lied to prevent him from jumping to conclusions. Anywhere in North Africa, "writer" is a doubtful job description. In Morocco, where news is censored, writers are lumped together with reporters, and foreign reporters may be confused with spies. I was neither. I worked for nobody, another touchy admission before customs. Rather than say I faced life with a pen, I decided to pass myself off as a tax-paying tourist.

"*Instructeur.*" The man wrote the word in a box on my entry card. "What is your subject?"

"Belles lettres."

"And this?" He touched the word processor.

"A sort of portable typewriter," I said.

"How does it work?"

I balanced the machine on my knee, opened the lid, and switching on the current, typed a line of numbers on the keyboard. When I turned it toward him, the ciphers glowed blue on a lighted screen. He leaned closer and closer. "Where does the paper come out?"

"It doesn't use paper."

He nodded. "And the plug?"

"It runs on batteries."

"Of course."

He left me there, stepped into a booth, and returned a minute later. "You'll have to pay a deposit on this," he whispered. "You'll get your money back when you leave Morocco."

"How much is the deposit?"

He glanced at the machine. "How much did you pay for it?"

Already I could see where this was leading. I didn't like it. I had a few thousand dollars with me, much of it from the last-minute sale of a fishing boat in San Francisco. The sum might last four months if I traveled cheaply. I did not want to park cash on a border.

"Is this deposit legally required?"

The man hesitated. The line was backing up behind us, and the other guards were staring. He said, "Not required. Just a good way to keep your equipment off our black market."

"I'm here to spend money in your country," I objected. "How can I spend it if you hold it?" I raised my voice so his friends would overhear. "Aren't there other ways to solve this?"

Raising my voice worked. The man became helpful. He waved at the machine dismissively.

"I suppose I could enter the serial numbers in your passport," he said. "That way when you leave, we could be sure you still had the item."

"Yes. Let's do that."

Momentarily he looked chagrined. Hard currency on deposit at a border can earn a guard more money overnight if he invests your cash in contraband. The man was perfectly placed for this kind of trading. Only the risk of being caught restrained him. Had he managed to take me aside, things might have gone differently. Perhaps he was lazy. I watched him pen the serial numbers into my passport.

"Don't sell the machine," he warned. "You must have it in your possession when you leave or pay the duties."

"How much are the duties?"

He named a sum five times the machine's price.

"Why would I sell it? I brought it to use it."

"Use it for what?"

"I'm keeping a diary."

"Don't sell the machine in Morocco."

"I won't."

This exchange seemed to satisfy him. He chalked pink *x*'s on my bags and passed me on.

*T*angier is the westernmost city in the Islamic world. After Damascus it is also the oldest continuously inhabited site on earth. Built on a series of rolling hills, it stands at the Pillars of Hercules, eleven miles from the coast of Spain. In ancient times these "pillars" (Gibraltar in Europe, Jebel Musa in Morocco) were popularly known as the Gates of Hell. Ulysses sailed his black ship past their peaks to interview the dead and learn his fortune. For Homer they marked the end of the known world.

A hard, warm wind was blowing as I taxied into town. Polished gray clouds covered the harbor. I went directly to the Hotel Atlas and took a third-floor room on an alley. When the bellman, an impeccable old gent named Bouselham, threw back the shutters, the Muslim call to prayer poured past the sill. I leaned out the window. A neighborhood mosque stood a few blocks up the street. Today was the first Friday of Ramadan. Waves of recognition ran through me.

I had formally embraced Islam the year before in California, after a decade or so of thinking it over. Every Friday since, it became my custom to attend noon prayers at a mosque in San Jose. This congregational *jum'a* service marks the high point of the Muslim week. Attending it meant a thirty-minute drive over a mountain, but I always made an effort not to miss it. In Tangier, I felt more vulnerable.

For one thing, Western faces were not common in the mosques here. And I hadn't been a Muslim very long. In the months leading up to Ramadan, I had tried to build knowledge and confidence by reading. Study brought me closer to Islam but not to being a Muslim in Morocco. One assignment actually put me into a panic—Mark Twain's account of a stay in Tangier, from *The Innocents Abroad*. Twain had written,

> About the first adventure we had yesterday afternoon, after landing here, came near finishing the heedless Blucher. We had just mounted some mules and asses and started out . . . when we came upon a fine Moorish mosque . . . and Blucher started to ride into the open doorway. A loud *Halt!* from an English gentleman in the party checked the adventurer; and then we were informed that so dire a profanation is it for a Christian dog to set foot upon the sacred threshold of a mosque that no amount of purification can ever make it fit for the faithful to pray in again. Had Blucher succeeded in entering the place, he would no doubt have been chased through the town and stoned.

Twain's account appeared in 1869—the first American travel book to impose a New World point of view on Europe. It is a wicked piece of

Yankee humor, fueled by bombast and exaggeration, and I knew better than to use it as a guidebook. The scene at the mosque remained accurate, however. Especially here, in the north of the country, non-Muslims are still not permitted entry.

I had time to reach the *jum'a* if I hurried. Recalling Blucher made me hesitate. I had not eaten since 3:00 A.M., and I felt shaky and unsure what to do. On the one hand, I was certainly a Muslim. On the other, I did not look at all Moroccan. My height was wrong, my hair too light, my eyes were hazel. In theory there was nothing to prevent me, only exhaustion in the face of a confusion and the probable demand to explain myself. After eight thousand miles of flying, I couldn't face it. I closed the shutters. I unpacked my bags and took a bath.

*E*very year for about a month adherents to Islam abstain from food and drink, sex and smoking during the daytime. Named for the month when it occurs, the fast of Ramadan is observed by hundreds of millions of adults around the globe. For Muslims the practice has a double purpose: to purify the body and to remind the individual that the real source of sustenance is spiritual.

The rough part of daytime fasting is not the lack of nourishment. (Every night, starting at sunset, one must eat.) It is the willed postponement of satisfaction. A fast calls normal behavior into question. The mechanics of appetite are broken up. The mouth waters, the hand reaches. A shadow falls between response and need.

I had been fasting for about a week when I reached Tangier. This was my first Ramadan as a Muslim. Like a lot of things I undertook that spring, I submitted myself to see whether I could do it. Beginning had been the worst part. To restrict one's intake after a fixed date, then maintain a month-long siege against it took the nerve of a soldier going to battle. I began to see the fast as a mental war with my throat for a crossroads. Self-respect lay on the line every time I salivated. Food was hard to forget and a pain to remember. I looked at a clock and was always amazed. When time didn't drag, it raced.

The hardships of fasting are easy to describe. The payoffs were more subtle. Days passed before I noticed. Beyond the obvious gnawing gut, I began to feel a surprising independence. The sensation was indefinable at first. Later relief came into it as I saw that survival did not depend on steady streams of food. The fast did not become easier with time. My energy flagged every afternoon. I napped late and occasionally was dizzy. Only I noticed less the difficulties. More and more my light-headedness was accompanied by a sweet taste in the mouth. For longer periods I felt pleasantly adrift. The fast was becoming a tentative adventure. I left off living for sunsets. I napped through lunch. I breakfasted at dinner.

I stayed in Tangier just long enough to lighten my bags and claim a friend's apartment. Rodrigo Rey Rosa, the Guatemalan writer, had rented part of a villa outside town. I found him packing up that afternoon, on his way to take a five-month job in Paris. He showed me a hole in the wall where a key lay hidden. This gave me a place to return and a safe spot to leave things. I had lived in Tangier myself many years before, and I had a few friends here: Mohammed Mrabet, the Moroccan author; Paul Bowles, his translator; and one or two others. But no one was expecting me for months.

❖   ❖   ❖   ❖

*D*owntown the streets were unusually quiet. At all the busiest hours of day people were in the mosques or at home resting. Even at noon the main roads through the heart of town lay deserted. Only at night, after eight or so, did people begin showing up in public. The turnout increased dramatically on Fridays after dinner, when families made their Sabbath promenade.

I joined the crowds on boulevard Pasteur. *'Isha'*, the final prayer hour, was approaching. As I went uphill, the scattered voices of many muezzins sang out the call to prayer across the city:

> *Come to prayer!*
> *Come to prosperity!*

> *God is great!*
> *There is no God but God!*

The amplified verses bounced between the hillsides as I walked. By the time they stopped, the town had grown quieter.

Near the big Kuwaiti mosque my conscience nagged. There was more the matter than missing a noon prayer. I had finally arrived in a Muslim country; I was here to enlarge on experience, after all. I knew the town well, yet I had never set foot in these fabulous interiors. Now, for a second time, I was hanging back.

On a narrow strip of lawn beside the mosque I noticed a young father and two sons, praying in their stockings on the grass. From the crowded road their isolation looked appealing. I still felt too out of step to enter the building, but a toehold on the lawn might be enough. At a break in the box hedges I stepped through.

No stone-throwing locals leapt from the bushes. I crossed the lawn to a rose garden, where the little family stood. The boys wore blue jeans. I removed my shoes and joined them, facing Mecca. The grass was damp under our feet. A month from now I would look back on this hedge of mine and laugh. Inspired by a conditioned apprehension, it had nothing to do with Morocco, I discovered. Tonight it controlled me.

I stayed on the lawn until the others left, then laced up my shoes and continued walking. It rained all evening. In the morning I bought a train ticket out of town. I would come back later. Today I needed to get away to drier country and to a more congenial setting for the fast. I had been in touch with a Moroccan friend in Marrakesh. Perhaps he could help me. Farther south it would certainly be warmer. In spite of Twain and Blucher, I wanted to feel at ease inside these mosques.

CHAPTER TWO

Are You Experienced?

*M*arrakesh stands on a broad field of terra-cotta soil at the foot of the Atlas Mountains. Its buildings are made of the orangish clay they rest on. Its color and the landscape's are the same. The night I arrived, a French poster pasted to a column outside the train station called the city Marrakech la Rouge.

From the backseat of a cab heading into town the flat-roofed dwellings on the boulevards appeared more salmon colored in the streetlights. In their coats of hand-troweled plaster the buildings looked organic, grown, not made. Roofs rose like rounded loaves coaxed up from nature, smooth and seamless. The skyline looked patted into shape.

The color of Marrakesh depends on sunlight. By night a name like the Red appears touristic. To get the meaning, you have to see the city around sundown, set against the white-capped Atlases.

These are North Africa's biggest mountains. Beginning in cedar forests forty miles from town, the green hills mount to headlands above tree line. The peaks beyond (to thirteen thousand feet) sit wrapped throughout the year in shawls of ice. Between their shoulders torturous switchbacks crisscross the higher passes, passes with names that call up dizziness, names like Tiz-n-Tichka, Tiz-n-Test, leading down by potholed, half-lane bends to the first Saharan palm groves of the south.

This geologic blend of fire and ice demands only a grain of imagination. The nearest dunes are a two-day drive from town. The roads up to the passes, at a distance, disappear like black threads in the rock. The snowfields are visible, however, from any rooftop in the city. All winter they form a whitewashed wall running up the map as far as Algiers. Their bleached faces sweep north like blown linen, forcing even locals to catch their breath. Cold causes the surrounding air to quiver. The snows add fire to the sunsets. The sunsets stain the city oxblood red.

The desert, out of sight, a two-day drive behind these peaks, is ever present. Even at street level in the springtime its breath can feel hot across your cheek. It is the largest of all deserts in a world by now half desert, and its borders are not easily defined. Even this side of the mountains you see hints of its nearness on the street, in the billowing gold turbans old men wear here and in the faces.

The population of half a million looks less Arab and more Berber in its features, with a strong admixture of Saharan blood. If parts of Tangier appeared more like Marseilles, that was because on a clear day Tangier is visible from Europe. Marrakesh owes more to the oasis. Built entirely of sunburned mud, it feels less like a city than an enclave of Saharan villages, enclosed behind eight miles of clay wall. Flanked by dunes and orange groves, it proved to be in the coming weeks a real desert crossroads and a perfect labyrinth for getting lost.

In Marrakesh, I tried to find Mostopha.

It was night and the middle of Ramadan, and the Djema el Fna, the central square and entrance to the markets, was triple packed with after-dinner strollers. My cab's headlights pushed through crowds. The square we entered was ringed by ancient ramparts, pierced by wooden gates whose double doors, into the 1960s, stood bolted after dark and watched by sentries. Today the roads leading into the square are paved, and cars (mostly vintage European models) slip through unnoticed. The cars don't get far. Inside the walls a driver must park and go on foot. The design of the ancient *medina,* or quarter, is medieval. Inside the Kasbah, 90 percent of the streets are twisted alleys barely wide enough for carts.

The cab rolled into a lot at the edge of the square. I got out and paid the driver and walked my bags a hundred yards to the CTM Hotel. Here a bed and shower cost eight dollars. Upstairs I locked the remainder of my luggage into a one-bulb room, using a key too big to fit my pocket. Then I went up to a terrace on the roof.

Mostopha's shop was not far from here, perhaps a quarter-mile walk, through one of three arches behind the *djema.* I could not remember which arch it was, however, or even see the entries at street level. The rooftop was a good place to get started. Looking down at the square, you saw what engulfed you: a shore of lights, a sea of shoulders, a heaving wash of shapes in floating clothes.

This thousand-year-old oblong acre of semipaved piazza was once the absolute center of the city. Here traders from desert tribes as far away as Mali have mixed, since the early Middle Ages, with polished Arab merchants of the north. The square was a thriving book mall, a social hive, and a military stage when Moroccan armies rode out through these gates to conquer Spain.

Guidebooks render Djema el Fna as "Square of the Dead." The square has been used in the past for executions, but the name refers more directly to a building—Djema (Square) of the Mosque That Came to Nothing. In 1194, Sultan Mansur had a mosque built on this spot, which among its other failings, lay inaccurately oriented toward Mecca. As the error of a compass point may invalidate the construction of a mosque, its walls were no sooner raised than he tore them down. The square remained the city's social nexus. The mosque was reconstructed a few blocks south.

As my eyes began to adjust to the plaza's contents, smoky grills and picnic tables emerged about its center. Cafés ringed the edges on three sides. You could separate men from their shadows at this height and sometimes pick out a face in the arc of a lantern. Down on the street vendors hawked clay bowls stacked up on blankets or touted herbal cures from wooden stalls. A heap of what looked like shoe boxes had been dumped down on the pavement to my right, at the feet of a rough-voiced barker. The light behind the man gleamed like a Rembrandt. Down the way on stools sat a row of Gambians selling cotton T-shirts off a rack. Pushcarts of fruit fenced the fourth side of the square. Under hissing lanterns Moroc-can boys in white shirts stood on boxes, hawking tall glasses of orange juice. Their carts formed a citrus curb to the traffic lanes.

The core of the *djema* was taken up by entertainers: drummers, pipers, conjurers, a fire-eater, a sword-swallower or two, mimes, shell readers, storytellers—the usual constituents of a medieval circus. Each act had its circle of onlookers who paid small coins to watch the show. The *djema* has always been home to these performers, who work the passing crowds for bits of change.

From the hotel roof I could just make out Bab el Ftah in the back-ground. As this gate looked familiar, I went downstairs and crossed the street. I waded toward it, armed with Mostopha's calling card, but before I reached the other side, my recollections of the route grew smoky. The shops lining rue Semarine were mostly closed now. None of their look-alike, roll-down doors was numbered. The lane beyond debouched into a maze of cobbled alleys. The light was bad. The souks were shut. The card proved worthless. I poked around for thirty minutes and got nowhere.

*M*ostopha's bazaar lay near the hotel, but I hadn't been there for a decade. I remembered the man in fragmentary highlights. His face with a point of beard at the chin, for example, was reduced in my mind by now to a cluster of triangles. I still could name his two favorite guitarists: Django Reinhardt and Jimi Hendrix. I knew he was capable and ran an honest shop. He had invited me into his life for a couple of weeks some years before in the offhand way that makes a guest feel welcome. When I recalled the night-long Genowa dances he'd slipped me in to see in the Arab quarter, I still felt grateful. But I could not recall the location of his shop.

Braced by predawn Turkish coffees, I tried again, milling around Bab al Ftah for twenty minutes before I engaged a three-dollar guide named Omar. Omar wore a butterball-yellow tunic. He was short, stout, with a built-in smile and regarded the world through Coke-bottle lenses—never a good sign in a dragoman. We spoke French when it came to the money. As I explained my situation, he grinned and touched the badge on his lapel.

"Official."

"Expensive?"

"Not so expensive."

By now a circle of street kids stood around us. They swam up out of the morning light at the first sign of confusion; each one was ready to show me the way for less than Omar was asking.

"Suppose I take one of these others?"

Omar shrugged. "If you do, you'll just get him arrested. No harm to you, of course, but no great bargain, either. *Et regardez, on est même perdu!* You'll have paid good money for nothing. You will still be lost. Let me see the address."

He took the card and raised it to the light, as if looking through it. The boys retreated to the shade.

Omar led me back to the square and put me into the rear seat of a taxi. We made a circle around the sprawl of the *djema,* then entered the souks by a street running through a gate carved into the ramparts.

Every third store we passed was named Ben Yusef.

"The road ends at Ben Yusef's mosque," Omar explained.

The pavement cut through a square of chicken vendors. Beyond lay a block of jewelry shops. Each had a small grille window with many gold chains and pendants pinned on felt. Gold, dispensed by the gram, was the only fixed-price item in the markets. Omar said, "My wife thinks of nothing else."

The passage narrowed down and the taxi lurched. We had three inches of room on either side, then two, and then the right rear fender scraped on stone. A startled woman in a green burnoose jumped off a motorbike. She flattened her back to the wall to let us pass.

The driver refused to continue.

Omar cracked open the passenger's door and gingerly worked his girth into the street. I followed him down an alley into a spice market.

Lined on three sides by apothecary stalls, the Souk al-Attarine was a riot of heaped-up colored powders, fennel stalks, lizard teeth, bat wings, and glass jars. Lady Macbeth would have felt at home here. It was difficult to walk. The stones were checked with vendors seated on blankets with their wares. Faces swam out of frame in the constant jostle. Here and there a buyer squatted like a boulder in a river. As I tiptoed on, Omar glided ahead down the jagged rows, holding up two fingers.

I caught up to him under a stone arch hung with carpets. A stream of Moroccan shoppers clogged the passage, pouring under the arch like beans through a funnel. Omar leaned on a wall, looking out of breath. I joined him in the entry of a shop festooned with foxtails. As he moved to make room for me, his magnified eyeballs darted. A quick discussion confirmed that he was lost.

He still clutched Mostopha's card. I took it from him and showed the address to the foxtail vendor. This man had an intelligent face and spoke, it turned out, four languages. But he could not read. I complimented the quality of his furs. He asked Mostopha's family name, and I gave it. His face ignited.

"The cowboy?" he cried.

"No, I don't think so. He's from Casablanca."

"Mostopha! The cowboy! I know him from *futbol.*" The man's English was breaking apart in the excitement.

Omar tossed me a withering glance and turned into the traffic. He seemed miffed that I would betray him. The fact that he had no idea where we were going did not matter. Tourists had rules, too. One did not hire a guide, then ask second opinions. Not that I put much stock in the foxtail vendor. The idea that his Mostopha might lead to mine through a full-tilt melee seemed preposterous.

"I know him! You'll see!" the man cried as I left his bazaar. "I'll bet you two coffees!"

The souks in this part of town were arranged by guild. First we passed into a colonnade of woodworkers, where cedar smoke and wood dust rode on sun shafts and finished tables stood stacked at every door. Down the lane the bang of mallets gave way to tailors' treadles. Inside each stall a single gowned man sat under a light bulb, bent on feeding cloth through his machine. From there we passed into a field of leather shoes and cobblers' blocks.

Omar paused in a kaftan glen to get his bearings. I watched him peer to the right, down a block-long alley lined on either side with small bazaars. I dismissed it as insignificant—just one more feeder lane off the main concourse. I was tugging at Omar's sleeve to move him along when I saw Mostopha.

The mustache was gone, but the point on his chin remained, and he still wore blue jeans. We embraced and shook hands and moved to the back of the shop. Omar followed. Mostopha produced three wicker stools to sit on.

"You hired a guide?"

"I forgot the way."

"What route did you take?"

I told him.

Mostopha, I now remembered, abhorred incompetence. He had in-stant reactions whenever it cropped up. Today, in a half-joking voice that softened the blow, he was taking Omar to task before we were seated. The cab had been a mistake and a waste of money. The Ben Yusef route was ridiculous—we could get here on foot from the *djema* in ten minutes.

"You picked the worst guide in Marrakesh," he said. "I know this man. He always gets lost. Don't you, Omar?"

When Omar nodded, Mostopha laughed and thumped him on the knee. "Have you paid him?"

"No."

"Give him ten dirhams."

"Twenty," said Omar, reviving.

Mostopha shrugged. He opened a drawer and slipped a bill from a box into Omar's breast pocket, patting the cash as if pinning a note to a half-wit.

He turned in the doorway. "I'm going to show him the quick way here for next time. I'll be back in a minute."

He nudged the guide from the stoop into the street.

❖   ❖   ❖   ❖

*M*ostopha's bazaar was a typical Marrakeshi storefront.

A metal roll-up entry door gave onto a single room with twenty-foot ceilings. The stall was surprisingly deep but extremely narrow. One could easily touch the side walls with two hands, yet the depth allowed for quite a lot of display space.

Every inch of open wall was lined with running shelves full of brass teapots, ceramic bowls in Andalusian patterns, fake pirate pistols, inlaid ivory boxes, kohl dispensers, belts, and serving trays. To this Mostopha added Berber jewelry, of which the more expensive-looking items hung in a big glass case on the back wall. On a desk beneath the case sat a cut glass lamp, a dozen music cassettes, and a ghetto blaster.

There were hundreds of shops like this one all over the city, holes cut into the walls for making money, jammed with the usual local tourist fare. It sat at the top of a gently descending alley. Across the way a tailor's cubby butted against a stall selling leather jackets. Next door lay a carpet store. Down the way were a dozen more bazaars dealing in brass trays, ceramics, tea sets, or clay pots. One small shop the size of a closet, across from a café, specialized in nothing but mock curved daggers.

The air felt fresh and cool on Mostopha's side street. The cobbles had been swept and watered down.

Inside, on the little desk, I spotted a dog-eared letter jutting from an airmail envelope. Beside it sat a Hendrix cowboy hat. I recognized the letter, of course. It contained a recent snapshot of myself and a short note posted in March from California, telling Mostopha that I would try to find him. I picked up the hat. It was covered in tin lapel pins with rock and roll slogans: DIG IT! SUMMER OF LOVE.

All at once a tall, thin man with a famished face from several weeks of fasting swept into the shop and kissed my cheeks. I didn't know him.

"*Salaam aleikoum!*" ("Peace be upon you!")

"*Aleikoum salaam.*" ("And on you, peace.")

"Abd al-Majeed! You look like your picture!"

Abd al-Majeed was the name I had signed to my note. It means Servant of the Glorious, with about the same force that Michael means "Who Is like God?" I had picked up the name at the mosque in San Jose, to simplify things for people there, who had trouble recalling "Christian" names.

The man was bird boned, with the posture of a crane. He pointed across the road at a stall full of leather goods. He worked there, he said, selling bags and jackets. His name was Sharif. He spoke arabicized English in a nasal, insinuating whisper that reminded me at first of Peter Lorre: How-uh l-o-o-n-g are ewe going to bay here? This and a habit of watching the ground while he spoke added a hint of conspiracy to his questions.

"How long will you be here?"

"Through Ramadan, at least."

"A good decision. The Prophet did not require travelers to fast. You need a stable home, you need a kitchen. Was it hard for you in America?"

"Hard?"

"To fast."

"Well, there aren't many Muslims."

"How many?"

"Four or five million."

"That's a lot."

"It's a pretty big country."

"You can relax now," he said. "You're in Dar al-Islam. It's bigger." He joined his palms and rubbed them.

Dar al-Islam, "the Realm of Islam," is a popular Muslim catchword for a swatch of lands that covers most of the planet: stretching west from Morocco across North Africa to Egypt, rolling on over the Arab Middle East, north into Pakistan and Sino-Russia, south across India, Indonesia, Japan. Allah's realm has many mansions and about a billion souls. One did not have to ponder long to form a mental picture. The scale of the area is vast, and yet at root the image is domestic. *Dar* also means "neighborhood" and "house."

Sharif confessed he'd been making plans since seeing my letter. An American Muslim headed for Mecca was rare news in Marrakesh. He wanted to take me under his wing, to prepare me.

"A month is not much time," he said, rubbing his palms like a tanner preparing to stain a hide. It made me nervous. "You must come to the mosque this afternoon," he said. "I'll show you a place where men take thirty-five minutes to say their prayers. In some of these places they do it in two minutes. I'll show you everything and make you correct. You have to be correct if you're going to Mecca."

I smiled broadly. But I wondered.

Events of the past three decades had conspired to throw up thousands of young Moroccans like Sharif, born to Islam, then fallen away, lured by Western ways but now repentant. For them Islam provides an aim and a challenge. In Sharif's case, this meant making up lost time. His fervor took the form of proselytizing, and he had a born-again flare for pedagogy. I instinctively resisted being his prospect, yet I liked him. In the next few months, I often felt sure he knew a thing or two, but I was not the one to memorize it.

His next remark stunned me.

"I have some videos you'll need to see: Jimmy Swaggart discussing Islam with an imam. And another of Cat Stevens, in a beard. You know this man?"

I nodded.

"We call him Yusef."

Cat Stevens had been a Muslim for years. It was not a rock-star convert that surprised me. It was the presence of video players in the souk. Since my last time here, a media revolution had swept the lower classes of Morocco. Today you found cable news in most cafés and many fewer Moroccans attending the movies. Large parts of the population had gone from illiteracy to global awareness in a decade. I had read learned articles about this in academic journals, laments of TV's effect on the tribal fabric. But no one had mentioned Islamicized VCRs. And then there was the shock of Jimmy Swaggart.

I was just getting over it when Mostopha returned to the bazaar. He greeted Sharif and busied himself, aligning jewelry boxes on a shelf.

When I expressed an interest in seeing both cassettes, Sharif was delighted. He would bring them to his shop in a day or two, but he warned me not to mention them in public. "Not everyone approves of these men," he said. "The videos are risky." And he raised a dramatic finger to his lips.

Mostopha watched with a bemused expression. When Sharif was gone, he turned to me and smiled and tapped his forehead.

"I saw those tapes years ago," he said.

❖   ❖   ❖   ❖

*M*ostopha was born in the early 1940s in Casablanca, the hardest working port in Africa. His father, a small businessman, earned more than most Moroccans, and the first few years of Mostopha's life were settled. The family lived in a modern flat in the Anfa district. He did not remember this period very clearly. His mother died in childbirth when he was four.

Mostopha's next ten years were split between the Casablanca flat and seasons spent with his grandparents on a farm. In the countryside he learned to shear sheep and buck hay. In town he went to school when he felt like it. He cooked for his younger brother and discovered street life. He became obsessed with matinees, with double feature movie bills, with Gable, Bogart, Garbo, and Jack Palance.

General George S. Patton described mid-forties Casablanca as "a city combining Hollywood and the Bible," a tough palm-lined skyscraper of a city where men still strolled about in flowing robes. Today its boulevards are six lanes wide. Fifteen-story gray apartment buildings crowd the skyline. The extensive urban sprawl is larger than Paris, but organically the city is a hoax. Casablanca was laid out on European lines by nineteenth-century French investors. It has no relation (as do most Moroccan cities) to the kingdom of a thousand years ago. Tourists mind this more than Casablancans. Twenty thousand Moroccans lived here in 1900. Today the population is three and a half million.

By age fifteen Mostopha knew all the boulevard cafés. About that time he found a steady job, as a film projectionist at the local Bijou. The night work kept him out late and later led to trouble, but he liked it and he saw movies for free. This was during the years (he said) before filmmakers learned how to strip a girl, fire a pistol, get the results on film, and award it an Oscar. Mostopha saw *On the Waterfront* fifty times. He became a film buff, able to list Liz Taylor's marriages or Edward G. Robinson's gangster roles in order. He also began to smoke and to test life's limits. He bought a motorcycle. He met some Americans.

In the early 1960s, Morocco's Atlantic seaboard experienced a peculiar innundation. Unlike previous generations of tourists, this flood was composed of young malcontents and self-styled gypsies. Those drawn down from Europe by winter sun and cheap hashish arrived by bus, in campers, on the trains. Those from the States took cut-rate flights to Casablanca or floated into the port on budget freighters. However they came in, from whatever quarter, a smaller, matching wave of young Moroccans like Mostopha was usually there to greet them at the gates.

These new arrivals did not look like normal tourists. Their hair was long, their pace relaxed, their music not the average French vacationer's. Their novelty was not confined to dress codes. Unlike the French, they were not colonially aloof. They sought out Moroccans to travel with, to talk to. They did not isolate themselves in large hotels. They flocked to campsites, slept in tents, put up in hostels. They were romantics, that is, enthusiasts, and their stories betrayed a common theme: they had left behind their homes, jobs, schools, to taste a larger world.

They were footloose, independent; at the same time they did everything in groups. This combination matched the style of many Moroccans. Moreover, they were in no rush to leave. They had loose schedules or no schedules at all, no pressing need, it seemed, to return to a job, a family. They did have money, they did need guides. These things were attractive to young Moroccans, yet the effective side of this tidal wave was social. They carried news from a more dynamic quarter. Apparently they wanted to be friends.

One spring Mostopha followed them to Essaouira, where a wide expanse of beach sweeps south and sandbars and rocky islets break the shoreline. On the beach a fort with turrets rides the surf. The harbor town that frames all this has an ancient, mesmerizing beauty. Above its streets run Roman aqueducts.

The year Mostopha arrived, a different history was brewing. Crosby, Stills and Nash had recorded "Marrakesh Express." The Vietnam War was turning to televised slaughter. Generational rebellion was afoot. A banner above a yogurt stall read TURN ON, TUNE IN, DROP OUT in seven languages. Thor Heyerdahl launched a reed boat from these beaches. In town the Living Theatre rented a house and began "rehearsing." Jimi Hendrix came down one week from London and tried to buy the fort of Diabet. At the height of the mayhem several thousand campfires lit the sand dunes. Acid rock music curled the surf.

Mostopha's taste for rock and roll dated from this period. So did the surgical scars and shattered bones suffered one night in a motorcycle crack-up. The accident sent him back to Casablanca, where he spent some months in a traction ward.

It was a curse and blessing, he said. At the hospital he met his future wife.

In the bed beside him lay an older man, a French Jew from Lyons, now a Casablancan. They shared their meals and the radio together, and every few days the man's adopted daughter came to visit. She was a Berber from the Atlases, named Qadisha. Her parents were farmers in a mountain village. The family was large, the soil poor. Unable to support a fifth child, they had arranged for her adoption by the Frenchman and his wife. The girl was now in her middle teens. Gradually she and Mostopha fell in love.

The day of his release he went to see her. When he felt well enough to travel, she led him to her village, Amizmiz, to meet her parents. It took weeks to persuade the family. They left the mountains married and settled in the Marrakesh *medina*. They saved some money. They opened a bazaar.

The first time I met Mostopha, in 1979, there were two sons. Today they had four children, one an infant. They owned a modest home. The shop was larger. They hadn't returned to Casablanca in many years.

CHAPTER THREE

Across the Bar

*T*he following morning, walking back to Mostopha's shop, I lost the way twice in a look-alike maze of *Pépé le Moko* arches and back alleys. It was Friday, the day of the Muslim Sabbath, and the streets were quiet. Mostopha stood locking the door when I arrived.

Sharif's leather stall was closed, too. The *medina* seemed set on quarter throttle. Occasional browsers slipped through the souks, but not many. Around noon the mosques would fill up for a service. The post office, schools, and banks would be closed all day.

We walked toward Mostopha's house to wash and dress. The cedar stalls in the carpenters' quarter stood idle. It was already after eleven and Mostopha walked quickly. I was trailing a few yards behind when an enormous man in a salt-and-pepper beard stepped without warning from an open door and seized my shoulders. I swung around, ready for anything.

"Abd al-Majeed!"

I stared up at him. Mostopha came back and introduced us. Medhi, he said, had seen my picture, too. Medhi was a broad, dynamic man in his early forties with heavy-lidded eyes, a playful grin, and an intimate way of leaning forward to address you. He spoke fine French, a crystalline barrage that marked him off from the rank and file merchants. His expansiveness contained a comic aspect, and he knew it. He and Mostopha had been friends for years.

"Friday!" he sighed. "There is no day like Friday. I wait for this one day six days a week! You see me the other days, I'm wearing blue jeans. Today, voilà, I'm dressed to meet the King, the Lord of the Worlds, *Rabbil-'aalameen*! I like your country, *mon ami*, but it suffers in the area of clothing. Look how we dress! Only your judges and choirboys can do this. Here everybody floats about in robes. We lie on long banquettes like ancient Greeks!" Medhi plucked from the air an invisible grape, popped it into his open mouth, and winked. "Thank God for Friday!"

"Thank the Prophet, peace upon him," Mostopha said.

"Indeed," said Medhi. "He was wise. The Jews have Saturday; the Christians, Sunday. The Prophet gave us our own Sabbath. We pray a day before them. This is right. Wait till you get to Mecca. It is always Friday in Mecca."

"Have you been to Mecca?"

"Of course! When I was ten, my father took me. The pilgrimage is in every Muslim's blood. And especially for Arabs. No matter how tragic life becomes, an Arab still believes travel will save him."

"I believe that, too," I said.

"Alors! What mosque will you go to today?"

"Ben Yusef," Mostopha said.

"Do you have your *wudu*?"

"No, not yet."

Medhi glanced at his watch. "You'd better be going."

After shaking my hand, Medhi drew back his palm and touched his heart. I had omitted this traditional Moroccan gesture. He called me on it: "When you shake a Muslim's hand, you do it this way. You take a bit of the person with you then. Not the way they do in Europe," and he imitated limply, letting his right hand fall away like a piece of meat.

✧ ✧ ✧ ✧

W*udu'* is an Arabic term with two principal meanings: on one hand, it refers to a set of ablutions Muslims use to cleanse themselves for prayer; on the other, it designates a purified state of being. The act, that is, results in a condition of the same name. When you wash, you are said to perform *wudu'*. Having finished, it is something you possess. You have *wudu'*, as you have a state of mind. Until you break it—by falling asleep, for instance, after which the state should be renewed.

Wudu', like all the Muslim rites, begins with a silent statement of intention, or *niya*. Alms, fasting, and pilgrimage require a preface, too. The phrasing varies. What matters each time is making a mental note to describe your purpose. "Now I shall offer the morning prayer" precedes the morning prayer, or it is worthless. The same holds true for *wudu'*, with good reason. For practices repeated daily, the offhand, the rote, the mechanical are pitfalls. *Niya* forestalls the paralysis of habit. It is as central to ritual action as a wick to a candle. Without it rites like *wudu'* become empty.

Wudu' cleanses a Muslim's public person. It is much more than a splash of holy water: the hands, face, and feet are washed three times. The mouth, nose, and earlobes are gone over. "Being clean is half of religion," the Prophet said, and he frequently compared prayer to fresh water. Medhi had joked that on Fridays Moroccans dress like ancient Greeks. They bathed all week more frequently than Romans. And not only Moroccans: from here to Indonesia, all over Dar al-Islam, few men think of praying without *wudu'*. Where water cannot be had, clean earth is used.

At Mostopha's we removed our socks and shoes and crouched by a drain in the courtyard. Facing each other, we took turns pouring water from a kettle. I poured first.

Starting from the right side Mostopha rinsed his hands three times, cupped water to his mouth and spat it out, snuffed a few drops up his nose and snorted. The arms came next, three times from wrist to elbow, then the head from neck to brow, and last, the feet. The kettle was still half-full when he had finished.

We switched positions. Mostopha started out handling the kettle while I washed. I had gone through this sequence hundreds of times at home in a Western setting. I rinsed both hands; I cleaned my mouth and nostrils, cupping my palms each time as Mostopha poured. But when it came to rinsing the arms, he stopped me. I looked up, vaguely put out but then befuddled: for somehow, without even noticing, I'd managed to get the kettle into my hand and was busy tipping a steady stream of water down one elbow.

"You're doing it backward."

Of course, he was right. With this method, the water ran too quickly off the arm, draining away before I could set down the kettle. This left no time at all to scrub the skin. Figuring I'd have to work more quickly, I reached to pour more water down the arm but again was left with no free hand for scrubbing. It was not a method. I was using the kettle as though it were a bath tap. The results were awkward, confusing. And *how*, I had to ask myself, did I come to be holding the kettle? Mostopha, during his turn, had not touched it. Seeing what I'd done, I felt embarrassed. On the other hand, I could not seem to improve.

"And you're wasting water. Look!" The tiles glistened around me. The kettle was empty.

As a man over forty taking points on toilet training, I had to remind myself I was here to learn. Mostopha refilled the kettle and squatted beside me. His own approach to the arm was humbling, economical, like Zen. There were three parts to the maneuver. First he poured from the kettle, using his left hand. Next he cupped the water in his right and set down the kettle. Finally, this palming action allowed him to raise the arm, letting water roll down to the elbow while he scrubbed. I tried it myself. It was simple.

When the washing was done, Mostopha lent me an emerald green djellaba. This trim-lined full-length robe, in different styles for men and women, is Morocco's universal overgarment. The weight of the cloth may vary with the season, but its sleeves are always long, a triangular hood hangs off the back, and if it is a good one, the pipings down the front are double sewn. This was a good one, in wool of just the right thickness to keep skin dry and cool in any weather. The Western academic robe is said to derive from this Quranic scholar's garment.

"I don't know," I said as he carried it toward me.

"What's the matter?"

"I've never worn one."

"Never?"

It was true. In the years I'd been coming here, I had never seen any reason to dress like a native.

Mostopha laughed. "But in those days, you were not going to the *masjid*.* There are no laws, my friend. But it is respectful to wear clean clothes there. And look, the cloth is green, the Prophet's color!"

He gathered the robe into folds and slipped it over my shoulders like a poncho. As it fell into place, it belled out around the ankles. My shirt and blue jeans disappeared.

Mostopha put on a sleeveless white *gandoura*. As an afterthought I slipped a prayer cap on my head. It was Friday again. Exactly a week had passed since the night in Tangier when I'd shied at the gates to a mosque and joined the children. Today we were headed for the front door in broad daylight. I felt relieved and full of a pleasant hunger. I had learned a trick or two about washing, too.

As we began to thread through the paved veins of the kasbah, other men joined us on the way. Approaching rue Semarine, I heard a brush of leather sandals on the flagstones. Ahead we saw flocks of men in their Friday best. There were no cars or trucks to block the passage. The crowd advanced freely, gaining a little speed as we left the souks, turning right at a junction, left under an arch, opening out all at once on a spacious plaza.

Here in the year 1125, Sultan 'Ali ben Yusef, whose rule extended as far as Lisbon, established a central mosque for his new *medina*. The structure (reportedly handsome) has not survived. The existing building, a replacement of a replacement, is half the size of Ali's original. It dates from the nineteenth century but looks older. Small shops on an opposing wall line the public square facing the complex. At other hours kids played soccer here.

Mosque is a French corruption of this word.

Today the square was filled a hundred deep with ranks of Moroccans packed shoulder to shoulder, shuffling toward a central door. The crowd was close yet calm. There was neither pushing nor shoving, nor much progress. Following Mostopha through the press, I noticed lined up just outside the gates a welcoming committee of six beggars. Old men in white caps and brown djellabas, expressionless of face with hollowed eyes, they stood chanting in unison for alms. I laid a dirham on the final blind man's palm and came to a stop at a shallow flight of stairs. The steps led down through a wall into a forecourt. The crowds descending flowed to either side—for the maw of the passage was blocked at waist level by a ten-foot cedar pole.

The pole, I knew, was there to bar non-Muslims. I'd seen ones like it all over the country and had read about them in books on architecture. Any of the older, venerated mosques had one. Up at Fez, in the mountains, in the mosque of Moulay Idriss, it hung by rusty chains from the first arch. Here it was raised off the ground on three-foot posts, leaving a gap at both ends to admit the faithful.

These poles had acquired symbolic force before my trip began. At home I had non-Muslim friends familiar with my journey who enjoyed predicting dire consequences. Americans make skittish travelers. And when it comes to going among Arabs, most of the population is ill informed. Those that knew better were sometimes the worst. Even recent letters from Paul Bowles, who after all had lived in Morocco for decades, were laced with forebodings. A few of my Jewish friends went overboard. They came up with ridiculous suggestions: I should darken my face en route with shoe polish; I should wear brown-tinted contact lenses to hide my hazel eyes. Deportation and evisceration were popular motifs at good-bye parties. I could not pretend to being unaffected. By the time I left home, the cedar poles had come to stand for all these nightmare hurdles, and I worried and even dreamed of them at night.

To be standing face-to-face with the real item was elating. I was ten steps short of Ben Yusef's mosque and closing. At home I had lived this scene a thousand times, with a mixed rush of excitement and apprehension. In most such armchair projections I had viewed myself as an isolated figure. I stood out, I looked white and Western, I felt inadmissable. Here, on the other hand, I blended in, another Muslim wrapped in a djellaba. This so relieved my anxiety about the pole that as the crowd pressed in on every side, I weighed my options for getting past it and very nearly made a foolish move. At home I had lived for a time on a cattle ranch. Being used to gates and wooden fences, my first impulse to beat the crowd was simply to duck the pole and take a shortcut.

No one ducked under. They hugged the sidelines, they shrank to patient groups of two or three, they slipped around the bar at either end, but they took no shortcuts. I managed to pull up in the knick of time, physically pull up and back, saving myself from a serious social blunder. I conformed to the flow of the crowd around the pole. In the meantime Mostopha had slipped ten feet ahead of me. This gave new direction to my worries.

At the foot of the steps a milling jam ensued as everyone bent down to remove his sandals. This was done swiftly, to keep from holding up the line, and then we spilled out onto an open courtyard—a flat, marble expanse of Olympic proportions. The effect was like passing through a needle's eye.

The outlines of any mosque create the borders of *haram*, a sacred precinct marked off from the world. Muhammad likened its enclosure to the woven cradle that bore Moses down the Nile. Others saw it as a cool oasis, a refuge in the deserts of the world. By whatever image, the *haram* imparts its mood to those inside, a palpable solidity of marble, water, and sunlight. It settled like an atmosphere around me. And then I lost Mostopha in the crowds.

The yard was expansive—I thought in terms of several football fields. Its airiness threw into contrast the narrow, thronged alleys of the town. A shallow, stone reflecting pool thirty yards across lay at its center. Balanced around the rim, hundreds of people bent to their ablutions. Mostopha had been right. There were no strict dress codes. Many men were in their best djellabas. Others, mostly younger, wore long-sleeved shirts and slacks or blue jeans.

Islam has no processional requirement, and the axial treatment of the Christian church, with its narrowed path to a theatrical pulpit, is missing. The Gothic use of height to point up spiritual ascendance is absent, too.

The structure of a mosque is horizontal. Space is a leveler anywhere one looks. Overhead, galleries about the yard create high planes around you. Below men drift through pillared hallways.

I drifted with them into the roofed *musalla,* the place of worship proper, where several thousand people sat on carpets. I recognized these long, straight rows from visits to the mosque in San Jose, but nothing could prepare me for the numbers. Ben Yusef's congregation was the size of a small town. Kneeling shoulder to shoulder, the worshipers looked east, facing a prayer niche shaped like a door pointing to Mecca. As in any mosque the only furniture consisted of a wooden laddered pulpit and carpets on the floor. Overhead a red-stained cedar ceiling threw the hall into shadow. The quiet hum below was solid, weightless. An occasional swallow blew in from the courtyard, swooped over the crowd, then flitted off.

Standing at the back of the hall, I scanned the carpets, looking for Mostopha, but rows of pillars fragmented my view. The simplicity of their arrangement was deceptive; the lines of the room were classic, apparently Romanesque, yet the columns made for visual confusion. Between each set of two an arch rose up, so that much of the space above shoulder height was curved. Also, the several dozen columns of the first rank were offset slightly in relation to the next, and so on across the crowded hall. This led the eye through a series of graded distortions, à la Escher, for which it was never quite prepared. Looked at on a diagonal, as I was doing, the perspectives set up between successive rows were bewilderingly varied, so that it was like squinting into a forest from the road. In the very first mosques, at Mecca and Madinah, these rows of columns *had* been formed by trees. Here at Ben Yusef old men sat crosslegged with their backs pressed to the bases, like picnickers inside an ancient grove.

Finally, I caught sight of Medhi's salt-and-pepper beard. As our glances met, he raised an eyebrow, then laid an open hand over his chest. Luckily he had caught my lost expression. He nodded down the rows toward Mostopha.

I crossed the room. Loudspeaker static crackled. From another part of the complex the muezzin was preparing to repeat the call to prayer. I sat down quickly on Mostopha's right, arranged the djellaba about my knees, and checked the straightness of my cap.

"Are you all right?" he whispered.

"Sure. Are *they?*"

"Who?"

"These people. About me being here."

He glanced at the prayer hall. "It's Friday," he said. "You belong here. These days Muslims die for stupid things. For border wars and British novels. If we had trouble over you, it would be worth it." He patted my knee. "Don't worry. Someone like yourself is a big thing here. I've just been thinking: we met one day, what? eleven years ago. You were lost in the Souk al-Attarine, and you came to my shop. You asked for a glass of tea. I gave it to you. Now we're sitting in a mosque together. Fantastic."

When the voice in the tower called out, he looked relieved.

The public call to prayer is a drawn out aural arabesque. Its eight repeated parts mount and descend a scale that sounds elusive to Westerners. The effect is come-hither. The meanings are simple, clear:

> *God is the greatest.*
> *There is no God but God.*
> *Muhammad is God's prophet.*
> *Come to prayer.*
> *Come to prosperity.*
> *Let the prayer begin.*
> *God is great.*
> *There is no God but God.*

Each call repeats the religion's fundamentals.

As it ended today, a rustle of cloth filled the building. The congregation got up on its feet.

A barely visible figure stood near the prayer niche. His back turned to us, the man faced east. He cupped his palms to his ears, and the crowd did likewise, but he wore no special clothes and was not a priest. There are no intercessors in Islam and no established priesthood at a mosque. Nobody stands between a man and Allah. The imam, whose head I could not see, was simply the one most conversant with the Qur'an in this assembly. As we followed his amplified voice through the opening verses, no one paid him particular attention. Nor was anybody watching me.

I had learned the prayers by rote a year before, from a novice handbook, *The Elementary Teachings of Islam*. Its interlinear translations into Pakistani English were accompanied by photos of the postures. The phonetic approximations of the Arabic seemed correct. I read the sounds aloud and I wrote them out. Then one day in December, I set the book on a music stand, positioned the stand near an east-facing window, and started to practice. I memorized the first chapter of the Qur'an as I had memorized Greek poetry in college—more or less blindly, led by the beauty of the sound. Next I began to fit the postures to the words. After a couple of weeks of this I noticed two things: the lines had distinctive rhythms and very often end rhymes; the postures relieved an aching back.

There is nothing very mysterious about the Muslim prostration. Its four alternating postures comprise a unit called a *rak'ah*. Salat, "prayer," is in turn composed of two to four *rak'ah*s, depending on the hour of the day. You stand, you bend, you kneel, you press your forehead to the earth, reciting specific verses at each juncture. To translate *salat* as prayer can be misleading to Westerners. The word *prayer* derives from *precarius*, "obtained by begging." *Salat*, on the other hand, means "to bow" and leads, in the Muslim view, to a state of *salam*, "uninjured peace." Conventionally one prays five times a day: before dawn, around noon, then late in the afternoon, soon after sundown, and later on that night. The muezzin calls the public to these occasions. On most Moroccan minarets a blue flag is also run up to alert the deaf.

> *Praise to God, Lord of the worlds*
> *Beneficent, merciful*
> *Owner of the Day of Judgment.*
> *You alone we worship.*
> *To you we turn for help . . .*

My eye ran out over this crowd of several thousand kneeling people, a quiet lake of caps and flowing robes. Mostopha was right: I belonged here. The Arabic name, the foreign clothes, and words I was starting to understand were a means of delivery, not a masquerade. If steadiness was what I sought, I found it in a building full of strangers. A few more swallows flitted through the hall. We bowed, sat down; the Qur'an was read; a second imam delivered a brief sermon; then we bowed again and it was over. At about one-thirty, holding our sandals above our heads, we inched through the crowds out of the mosque.

CHAPTER FOUR

The Food of Love

For a couple of hours on Saturday, I took a bike ride through the Aguedal, where olive groves ran on for miles and irrigation channels fed the trees. Even when the streams were out of sight, one still could hear their plashing—a rare experience in the pre-Sahara.

I pedaled along a broad dirt track, past stone walls and purple bougainvillea. The track continued up a steady rise. It was shirtsleeve weather. Bit by bit the sun began to beat, and brilliant finches flitted through the palm trees. When the hill grew steeper, I got down and walked the bike.

Halfway uphill I passed a palace tucked into the groves. Its grounds were extensive, the red walls punctuated by tall towers. The effect, without a car in sight, was feudal. The king of Morocco sometimes wintered here.

At the top of the hill lay a rammed-earth reservoir. Inclined toward the groves, it fed the channels. At the entry gates I met a young man carrying a book bag, who offered to show me the water for a dollar. Morocco is full of invented jobs like this one, car watcher, beach guard, dreamed up on the spot by its unemployed. Sixty percent of the country is under twenty years of age; a third are jobless. The Moroccan economy has been accurately compared to a bucket brigade in which everyone sips from the bucket as it passes. I gave the young man the coins, but I did not need him. I could see the water behind him, in plain view.

The gardens around the pool were full of students. It was exam time, and they had come here not to relax but to cram and read. I knew firsthand how Ramadan gnawed at will power. It impressed me to see them seated under trees, bent over notebooks, or declaiming speeches in French for a diploma. I tried not to wonder who would employ them after graduation. They looked better off here than in the libraries of Paris, and they did not need my imported lamentations.

After a while I made a circuit around the pool and pedaled back to town.

✧   ✧   ✧   ✧

*R*amadan is enjoined on every Muslim, in the second and longest chapter of the Qur'an. For one lunar month, during the evenings, one may

> *eat and drink until the white thread*
> *of dawn appears clear from the dark line,*
> *then he must fast until night fall.*

The Qur'an goes on to list the rules for social conduct during the period, with references to sex and economics. It then defines the means of expiation for those who variously cannot keep the fast. Illness and travel are high on the list of excuses. In Marrakesh, I read this passage with new interest.

A week before the end of Ramadan, I woke at dawn with burning lungs. In the shower I felt dizzy. Later on I went for a stroll and barely made it back to the hotel room. The hot spots in my chest felt like the first signs of pneumonia. The accompanying light-headedness depressed me. Long months of travel lay ahead. Rather than be brought low now, I decided to treat the problem before it worsened, with a course of antibiotics.

At a *pharmacie* near the spice market a salesgirl in a nurse's outfit sold me a vial of ampicillin. She advised me to take three pills a day, and never, she cautioned, on an empty stomach. Her warning made me remember the last time I'd ignored the same advice. Ampicillin turns empty stomachs inside out. The cure could be more gut-wrenching than a virus. Back in my room I opened the vial and laid out eighteen tablets on the bed stand. If I took them, I would be eating for six days.

I took the first pill and felt disappointment. From dreading the fast at home, I had come to like it in Morocco. If misery loves company, I had a whole country behind me. Even on the streets I found support. One day in the market an eighty-year-old onion vendor asked me whether I found the fasting hard. "Late in the afternoon," I confessed, "I do." His eyeballs twinkled. "It's easy!" he told me. "It cleans the gut. You live longer. When the month is over, I find it hard to stop." This unity before hardship proved contagious. In a way it was more nourishing than food.

Ramadan turned schedules upside down, threw habits into sharp relief, and added several hours to your day. It lent perspective to thirst and hunger and left an odd, sweet taste inside your mouth. My first attempts were going better than expected. With a week remaining, I hated to give up my regime. It felt like falling off the wagon.

The only food to be had before dark was served in the Ville Nouvelle, the so-called New Town. This modern French adjunct to the *medina* spread west from the ancient town. It had broad streets laid out in radiating star patterns. Most of the avenues were tree lined, paved. The mood was European. The five-minute ride in a cab between these different-looking worlds provided an exercise in time travel. Their coexistence never failed to impress me. For sixty cents and little effort one could cross centuries and never leave the city.

The New Town had clean markets, European restaurants, travel agents, a movie house, and not much else to recommend it. Gueliz, the best of its residential districts, looked like an ochre version of a French provincial *ville* without the plane trees. If you wanted food during Ramadan, you had to poke around.

The cafés and restaurants were mostly Muslim owned. Although they did not close during the day, their only paying clients in Ramadan were travelers and Christians. The fast did not keep Muslim habitués from sitting on the terrace. They could not order food or drink, but some still came. Even on empty stomachs Moroccans are great observers of the street.

The only places with working kitchens were the hotels. Dozens of these in the three-star range were set on back streets off the boulevards. They catered, whenever possible, to package tours. This meant serving three square meals a day on a timely basis no matter what the natives might get up to. The kitchens, of course, were staffed by fasting Moroccans. The meals still managed to get through.

I hit by chance on the Hotel ben Tashfin. Here food could be ordered in broad daylight, the meals were passable, and no one knew me. I ate. I took my pills. I read newspapers.

❖   ❖   ❖   ❖

I recouped and took my meals in the New Town, but the *medina* remained more interesting. I still passed most of my time there, in the souks. I loved their endless bamboo-covered alleys. Although I was frequently lost in them, it didn't seem to matter. Except for Mostopha's familiar lane and three or four bazaars, I had nowhere in particular to go. It freed me completely. I could ride the flow of a crowd for miles through the vascular *medina*, down lanes lined with open shop fronts where vendors waved at every other door. I could stop and chat or pass them by. Sometimes I even bought things.

The multiplicity of goods went on for acres. There was a district of three or four blocks that sold nothing but *belra*s, the backless leather slipper with pointed toes that Delacroix made famous in his sketches. The *belra* souk bled into the fabric market. These shops all had counters at the door where vendors could unroll great bolts of cloth for your inspection, then direct you to the tailors' square.

One day at the entry to this maze I passed a collection of blind men in gray robes. They were not the same men I had passed at Ben Yusef's mosque. These carried copper bowls and chanted together. Elias Canetti described a similar contingent in a short book on his visit here in the 1960s:

A group of them . . . stood close together in a row in the market, and their hoarse, endlessly repeated chant was audible a long way off. . . . Each man held out a wooden alms dish, and when someone tossed something in [to it,] the proffered coin passed from hand to hand, each man feeling it, each man testing it. . . .

All the blind offer one the name of God. . . . All their cries contain a declension of His name. . . . But the cry is also a multiplication: the rapid, regular repetition makes of each beggar a group. There is a peculiar energy of asking in it; he is asking on behalf of many and collecting for them all. "Consider all beggars! Consider all beggars! God will bless you for every beggar you give to."

It struck me as I listened that the chanting had not changed in thirty years. The same "multiplication," the same "peculiar energy of asking" had survived through time exactly as described.

Later I learned these men belonged to a guild named for one of the city's patron saints. Sidi Bel Abbes died in 1205, but his acts of charity won him veneration, and his shrine remains a center of good works. Fifteen minutes from Mostopha's shop, it served free meals every night and parceled out donations to the sightless. Eye diseases are common in Morocco. Glaucoma can run rampant in the south, and river blindness, carried by a blackfly parasite, is no stranger. Half the families I knew here had one or more sightless relations. The count had been higher twenty years ago. It was not hard to imagine a file of blind men stretching back through time, the little group by the market gate part of a much larger operation, pre-dating Western travel books by centuries.

The ampicillin did its job. I walked more each day, took lighter snacks in the New Town, and dined with Mostopha's family every night.

The end of the fast at dusk is announced in different ways in every city. In Tangier a cannon is fired in the kasbah. In Casablanca air raid sirens wail. In Marrakesh the mosques perform the job. Every night around seven the speakers clicked on in Ben Yusef's minarets, and a muezzin gave the call to prayer. Within minutes a hundred mosques had picked it up. The sky filled with darting swallows. Doors banged closed in the bazaars. Store owners hurried through the streets, dodging carts and vanishing down alleys. The souks emptied out. Night came down. The city rushed indoors.

I did not discuss my lapsed fast at Mostopha's. The first night I'd been too weak for explanations. I also felt guilty. Ibrahim, a fifteen-year-old, was fasting. Qadisha, nursing a newborn, fasted, too. Many Moroccans referred to the fast as armor; it clearly gave Mostopha's family strength. I admired their persevering humor and did not want to watch Qadisha cook me food nobody else could eat. For this was what would happen the moment she heard about my pills.

"Avoid any act that requires an excuse," the Prophet said.

Maintaining silence was not difficult. Moroccans I knew did not lament the hardships of fasting, except to excuse some failing in the system. If a shop closed at noon, if the mail slowed down, if a fight broke out in the market, these things were ascribed to Ramadan. Discussion of its hardship was avoided. The evenings were too precious for complaints.

I usually reached the house in time for *harira,* the soup Moroccans serve to break their fast. The stomach, they say, should be treated like a child at Ramadan, and the soup was gentle and only lightly spiced. Qadisha served it with mint tea and three or four kinds of bread, which emerged still warm from her tiny downstairs kitchen. We ate from a low table in a long salon upstairs, called a *sala.* We watched the evening prayers on television.

This program was broadcast from the king's palace in Rabat. It featured King Hassan and his royal court performing their *rak'ah*s in a gorgeous mosque. The camera work was passive, looking on. This window on the sultan's world intrigued me. Prayer in the West is a more private thing. Here, during Ramadan, it became a public function. These humbling scenes of prostrate dignitaries, including army brass, seemed politically healthy. Later on we watched sports and news, then French programs from Paris.

During my first trips to Morocco, in the 1960s, TV had been a bland affair, dominated by dreary orchestral performances and soccer. These days the programming was more varied. We watched historical melodramas made in Egypt that often ran for three hours at a stretch. We watched contemporary thrillers from Casablanca, which despite their shaky camera work contained more realism than crime shows in the West. And we watched *Roots,* beamed that month on Wednesday nights from Paris. At home I had missed the epic miniseries of Alex Haley's paperback best-seller when it played to record audiences in the seventies. Now I had good reasons to catch up. First, I was watching in Africa, where the initial two shows were set. Second, in the Paris broadcasts, the characters spoke French. This provided an unexpected chance to hone my speaking skills on Kunta Kinte.

Around 10:00 P.M. we ate a second meal of many courses: mixed vegetables, lamb stew, a mound of couscous on a platter; three types of salad; pots of sweet mint tea; mixed fruit; and for dessert, cakes with powdered sugar at the edges. This repast was meant to tide us over until the final meal at 3:00 A.M.

Feasts like these revealed the second face of Ramadan. I'd been familiar with the fast as a form of abstinence. Now I saw it was also a matter of deferred bliss, carefully prepared and executed in the long hours between dusk and dawn.

I never made it through to the third sitting. By midnight I had always had enough. Then Mostopha (when he could manage) or Ibrahim (if not) would lead me home through the vacant *medina*. I protested this formal escort as time went on but could never shake it. Long after I knew my way, they still insisted. It seemed to be part of a formula for fair treatment of guests. It taught me new routes through the narrow alleys.

The hours after midnight reduced the *djema* to a campsite. The milling crowds were home in bed, awaiting a last meal before sunrise, and the cobbles were taken over by scattered circles of performers drawn up on blankets around lamps. The moon came down and dropped behind the ramparts. Scraps of music drifted on the square.

Here one night I came across a group of eight musicians seated on strips of cardboard to keep off the damp. While singing softly, six of the men clacked iron castanets. These were not the dainty finger cymbals of southern Spain but eight-inch pairs of iron clackers knotted at the ends with heavy twine. Each pair weighed a pound or more and produced a sound like hoofbeats. It took great strength to keep them going. Behind their racket came a quiet drum and a line of jazzy notes plucked out on a *ganbri*, the indigenous three-stringed Moroccan lyre. The words were simple, the rhythms unutterably subtle.

> *Salaam aleikoum, Moulay Muhammad.*
> *Salaam aleikoum, Moulay Muhammad.*
> *Rasullah nabi, Rasullah nabi*
> *Moulay Muhammad . . .*

The men wore tattered robes and in the daytime worked as minstrels. The ballad was a greeting to the Prophet. Playing for themselves tonight, they broke into grins from time to time as they hit upon some fresh change in the music.

I thought I recognized the *ganbri* player. Years ago Mostopha had invited me one night to a large house deep in the *medina*. The occasion had been a ceremony where several dozen men and women danced and sang and entered into trances, moving to music played by men like these. They were called Genowa, an African name for a local cult of mystical adepts who heal the sick with therapeutic dancing.

✧   ✧   ✧   ✧

*A*lthough I had not resumed my fast, it did not stop me from spending time with the orthodox Sharif.

Most people called him Moulay Abderman, but because the shorter family name implied connections with the Prophet, I assumed he preferred it. In his forties now, he bore the weighty faith of a recent convert. His face betrayed the marks of alcohol. His lower teeth were completely gone, and his cheeks were mottled. He had, he confessed, stopped drinking one night five years ago and come back to Islam forever. "I weep when I think of the years I've lost," he said. Sharif had, of course, been born to Islam, but that, in his opinion, did not matter. What mattered was how one lived life as an adult. "A baby," he said, "is an automatic Muslim. Later on a man must make a choice."

Sharif neither denied his past nor reveled in it like some ex-drinkers. He did distort the date of his conversion, as I learned by discussing his story with Mostopha. Mostopha claimed that Sharif had stopped drinking about a year ago. Mostopha had found him one morning, passed out on the floor of his bazaar.

"Really?"

"Last March."

Perhaps it seemed much longer to Sharif.

His bazaar sat kitty-corner to Mostopha's. Over the door hung a metal rack packed tight with leather jackets. We were sitting in their shadows on foot-high stools one morning when I happened to ask Sharif if he had kids.

He raised three fingers, then waved the whole hand at his future: "Later, *insha'Allah,* God may bring me more."

I wondered how many kids he planned on having.

"That's none of my business."

Most Muslims left this question up to God. In Sharif's case, it meant he was expecting the normal small army of a family that in ten years had increased the census here by 35 percent.

"One day the whole world will be Muslim," he offered.

"Don't treat it as a one-man job," I said.

The Qur'an takes a split view on procreation. In some suras it advises nonintervention; in others it advises couples to think ahead, to "take account of time and place." Sharif saw having children as a duty. When he cited a famous verse to back this up, I invoked a different quotation to oppose him.

Brahim, who ran a carpet shop next door, overheard us talking. Now he came over.

Milder than Sharif, with a fuller face, Brahim often glanced at the sky when he addressed me. His French was letter-perfect, and he knew more than Sharif because he loved reading. He had heard about Sharif's aims to improve me. Seeing us together, he came to help.

"Of the five things only Allah knows," he said, "the first concerns the origin of children. Only Allah can know when one will come."

I had not heard this *hadith* before. But such reliable reports of what the Prophet said or did are voluminous; those gathered by al-Bukhari run to nine volumes. I asked what the other four things were.

Brahim ticked them off on his fingers: When it will rain. What tomorrow will bring. When your life is going to end. And the origin of children.

It was a sweet list, neatly put and thought provoking, and we could barely wait to begin discussing it, which only added to the moment's tension, for the list was short by an item: the bit about the children had been repeated. Brahim stood tugging on his little finger. We sat and watched him reassess the list, attaching an Arabic term this time to all four entries. It was hopeless. No one could remember the fifth thing.

What is it that only Allah knows? It seemed like a pleasant way to pass the morning, but when I ventured a few guesses of my own, the attempts were rejected as heretical.

Brahim proposed a more devout approach. "We don't know what the fifth thing is. But we do know it's *something, one* thing, not just maybe. *Donc,* it is better to wait for the truth than waste time guessing."

With this pronouncement five hundred pages of Descartes flew out the window. It seemed like nothing. We let it pass.

The missing item was only a momentary setback. Within minutes Brahim was drawing fine distinctions between amniocentesis and God's knowledge. He'd read about it in a magazine. "The Americans put a needle into a pregnant woman's womb and tell you the sex of her child before it's born. But this is nothing. It only tells us what's there before they can see it. It's good to know, but Allah's eyes are stronger than these people's. He knows from the beginning what will happen."

I was about to respond when an elderly man in a scruffy beard and turban passed the storefront. Brahim waved the man inside and asked him a question. I did not need a translation to see what this was all about: the man began to shout and count on his fingers, enlightening his juniors on the fine points of Islam. Sharif listened closely. Brahim politely thanked him. The man reached down and shook my hand, as if commiserating with me. He was gone in a moment.

"He welcomes you to Islam," Sharif explained.

"What's the fifth thing?" I asked.

Brahim looked sheepish. The final bit they could not recall was when the world would end.

* * *

I could chuckle over my meetings with Sharif—the intent to perfect me burned in him, the instruction proved so shallow, but our positions were not so very different. Beneath the *gandoura* he was another fledgling Muslim. We each had put in a serious year at it. If Sharif had grown up in Morocco, if I had read a few more books, it did not mean that either of us knew much.

In one way being Moroccan handicapped him, for his background left him open to popular and benighted misconceptions. For example, both he and the carpet man Brahim were literate in Arabic, yet when we got around to it, Sharif's translations of even the best-known prayers were weirdly flawed. For example, he claimed initially that the last lines of the Fatihah,

> *Guide us on the straight path . . .*
> *Not the path of those who have gone astray,*

meant simply "don't behave like Jews." The problem went beyond vocabulary. So many Muslims compared themselves so favorably with Jews that before I'd been here very long, I began to suspect Islam would be lost without them.

Sharif backed down when I questioned his translation, but I knew again that I had not found my teacher. A teacher, in any case, wasn't on my mind. What I wanted was more instruction in the basics, a finishing course in Islam, to brush up and prepare myself for Mecca. Without it I ran the risk of mere tourism.

Islam is mostly a matter of the heart. It has no priesthood, no effective hierarchy. Every person faces God alone. Desire backed up by intention was all one needed. I could now recite the most common prayers by rote and understand them interlinearly. I had read the Qur'an in numerous translations. I felt at home in Moroccan mosques, when with Mostopha.

On the other hand, I was aware of a vast tradition of scholarship, of wit, of mysticism whose surface I had not even scratched. Because of this I still felt like a novice. I had been counting on travel to improve me. Sometimes I felt I was getting nowhere.

I continued to visit Sharif and Brahim. I took my evening meals at Mostopha's, but I saw I would have to wait for more instruction. With a little luck I might find someone. Or perhaps he would happen by, the way the old man had happened by to fill in Brahim's list when it was needed.

✧   ✧   ✧   ✧

*Q*adisha continued to load the boards each evening. Between fasting and nursing an infant son steady streams of dishes poured from the kitchen. She drew on some hidden reservoir for power, like the rushing channels in the Aguedal. Her endurance seemed to penetrate the food and issue from it. A few nights of this and I felt stronger.

With two days remaining in Ramadan, I tossed out the rest of the ampicillin. That night I told Mostopha what had happened.

"I broke the fast," I said. "I picked up a virus and had to take pills. They're like poison on an empty stomach. I've been eating."

"How long?"

"Four days."

"And now?"

I said, "It's over."

Qadisha had an uncle, Omar Adnas, in the mountains, who kept an office at the mosque in Amizmiz. Omar Adnas was a Quranic scholar and a local authority on Islamic law. When a villager had a question, he went to Omar. When Mostopha had a question, he asked his wife.

The two conferred in Arabic for a minute, after which Qadisha began to laugh. She often laughed over anything I'd done. Then she spoke fast, straight at me.

"She says you should feed a poor person for four days. She says if you do this and fast again, you'll be fine. She says Allah never burdens a sick person."

"That's all?"

They nodded.

"How do I do it?"

"Qadisha will do it."

The image of Qadisha whipping up extra dinners was nightmarish.

"No, no," he said. "You give her a few dirhams. She will buy the *fotra* and take them to the mosque."

Fotra are sandbox-size tin pails that people fill with grain for charity. I remembered seeing men selling them in the market.

Although the solution absolved me, its simplicity raised new doubts. That night at the hotel I checked the Qur'an in greater detail. Finally, I discovered what I was after:

> *Those who find it hard to fast should*
> *expiate by feeding a poor person.*

In the morning I brought Qadisha thirty dirhams.

Set against the Gregorian system, the Muslim lunar calendar "loses" eleven days each solar year. Because of this lunar years appear to move backward. The effect from one year to the next is not pronounced. Over fifteen years, however, Ramadan may circulate from April to October, passing through December on its way. In fact, a specific lunar date will recur in the same decan once every thirty-three-odd years. Even then its solar date may differ, for Muslim months do not begin or end at a fixed moment. They are announced on the appearance of the moon.

This explained why no Moroccan could tell me either when Ramadan would end or when the feast of 'Id al-Fitr should start. The consensus favored Thursday, if not Friday, but Wednesday was not out of the question.

My briefcase contained a calendar that neatly joined the solar and lunar dates. It showed a printed crescent moon in the box for Thursday, but as the hours ran down I kept my mouth shut. Exact predictions were beside the point. The point, for any Muslim, was simple: the fast would end when the new moon was sighted. *Vision and experience led to nourishment,* that is. Any other method was irrelevant.

On Wednesday night, while we were watching *Roots,* a voice interrupted the show with an announcement: the new moon had been sighted at Figuig.

Figuig was an old foreign-legion post at the edge of the Sahara. On a clear night from any of its rooftops the moonlight ran like rivers through the dunes.

" '*Id mubarak!*"

" '*Id mubarak!*"

" '*Id mubarak!*"

We exchanged our congratulations and shook hands across the table. No one said much. There were no effusions, no Western-style backslaps at having pulled through. The mood was nearer idle pleasure, like a walk in the woods at the end of the month, or a picnic. I was shocked by how quickly the station returned to *Roots*.

*Q*adisha spent the evening baking.

When I returned for breakfast in the morning, thirteen plates of different-looking cookies graced the table. Before we ate, Mostopha took a photo and passed out presents. The boys received new shoes. Nishwa, the four-year-old, received a party dress, which she immediately modeled. Mostopha had on a new djellaba.

"After this let's take a walk," he said. "We'll go to a café."

"And smoke cigarettes in the daytime," said Qadisha. She poured hot mint tea into glasses and passed the tray. Mostopha flicked on the TV, thumbing by remote through a dozen channels.

The program he settled on looked at first like another prayer hour with the king. Familiar flocks of meditative dignitaries sat neatly posed by rows in a vast hall, but when the camera pulled away, we were not in Morocco at all. We were in Mecca, at Islam's most famous mosque. I recognized the fields of blue-white marble from still photos, the acres of columns, the slender minarets. Now I saw the place in action.

The House of God, the Bayt al-Haram, is the Muslim sanctum sanctorum, the lodestone of Islam, the point of prayer all mosques face, and the final goal of every pilgrim. In modern times the Saudis have lavished untold petrodollars on this structure, and its scale and proportion beggar words. A pair of granite mountains sits enclosed within the building's eastern wing; two million square feet of floor space accommodate enormous congregations. The world's largest mosque, it is active night and day throughout the year, with two high seasons: Ramadan, and Dhu-l-Hijja, the month of pilgrimage.

Today the inner galleries were packed with hundreds of thousands of visitors. Hundreds of thousands more filled the nearby roads. Besides the crowd's vast size, its pace was remarkable: a slow crowd, almost viscous at a distance, growing more stately as the cameras drew away, for everyone wore white robes, and they were praying.

Qadisha's powdered pastries sent a blast of sugar through us. Mostopha and I went out to walk it off. He led the way to the Djema el Fna. We were passing through a block of dried-fruit stalls when two policemen stopped us, asking to see Mostopha's papers.

"What papers?"

"Your guide's license."

Mostopha touched the policeman's arm. "You don't remember me? You came to my shop last month to buy some jewelry for your wife."

The officer nodded.

Mostopha quickly introduced me. "An American Muslim, on his way to Mecca."

"Ah, Muhammad Ali!" the policeman grinned.

We talked for a minute or two, and then they left us.

"What was that about?" I asked.

Mostopha laughed. "They thought I was guiding you."

We went to a small café set off the square. It was shaped somewhat like a horseshoe pitch, with half a dozen tables on a pad. Mostopha lit up a Winston. We ordered coffee.

"Is guiding illegal in Marrakesh?" I asked, half joking.

"Of course not, but you have to have a badge. You have to take a test and pay some money. Some beginners start without a license. It's possible to make a lot that way. There are ten-year-olds who earn a thousand dirhams off one tourist. But in the end the policeman gets you. A policeman earns a miserable monthly paycheck. To even the score, he will shake you down for a kickback or put you in jail."

"What did those two want with you?"

"To pay them for walking you through the markets."

A man four chairs away in a brown *gandoura* seemed to be smiling at me as we talked. Because he was slightly walleyed, I couldn't be certain. I had grown used, by now, to deflecting sidelong come-ons from perfect strangers, and I ignored him. Finally, he came over and sat down.

Mostopha seemed to know him. They began to talk in Arabic.

"He says he saw you in the square the other night."

It was the *ganbri* player from the Genowa troupe in the *djema*. I hadn't recognized him in the daylight.

"He could see you liked his music," Mostopha said. "He says if you want to watch some night when he's playing for real, he'd like you to see it."

"For real" meant the performance of a *laila*, one of the healing evenings that went on until dawn, with twenty dancers dropping into trances. I said I would like that.

I bought them each a coffee. While they talked, I watched the square. Overhead stray scraps of paper swirled above the rooftops, riding funnels of warm air. After a week of sun the sky looked hazy silver. I shook my head as the paper spiraled higher.

The fast is over, I thought. Now it's going to rain.

CHAPTER FIVE

Electric Minarets

*T*hat night I moved my bags into Mostopha's. After dinner I went to bed upstairs on a long banquette softened with sheepskins. The room, lime white and rectangular, had a tall, grated window in one wall that looked down onto a central courtyard. The courtyard was roofless. The rooms of the house all faced it, Roman style.

Several times in the small hours of the morning showers hit the pale tiles downstairs. Imagining the streets swept clean by rain, I woke before dawn and planned an early walk.

When sunlight touched the gratings, I got up, put on a sweater and pants, and slipped the green djellaba into a knapsack. Mostopha had agreed to show me the city's major mosques. Today we were going to visit the legendary Koutoubia. We planned to meet in the *djema* at noon. This left five or six hours free for walking.

That year Barnaby Rogerson had published a good guidebook to Morocco. I had already starred one passage, on a small palace named Dar

Si Sa'id. For some years it had housed the mad younger brother of Bou Ahmed, a nineteenth-century sultan's vizier. This modest building, reportedly exquisite, was said to be joined by tunnels to the enormous Bahia Palace up the street. I rejected Bou Ahmed's Bahia as being too big, too exhausting, therefore pointless, and drew a line at the idiot's smaller apartments. These days the Dar Si Sa'id was a museum.

The only way out of Mostopha's house was by the big front door, a three-inch slab of ancient wood with rusty steel jambs, slung so low you had to duck to get through it. There was a bolt lock on the inside and a loose knocker without, of heavy iron, forged into the shape of a woman's hand. Unless you pulled the bolt back very gently, the knocker rattled. I was still working the door when a hand touched my shoulder.

"*Un moment.*"

Ibrahim, Mostopha's teenage son, pointed past the door into the alley. His lids were still crusted with sleep. He crouched to the floor to tie his laces. He was coming with me.

The rains had worked a quick change in the alley. What had been a hardpan lane was now slick mire. In the low spots, patched with stone, puddles brimmed over. The byway was very narrow—an adult could reach out and touch both walls in certain places—and right now it resembled a long sluice: trickling during a light, dawn shower, but with the means to flood at any time. It meant the maze of alleys farther on, connecting Mostopha's home to Mostopha's shop, would be a mud bog. This time I was glad to have a guide.

We walked a hundred yards to a forking path, but rain had turned the shorter route into an impasse. We returned with muddy cuffs through a pink arched gate, taking a back way into the bazaars.

Near Mostopha's shop we reached high ground, and Ibrahim left me. I struck out on my own toward the *djema*. Rue Semarine was a cobbled thoroughfare, but even this main artery was empty. A stray cat fed on refuse in a corner. Far away I heard a radio.

The rain had stopped, and broken spears of light fell through the trellis. Close to the square a few bazaars were opening for business. I passed three adjoining kaftan shops with hangered garments hung high in the doors. Inside each shop stood a single man—one bronze, one black, one white, the three main races of Morocco.

The bronze man's lineage went back at least three thousand years. His people were indigenous Berber tribesmen. Like Qadisha's parents, many worked small farms throughout the hill country. Today they made up 40 percent of the population. They spoke their own language, in three main dialects. Some knew French and Arabic as well.

The white man one stall over was an Arab, descended from the millions of Caucasians who came here from Arabia in the seventh century, bearing the Qur'an and Arabic. Compared with the Berbers, they were new arrivals, though not nearly so recent as the blacks.

The blacks were brought north as slaves, from the Niger River, beginning in the sixteenth century. Today many Marrakeshis show Negroid features—a flatter nose, the smoother lips, spring-curled hair. From the beginning the progeny of marriages with slaves were treated as children of the household and regarded as Moroccans. Intermarriage was not an unusual affair. Even at the palace some of the great sultans have been jet black. Today I saw no distinctions based on skin color. A rich man, a poor man, a cabinet official might be any color.

There was nothing extraordinary about these vendors. Men like them worked side by side all day and often were family or blood relations throughout the country.

The *djema* was in transition. The rain had washed away the dust; the night troupes and musicians were packing up now. Meanwhile basket ladies and grilled-meat vendors had started setting up their stalls and wooden tables. In one corner a family of snake charmers brewed their morning tea. They drank it while seated on wooden boxes with air holes poked in the sides and heavy locks. Only one café was serving at this hour. I sat down on the terrace and ordered coffee. As the waiter returned, I saw Brahim wave from across the square, then come toward me.

He had a man about seventy on his arm, in a white and gold turban. Shaped like a fireplug, this man was anything but frail. Halfway across the *djema* he broke into a grin, dislodged himself from Brahim's arm, and strode to the table. Brahim introduced him. They sat down.

Si Hadj Mallek had been to Mecca several times. According to Brahim, the man was *hafiz* Qur'an, meaning that he had learned the whole book by heart. Si Mallek spoke fractured French, but he started right in on me. First I was welcomed to Dar al-Islam, then I was quizzed—the usual opening I met with as a Westerner, half-charitable, half-testing, a quick run-through of the Muslim fundamentals and a shield against impostors. As he ticked off Islam's five pillars, I managed the appropriate replies.

Si Mallek gave short shrift to three pillars: Ramadan (the fourth) was over; the pilgrimage (the fifth) was still a few months off; almsgiving (the third) took a backseat to prayer and declaring God's Oneness.

> *Qul huw-Allahu Ahad,*
> *Allahu-samad,*
> *lam yalid wa lam yoolad,*
> *wa lam yakun*
> *lahoo kufuwan ahad.*

> *Say: He is God,*
> *The One, unique*
> *Whom no one forgoes,*
> *Whom everyone is seeking.*
> *The One never born*
> *Who never gave birth,*
> *The One beyond compare.*

Si Mallek sang the lines and raised two fingers. I knew the words of the Ikhlas, they were famous, but his exposition eluded me. It was gently insistent, with many mentions of the number two. I glanced at Brahim when it was over.

"He's saying that everything but Allah comes in pairs. Good and bad; life and death; the poor, the rich. Even our families are divided. He says that on earth the sweet note and the sour note play together. We have wars and we have surrender. Nothing is hopeless. Nothing lasts forever. All life comes in twos, except the heart."

Si Mallek, I decided, was a mystic. The quoted verses were straight from the Qur'an, but equating Allah with the heart was a Sufi image. Its content went beyond orthodoxy. Or might have. Si Mallek moved quickly.

From Oneness he turned to prayer, for it was Friday, and he wanted, I think, to be sure I knew my lines. He started by repeating the Fatihah, the prologue to the Qur'an, which even Mostopha's unschooled daughter knew. He flushed like a tickled infant when I joined in. Then he motioned me to stand and perform the prostrations.

"Right here?"

Si Mallek nodded with enthusiasm. The terrace was still deserted. I stood up, flustered, and turned to Brahim.

"He says don't pray. Just go through the movements. He has something to show you."

I stood and placed my right hand on my left above the navel. I bowed at the waist and set my hands on my knees, forming right angles. From this position I sank down to the ground, then doubled over, touching my forehead to the tiles. "Alif, dhal, mim," Si Mallek said.

The words he pronounced were Arabic letters, corresponding to *a, d, m* in English. Prostrate on the terrace, I looked up.

"Alif, dhal, mim," Brahim repeated. "Adam."

The old man asked Brahim for pen and paper. Brahim had the pen. They called to a waiter, who brought a napkin. Looping on a pair of wire-rimmed glasses, Si Mallek set down stick figure drawings of the positions. When he finished, the napkin looked like this:

Beside the figures he had put letters.

As I took in the drawing, Si Mallek's face appeared ready to go to pieces from sheer pleasure. Brahim beamed, too; I'm not sure why. Did *they* see what I saw? Did they know that after a year of lip-synched Arabic, I had finally been given more than a stiff translation? All at once I was being informed that the words I had learned by rote *were contained in a larger word spelled out with the body,* a word I could read and make sense of: the collective name of Man.

The implications were astounding to me. If flesh could be formed into writing, did that not make the world a book? And if so, what sort of book was it? Were we sentences in it, as we sat here? And who would read it? Who *could* read it? Who was turning the pages?

Brahim interrupted. "He says you should think about this at the mosque today."

I got up from the terrace.

Si Mallek was already on his feet. We shook hands, and I watched them move away, growing smaller quickly as they crossed the *djema.*

The Dar Si Sa'id Palace lay in a carpet souk twenty blocks away. A palace wall formed one side of the alley. Over this, merchants draped their rugs. There were knotted Tazenakht carpets from the highlands, with vivid lozenges and diamond peaks, and fine kilims from the Middle Atlases, employing motifs I'd seen on plates in Qadisha's kitchen. There were woven Rabats of living room dimensions, based on thirteenth-century Persian patterns. The carpets hung within easy reach. The street was closed to traffic. I might have been walking through an open air museum.

This neighborhood had not always been so calm. A block away, in 1907, a French physician named Muchamp had wired a radio aerial to his rooftop. The appearance of this "electric minaret" raised the suspicion of local businessmen. Muchamp, one of a half dozen Frenchmen in the city, was noted for his commercial acumen. A few days later a mob of merchants marched to his door, claiming (rightly) that with his device Muchamp could divine the price of goods still on the dock at Essaouria and so strike deals before their arrival here. Muchamp was accused of sorcery, too, and hung by the neck for meddling and witchcraft.

This event had major consequences, providing France the pretext it had sought to occupy Morocco. A first fleet reached Casablanca two months later. It took five years to conquer Marrakesh.

Bou Ahmed, across the street in the Bahia Palace, was at the height of his reign when Muchamp was hanged; his idiot brother lay in the Dar Si Sa'id. I went in for a peek, but the grandeur was wasted on me. If the plaster faience was any good (a lot of the late work is clumsy), I could not judge. My head was too full of Si Mallek's words and drawings.

The one item that struck me was a cape.

Pinned open on a board in a display case, its prominent feature was the scalloped shoulders, which when the wearer stretched his arms, would make him look exactly like a bat man. Shepherds wore this garment in a part of the mountains dotted with many caves. The museum card called it a bird cape, suggesting that the huge eye at its center "probably served to ward off diving hawks." The rest of the cloth was dyed deep orange. The color scheme convinced me the card was in error. Anyone could see by its Halloween outlines that the cape had been cut to protect a man from bats.

✧   ✧   ✧   ✧

As I walked back to the square to meet Mostopha, the spare Koutoubia tower marked my way. This minaret, the city's tallest structure, has formed the town's hub since its construction in 1158. The Koutoubia takes its name from a bookseller's market that once stood here. It has a twin, the more famous Giralda, in Seville. As I approached, the three hundred feet of stone came and went around corners, dived behind walls, reemerged looking larger than ever, and doubled in size every few blocks. Each of its four huge faces has a unique decorative scheme, so that sometimes, reappearing at a new angle, I took it for a different minaret. This morning I felt an irrational urge to get up in it.

Mostopha was at a table when I reached the Genowa café. He showed me back into the tiny kitchen, where a teapot of warm water sat on the cookstove. After making our ablutions, I drew the green djellaba from my sack and slipped it on. The fabric covered the street mud spattering my knees. I felt immediately pristine. As we turned to leave, I remembered the prayer cap in my pocket. I put it on my head. Mostopha frowned.

He adjusted the cap's edge lower on my forehead.

"Why do you want to wear something like that?"

Men often wore caps at the mosques in California.

He said, "That's different. Here people wear them to prove something. They wear perfume or a pair of fancy slippers; they put on a cap, and they think it makes them better Muslims. On a foreigner it's worse. He buys the wrong cap. It makes him look like a tourist."

"Is this a tourist cap?" I asked.

"No, it's a good one."

I removed the cap. We left the café and crossed the square.

We were soon near enough the minaret to have to crane our necks to see the top. It resembled a landlocked lighthouse, or a military watchtower. Its first three floors were occupied by cloisters. The height of the sills would afford good views, I thought. I wondered whether hermetic scholars still used them. Perhaps a huge Qur'an stood at one of the windows. It reminded me of Thomas Merton's poem:

> *The monks come down the cloister*
> *With robes as voluble as water.*
> *I do not see them but I hear their waves.*

The inner courtyard of the mosque is different from Ben Yusef's. It looked broader and more open, and the reflecting pool was vast. The Koutoubia is one of Africa's great landmarks. But because it stands outside the *medina,* its buildings look stranded. The surrounding land is covered by a park with many paths, where the heads of huge cypresses hang nodding.

The prayer hall inside the building was a forest of white pillars. Six feet square at the bottom, set on piers, each pair of columns tapered to a massive horseshoe arch. The arches were everywhere. I stopped counting at one hundred. They interlocked in ranks to hold up ceilings and split the floor in checkered squares. Viewed on a diagonal, they formed dozens of telescoping tunnels. Straight on they created horizontal aisles. I never succeeded in analyzing the secret of these perspectives. My wife had once tried from a photograph to work it out on canvas and given up.

Several thousand people sat in rows between the columns. Mostopha and I found a patch of carpet at the rear and settled down. I made an attempt to collect my thoughts, but it was difficult. Over the public-address system a group of qurra was chanting verses with terrible vigor. *Qurra* are professional reciters trained in special schools to chant the Qur'an. Their phrases came out punctuated by crisp percussive explosions, like rattled teeth. The effect was riveting. When the chatter ceased, my head was ringing.

A moment later everyone in the hall was on his feet, lifted like a body on a wave. The imam began reciting the Fatihah. Each man repeated the prayer to himself, in a whisper, and then we moved en masse through the *salat.*

Today I performed the prostrations with greater clarity. My word-for-word grasp of the prayers had been blurred before, by phonetic approximation and stiff translation. Now, thanks to Si Mallek, I possessed an overview. The old man had cut me a perfect mental window. Through it I could look out on the crowd and read the word we were spelling. It was one more means to grasp the shape of prayer.

✧   ✧   ✧   ✧

Being by this time Mostopha's guest, I lunched in his *sala* every afternoon and slept there every night. It was the largest room in the house and the family's social center. It also held their only television. When I suggested that my occupancy might be an imposition, it took some time to explain the remark to Qadisha. The concepts of imposition and guest did not seem to cohabit in the Berber language. In fact, my question puzzled everyone.

I slept well on the sheepskins. I went walking every morning in the souks. When I returned from these outings around lunchtime, Raschid, Mostopha's second son, would often meet me in the courtyard with a water bowl and towel to clean my hands. Then we and his brother Ibrahim, Mostopha, and Qadisha bearing the infant Yusef on her back would go upstairs and settle on banquettes. Nishwa had usually preceded us. She liked my quarters and passed a lot of time there, singing and drawing.

Today Ibrahim was in the *sala,* too, playing with my shortwave radio.

I had lent it to him during the day, to help improve his English. We ate lunch and listened to music. After a while Mostopha told a story.

After his mother's death, he said, he'd been sent to his grandparents' farm in the country. This was the usual collection of rammed-earth huts and houses where a handful of large, tribal families farmed and lived. His grandfather Yusef, a big man with a white beard, had owned the first radio there. It ran off two six-pound batteries, each with its positive and negative cables. The batteries were expensive and did not last long. The aerial was tacked to a beam in a manger. The old man hooked up the receiver twice a week: on Friday afternoons for *jum'a* prayer and on Sunday nights for the news from Casablanca. On these occasions, before he turned it on, forty men from the hills were called to listen.

Technology arrived late to Morocco. Dry cell receivers were state-of-the-art in 1950. In 1980, Mostopha bought his first TV. By then the *medina* rooftops were thick with aerials. Many mountain villages had them, too. Ten years later he owned a VCR and thought nothing of it. He and his friends might wear togas and pray in thousand-year-old mosques, but the glow from their windows at night was modern.

For about a year his set had been hooked to a French cable network that carried movies, travelogues, and world news. It also brought the occasional bare nipple into his *sala*. France is a topless country, its advertisements and musicals are racier than most, and nudity does not end at the neckline. God knows how this affected the Muslim psyche of Morocco. I had passed, one day in the New Town, a pornographic movie house of the sort one finds in every Western city. The marquee announced *Les Plaisirs Interdits*. The ticket booth was empty. The stills in the glass display case had been doctored with tape.

Mostopha dealt with nipples very simply: he had a remote control for switching channels. When a breast or haunch appeared, he flicked a button. Temptation dissolved into a soccer game.

We watched a lot of soccer, and we often watched cartoons. Nishwa loved these mostly American vintage shorts featuring Popeye, Daffy Duck, or Uncle Scrooge. From France came Babar, the elephant-child adopted into a classic bourgeoise family. I never tired of Babar's comic predicament. It was, somehow, a mirror image of my own. Nishwa and I formed a rapid bond through this program.

In a matter of days I forgot about hotels. Qadisha's meals were the best I had ever eaten in Morocco. Their scheduled appearances put new order in my life, and the bed and board saved a certain amount of money. Most important, I felt at home. Even at the foot of the Atlases, in a land of dates and honey, the need for simple relations can sap you dry. Mostopha's bustling household kept me from pining away for my family. I chipped in for food. I brought the children sweets.

CHAPTER SIX

The Book of the World

Despite the rains, the town was growing hotter day by day, and many people began to take siestas. With a home to go to now, I did the same.

The hours after lunch were good for reading. The plates and trays would disappear downstairs. Mostopha returned to his shop, the boys to school, and the *sala* became quiet. Then I could gather my books around me and lie on the banquettes.

Nishwa would sometimes join me, too, climbing upstairs in a sweatshirt with HEAVYWEIGHT emblazoned on the chest, bearing a pint-size backpack of coloring books and crayons. Spreading her things on the wooden dining table, she would start to scribble, like a student preparing for exams.

I had some boning up to do myself. Si Mallek's revelations at the café had turned a set of tumblers in my thinking. The new information required consolidation. I resolved to use this time to order my thoughts about Islam, to come up, if possible, with my own sense of what mattered. The necessary materials were all in the Qur'an, a lot of it packed into one chapter.

The position of the Qur'an in Islam is akin to that of Jesus for a Christian. In Islam the book is the miracle. While the Gospels aspire to history, establishing a record and a context, the voice of the Qur'an is always God's. In contrast to his message, the prophet Muhammad was a mortal. He worked for a living, married, had children, established a faith, and died at sixty-two. Every step of his life has been recorded. His words and deeds are considered a guide by modern Muslims, and yet the book comes first. In place of the Word incarnate we have what might be called the Voice *inlibrate*. The Qur'an is considered Muhammad's only miracle. Nothing in Islam is more revered.

Chapter 2, "Al-Baqarah," contains all the essential meanings of the religion. It is the longest section, line for line, and topically the richest. Some say the grace derived from its recitation equals the other chapters put together. In classrooms all over Marrakesh children only a little older than Nishwa sit chanting "Al-Baqarah" every day, repeating its verses, chalking them on hand-held blackboards until they have the whole chapter by heart. It occupied forty pages in my translation.

Today I proposed to start with verse 255. Ayat al-Kursi, the famous Throne Verse, evokes in seven lines the majesty of God. But when I leafed toward it, I stumbled first on verse 136:

> *We believe in God*
> *and in what has been sent down to us,*
> *what has been revealed to Abraham and Ishmael*
> *and Isaac and Jacob and their offspring,*
> *and what was given to Moses and to Jesus*
> *and all the other prophets by the Lord.*
> *We make no distinction among them.*

Islam, a more recent extension of the Jewish and Christian traditions, sees itself as their continuer. That is,

The Qur'an is not a story that was forged.
It is the confirmation of what preceded it.

Two thirds of its chapters contain allusions to the Bible and its heroes. Adam, Noah, Lot, Jonah, Moses, Aaron, David, Enoch, as well as John the Baptist, Jesus, and Mary are frequently mentioned. In this particular passage the lines make plain that Allah and the Lord of the Flood are identical. This is not a literary trope. Muslims I spoke with on the streets explicitly acknowledged Islam's lineage. Jesus' name was never mentioned without a reverential "peace be upon him." People spoke in one breath of Muhammad and Abraham. They perceived Islam as the last in a series of covenants.

Children of Israel . . . keep your pledge to me,
and I will keep mine to you. Heed me,
and believe what I have sent you,
which verifies what is already with you.

The Qur'an is a book that comments on itself. It was "sent as guidance," a "perspicuous" message counseling "temperance" and "patience" in hard times and presenting God as nearer to man "than your jugular." It was not God that remained remote but the minds of people.

The Qur'an is an unstemmed outpouring of words. Muslims sometimes call it the Bible's final chapters. If that is so, the Narrator has closed a lot of ground with man since Job. This is not a godhead loathe to speak, as in the Torah, nor in any need of goading. The Voice is "inside your ear." The task of understanding lies with the hearer.

Let there be no compulsion in religion.
The way is clear.
He who turns from evil
and believes in God holds fast
to a handle, strong, unbreakable.

A second passage caught my eye as I lay reading. It spoke of a correspondence between the universe and knowledge, a correspondence partly obscured, like the fan of a peacock half hidden behind a rock. The passage has two parts:

> *Creation of the heavens and the earth,*
> *the alternation of night and day,*
> *and sailing ships that cross the ocean*
> *with what is useful to man,*
> *the rain that God sends from the sky, enlivening*
> *the earth that was dead,*
> *and the scattering of beasts of all kind upon it,*
> *the changing of the winds,*
> *and the clouds that remain*
> *obedient between the earth and sky,*
> *are surely signs . . .*

The first ten lines have a Whitmanesque roll. The eleventh line sent me scurrying to my notebooks in search of a quotation. It was only a single sentence from Emel Esin's *Mecca the Blessed, Madinah the Radiant*. It expresses a relation between the world and a book. Si Mallek's napkin drawing had pointed in this direction, too, but Esin's observation was more alarming. It ascribes to the Qur'an a description of the world as

> *a book, of which man can see the writing,*
> *but cannot understand the meaning.*

Esin did not cite chapter and verse, but I recognized the general point of view. It proposes a world populated by spiritual illiterates, men tantalized by imagery that they can read but not quite comprehend. The peacock is there, behind the rock. The eye affirms its feathers. The mind cannot quite get round the vision. It is a conundrum out of Borges: "The outer world—forms, temperature, the moon—is a language we humans have forgotten, or which we can scarcely distinguish. . . ."

An abyss of meaninglessness in the face of signs, a human grammar opposed to nature's syntax—it typifies the fate of Western man. As Saint Paul said, we see *per speculum in aenigmate*, "in mystery by means of a mirror," "through a glass darkly."

The Qur'an proposes the world itself as a route through this conundrum. Everything in it, every process, every object and event contains the secrets of its own creation—a surprisingly modern, scientific notion. People have eyes to see the signs that Allah shows them "on the horizon and in themselves." Imparting a shape to which life's mysteries conform—that, in Borges's view, is God's real business:

> What is a divine mind? the reader will perhaps inquire. There is not a theologian who does not define it; I prefer an example. The steps a man takes . . . trace in time an inconceivable figure. The Divine Mind intuitively grasps that form immediately, as men do a triangle. This figure (perhaps) has its given function in the economy of the universe.

The Qur'an positions itself at the heart of this matter: *ayat,* the Quranic term for "verse," is also a common word for "sign." The double meaning sets each of its lines on a parallel plane with the truths of nature. One of the Qur'an's many attributives for God is al-Haqq: "the Truth," "Reality," "the Way Things Are." This was the divine face I was after, not a bearded figure in the clouds.

My first interview with Si Mallek shook up my passivity as a novice and shed new light on the meaning of *salat.*

Later I discovered he was a tailor. Now and then when I passed his shop, I stopped to chat, but I did not seek him out to be my teacher. I wasn't in the market for a teacher. I preferred whatever my strolls delivered to me. (They had, after all, delivered up Si Mallek.) I saw myself as poking around in a gold mine, striking rich veins here and there and entertained between times.

The Teacher Who Knows and the ones who don't seemed fated to make awful chemistry, and I wanted to avoid the combination. I did not want to place myself in someone else's hands. Not that Si Mallek had offered himself in a role, but I was chary and preferred to follow my instincts. I was traveling, and I gave myself up to travel, to the countless twisting lanes of the *medina* and to the signs that popped up as I moved along. Si Mallek in his turban was such a sign, and I felt grateful, but to crouch beside a post because it offered good directions seemed misguided, especially in a place so full of signals.

> *The scattering of beasts of all kinds upon it,*
> *and the changing of the winds . . .*
> *Wherever you turn,*
> *Allah's face is there.*

I resolved to spend more time in the *medina*. I thought I would keep up my reading, too.

✧   ✧   ✧   ✧

I glanced up from the book and found Nishwa sleeping. Sunlight slanted through the window gratings. As I put on my sandals, I could hear the *adhan,* the call to prayer, coming from Ben Yusef's minaret. It was after four o'clock. I went downstairs.

The bazaars lay a few blocks away, and I reached Mostopha's shop in about five minutes. Across the way Sharif stood working with a wooden pole, lifting down jackets from the wall racks. A nail protruded from the pole, on which he hooked each garment. This was standard drill when locking a shop. Mostopha had already closed his doors. He stood waiting with impatience for Sharif.

"We're going to the Mouassin mosque for *'asr,"* he told me. "Do you want to come?"

'Asr is the third of the five prayer hours. The Mouassin was said to be a gem. Largely hidden by surrounding buildings, it gives up little to the passer-by. In a square to one side, however, stands an impressive three-bayed fountain, hinting at greater things inside. I jumped at the invitation.

"Sharif has a lot jackets," Mostopha sighed.

Brahim waved me to a wooden stool, and we sat watching the tardy Sharif haul down his goods. It was terribly silent. He worked with his back to us.

Brahim asked where I had gone for the *jum'a* prayer. I said to the Koutoubia, and mentioned the chanting I had heard there.

"What chanting?"

"As we were coming in. Ten or fifteen men, over loudspeakers."

"That *merde?*" he whispered. "It should be forbidden. It isn't sunna."

Brahim had lamblike, exophthalmic eyes and did not swear much. I inched my stool closer.

"The Prophet did not sing before the prayer," he said. "Then why should we? This is *bid'a:* 'adding on ideas invented after Muhammad died.' It isn't right. God gave Muhammad the straight way; Muhammad gave it to us. What do we need with these innovations?"

"Who hires the *qurra?*"

"How should I know! I think it is done to keep men from making speeches before the prayers. It keeps them from stirring up people politically. I don't think about politics anyway, not in the mosque. That would be *fitna,* you see: 'creating turmoil.' In a mosque one is supposed to think of Allah. This crazy singing makes it hard to do."

I asked where he had gone for the Friday prayer.

"The Koutoubia," he said.

"But I thought—"

"The singing is awful. But the imam's reading of the Qur'an is really good. He shows, by the way he reads, what it really means."

When I looked up, Sharif and Mostopha were heading down the alley. I caught up to them and walked beside Sharif.

Sharif went to the mosque as often as possible. He said that some nights he cried for the years he had wasted drinking wine, and he wanted to make up the lost time. He was also glad to get out of the shop, because working in a shop was "like eating fire." The simile, from the Qur'an, describes the consequence of overcharging customers.

"When a guide with the government badge brings you a tourist," he explained, "he will come back later for a cut. Most of the time they want fifty percent of whatever the customer paid you. Sometimes they take more; it all depends. You work this out beforehand, and the fees are put back on the tourists. It means you may handle more money than God allows."

I asked what was the limit one could handle.

"More than fifty percent and you're eating fire! I don't own this shop. I have no choice. I want a little cart where I just sell mint leaves."

The guides were often a curse for tourists, too. The worst of them dogged you outside the gates and preyed on your insecurity without mercy. It was true, as they said, that you might be lost without them, but taking one was a losing business, too. You were here, after all, to open up the secrets of Morocco. Whether German, Italian, Japanese, French, or English, you had probably spent too much on your airline tickets. Then, despite the advice of untraveled friends about killer germs and aberrant sexual behavior, you had very possibly brought along your wife. All this counted for nothing. Once inside the market, your guide, if you had a bad one, ignored the real landmarks, intent on visits to shops that paid big commissions. You were dragged along like a piece of bleeding meat through a white shark's gullet and wound up opening nothing but your wallet.

I found the guide subject boring—it was all most tourists discussed here and one of my reasons for avoiding them. I did not want to discuss it this afternoon, from any angle, but Sharif had raised it. To relieve his moroseness, I suggested that the existence of guides seemed natural enough; after all, I said, the souks were huge. Foreign business might never reach his door without them. Therefore, it seemed only right that he should pay them. I compared it to the price of advertising.

Sharif winced.

*T*hat night Mostopha asked if I had liked the Mouassin mosque.

"It was beautiful," I said. The cool galleries, the hand-decorated ceilings recalled Ben Yusef's.

Mostopha agreed that it was beautiful. "But did you like it?"

I said I had liked it.

"I didn't like it," he said. "The only people who go there own big shops, or they are *shorfa*, descendants of the Prophet. They try to outdo each other with fine djellabas. I know every one of them. I know this building, too. The place was built after a plague on a Jewish cemetery. Later on they were fixing the foundations and dug up some bones. A lot of Jews got angry. Even now some people won't go near it. The *shorfa* only go because they built it. The rich men follow the *shorfa* because they are blessed."

I wasn't sure how much of this to believe. Moroccans were exceptionally gifted storytellers. At the drop of a hat many had the skill to shore up private views with a rich supply of brilliant detail. The more you were after the truth, of course, the more this talent colored your reflections. Just when you suspected ulterior motives, your informant was apt to slip in a luminous detail, a bone, a plague-ridden city, to win you over. Having taken a personal interest in the mosques of Marrakesh, I checked Mostopha's tale against Rogerson's guidebook. Here is what I found:

> Right at the crossroads and 150m down rue Mouassin is the Mouassin Mosque, a monumental building established by the Saadian Sultan Abdullah el Ghalib in 1560 complete with baths, *medersa* and exterior fountain. The Mosque has an equivocal local reputation. It is named after a prestigious local *Shorfa* family, but during the building of the foundations a 14th-century Jewish plague cemetery was unearthed. This is considered to have reduced the sanctity of the site and rumors of a curse, released in disturbing the grave of a Cabbalist rabbi, began to circulate.

Either Rogerson had interviewed Mostopha, or the Cabala was alive and well in Marrakesh.

In the course of showing Qadisha my family photos, it came out that my wife is Italian. Tonight Qadisha reflected this fact at dinner: the main dish was spaghetti, Moroccan style. It tasted delicious, though not Roman. The gesture kept us chuckling for an hour.

While Raschid cleared away the dishes, I unboxed Sharif's cassette of the American evangelist Jimmy Swaggart. I had picked it up at his shop that afternoon. It was a copy of a show taped off a TV in Kuwait. A pilgrim had brought the original back from Mecca. The grainy picture, broken up in spots by bursts of light, attested to how often it had been dubbed. On the label, hand-printed in Arabic and English, Swaggart's name was spelled Gimi Swagarte.

The tape had been made at the height of Swaggart's fame as a TV preacher. During this time his sermons were being aired around the globe on a budget of a million dollars daily. The funds derived, it seemed to me, from huge donations by rich white southern crackers mixed with millions of nickels and dimes mailed in by trailer park Christians from places like Des Moines. He was another tarnished apple in the buck-mad Christian barrel. When he was photographed with a prostitute one night at a cheap motel in Georgia, no one was shocked. The media ground him to powder. (*Penthouse* interviewed the woman in question; her contract included a photographic spread.) By the end of the year the case was forgotten by everyone but Swaggart. He continued to do penance on the airwaves.

Sharif's cassette intrigued me because it was Sharif's. In California, I would not have watched it. In Morocco it acquired weird appeal. The program reprised the high points of a debate between Swaggart and Ahmed Deedat, an eloquent South African imam. The debate took place in a Cape Town hall. The audience, mostly Muslim, posed questions to both men, on a theme. The theme was the validity of the Bible. Deedat proved fluent in English and deeply witty; Swaggart appeared dogmatic and worn down, perhaps by jet lag. Deedat knew his biblical citations; Swaggart rarely mentioned the Qur'an. This was unfortunate. It allowed Deedat to typify the New Testament as an encyclopedic work by numerous authors, based on hearsay. The reverend's rebuttal was weak and uninformed. He lost the point. When it came to Christ's divinity, he failed completely.

We watched the debate from beginning to end. It appeared to be a victory for Islam. The forces of modern technology had been placed at Allah's service. Deedat defeated Swaggart hands down. If the beauty of a man is in his tongue, then Deedat was beautiful, but I could not imagine what would make the cassette illegal in Morocco.

"Who told you it was illegal?" Mostopha asked.

"Sharif."

"Ah, Sharif. Did you see him at the mosque today?"

I said I'd prayed next to Sharif. Of course, I had seen him.

Mostopha stood up. He spread his feet a yard apart, threw back his head, squinched his eyes, and clasped his arms below the chest like Rodin's sculpture of Balzac. It was a melodramatic parody of Sharif's prayer posture. I had to laugh.

"I've known Sharif for years," Mostopha said. "I like him. But as a Muslim he's just walked through the door. He's on the ground floor, but he wants you to think he lives in the penthouse. He thinks if he looks pious, people will reward him—maybe with a good job and lots of money. People watch him, but they see with different eyes. They see a man in a hurry, who takes up too much room at the mosque and talks like an imam at all the wrong moments. He gives you this tape and says its the only copy in the city. A friend of mine brought me this tape four years ago. I made a few copies and passed them around. Other people made copies of the copies. Finally, one gets back to Sharif. All of a sudden the tape is *interdit* and Sharif is the keeper of state secrets. His brain is the size of a baby's, like a peanut." Mostopha shook his head. "His brain is working harder than his heart."

I was caught off guard by the strength of this invective. "Does his name mean he's really *shorfa?*" I asked.

"If he wasn't, who would put up with him? They're allowed to be a bit crazy because they're holy."

This was true. Some people even said that if a *sharif* drinks wine, the liquor turns to honey in his mouth because of his blood links to the Prophet. No one I met believed this, least of all Sharif, but the title counted.

Mostopha said, "There are many kinds of *shorfa*. Five centuries ago if you had the money, you could buy a decree that made you a *sharif*. After that all your descendants were *shorfa*, too. Who knows what kind of *sharif* Sharif is? My wife Qadisha's family all are *shorfa*."

"They are?"

Mostopha nodded. "Her uncle Omar Adnas can heal children. I'm sure he's as much of the *shorfa* as Sharif."

This information shut me up completely.

An hour later I lay in bed, dialing my way through a hive of shortwave stations. In theory shortwave reception is best at night. The signals are bounced off charged particles in earth's ionosphere; and sunspots are disruptive. Marrakesh upset even this theory. It was midnight and I could not bring in London. The receiver's tiny red tuning light came and went in the darkness but refused to hold the station for more than a minute. Perhaps we were too near the desert. Perhaps the mountains interfered. I settled for Dakar and fell asleep.

I woke much later in the night. The radio was still playing. I cursed the waste of batteries and was reaching to switch it off when I heard a snatch of guitar that felt familiar. Adjusting the volume, I finally placed the music: a cut from an old recording by Frank Zappa's Mothers of Invention. Zappa's cogent mayhem could be beguiling; he did not let me down in Marrakesh. As a warm wind blew past the grating, Jimmy Carl Black ("the Indian of the group") joined Frank for a chorus:

> *Out, out through the summer breezes*
> *To the place where they keep the imaginary diseases.*

I thought of Qadisha's uncle healing children in the Atlas Mountains. I thought of Jimmy Swaggart. I thought of home.

CHAPTER SEVEN

A Parliament of Birds

*I*slept upstairs in the TV room, the largest in the house. It was not the only available bunk, however. My *sala* faced a smaller chamber across the hall, a tidy, blue cubby with double windows and nothing much in it but a few birdcages and a bed. A poster in French and Arabic pinned to a wall depicted a homing pigeon from three angles, with detailed information about the bird. Mostopha had once raised pigeons by the flock. When we met, in 1979, the room and its window loft had been aflutter with a dozen varieties from Belgium, Britain, and France, as well as a large collection of songbirds. Gradually he had sold these creatures off and now possessed a single yellow canary. The room's sole tenant, this male bird lived in a lath cage by the windows. His voice was sweet. His trills began at dawn.

I woke with the bird and often left the house before six-thirty. No market stalls were open at this hour; the lanes lay vacant. I could choose a fresh direction without hurry. Later on, when the streets began to fill, the *medina* developed capillary pressure—the wider alleys swelled with shoppers and the pumping action of many feet swept one along. If you knew

where you were going, the flow provided free propulsion. If not, you
wound up in a backwater, cut off.

One day I set out to visit the Ben Yusef *medersa*. Built in the 1300s, around
the time of Cambridge, this school once formed the southern link in a great
chain of colleges stretching across the Maghreb as far as Tunis. These
"houses of knowledge" were the earliest centers of learning in the kingdom.
Logical extensions of the mosque, their teaching methods shared some
ground with the Greek *Mouseion*, where dialogue formed the principle
mode of instruction. The *medersa*s also functioned as boarding schools. A
full-time student might pursue a complex course of study divided between
theology and science.

Ben Yusef was not the first *medersa* in Morocco, but by 1565 it was
the largest. Its simple, sky-lit cubicles housed nine hundred students in its
heyday. They lived here for up to six years, on stipends or at a minimal
tuition, receiving instruction from professors whose posts were philan-
thropically endowed. During summer vacations students wandered the
countryside, reciting the Qur'an at village fairs.

The line between student and teacher was often blurred in a *medersa*.
The same man might have a certificate in mathematics, give daily lectures
on scripture, and be pursuing studies in the law. Even the ripest scholars
attended lectures by notable colleagues at other schools throughout the
Middle East. This peripatetic system helped make knowledge public all over
the kingdom.

The Ben Yusef *medersa* was active for six hundred years. For most of
its history, the school sat kitty-corner to its mosque. After independence in
the 1950s, it moved to a modern campus across town. The original site has
been preserved as a museum.

I was told to knock at a wooden door beneath a covered arch in a
corkscrew alley. I passed the low door twice before I found it. Another
caller, a Moroccan vacationist from Fez, preceded me through a narrow,
sky-lit passage. Ten yards down the hall there stood a desk. At the desk sat
an official, squinting beneath a yellow turban. A money box yawned before
him. One hand rested on ticket roll.

"American?"

"Yes."

"You have come a long way," he said.

I passed down a marble hall into a spacious, open courtyard. A pool lay at its center, and mosaics ringed the walls. The second floor was screened with wooden galleries. Upstairs lay several floors of students' quarters set in groups of four around a stairwell. These rooms were wood lined, small in scale, with cedar lofts for sleep and storage. The atmosphere felt cool, subdued by Moroccan standards, unpuritanical. It looked like a reasonable place for a long vacation, and the tile decorations were unique. Amid the usual semifloral patterns I picked out shapes that definitely were dolphins, griffins, small heraldic eagles. Skylights overhung stairwells and fountains played below.

The corridors between the rooms were long and narrow, unbroken at times for thirty yards. On either wall, just below the ceiling, ran lacily carved bands of sacred verse. I followed these calligraphic friezes around three corners. I climbed more steps. Upstairs they continued, first in cursive, then in Maghrebi, flowing along like pages in a book.

Maghrebi writing was first developed in Andalusian Spain in the 800s. Distinctively North African, it preserves a blend of ancient Kufic with the "new" Omayyad script. The blockish Kufic resembles German Gothic; the agile Naskhi cursive flows like brushwork. According to Rogerson, countless other styles had evolved through the ages: graceful Taliq from Persia; the squat Riqa of the Turks; Tughra, a cryptic Tatar version; Ottoman Diwani, richly oppulent; Sayaquit, the secret script of Seljuk clerks. There was even a style called Ghober, designed for the tiny messages borne by pigeons, which required a magnifying glass to read.

This calligraphic tradition is vast and unexcelled in its subtlety. Not only does it embody the divine word, but it conveys a visual rhythm on the verse and supplies inexhaustible decorative richness. The Topkapi Palace alone contains two hundred thousand manuscripts. The Taj Mahal houses priceless Qur'ans, whose beauties lie mirrored in the walls around them. In Marrakesh, too, the building and the book go hand in hand.

I suddenly wished Sharif were here to see this. His urgent dream to escape the fires of commerce seemed part and parcel of the building's spirit. Peeking down on the courtyard through a screen, I looked into a forest of white pillars. Their trunks had been polished by centuries of teachers leaning back to question and address. It seemed a shame for the place to be closed down. Sharif with his hyperactive brain might have made a good scholar in the old days. I wondered whether he ever came here now.

The lunar year rolled backward as the warm weather came on. Now that Ramadan was finished, the hadj, that other engine of the Muslim calendar, began turning over. The rite would not take place until July, but a pilgrimage required preparation. The three-thousand-mile journey from Morocco to Saudi Arabia involved visas, reservations, and other arrangements. For many these plans were already afoot, and the hadj was becoming a topic in the *medina*. Every week the local papers carried more full-page advertisements for flights to Mecca. I began to meet a few pilgrims in the souk. They all were merchants.

Abd al-Hadi ran an electronics shop a few blocks from the *medersa*. He was fifty-five, a chunky man with baby-smooth skin and a hairline mustache. His store faced a busy square lined with vendors and fruit carts. I passed the place often. His floor stock never changed. In a storefront window misted with red dust were on display his few more modern items— three transistor radios, a videotape machine, two cassette recorders, and a color television. These never sold. Mostopha claimed that the shop did well because Abd al-Hadi could fix whatever you brought him. I never saw him sell a retail item. The real money, you felt, was in repairs.

Indoors, behind a waist-high counter, stacks of used equipment rose to the roof beams, and forests of wiring dangled everywhere. Vintage amplifiers sat balanced on torn speakers at odd angles. Empty TV consoles, rainbows of circuitry poking out the backs, leaned against piled crates of picture tubes. Because the dirham abroad is all but worthless, Moroccans (who save the flints from disposable lighters) do not easily part with imported goods. No matter how outmoded, when a piece of equipment fails, they bring it into stores like Abd al-Hadi's. The entire shop was twenty-five feet square.

Although he went to Mecca often, Abd al-Hadi was only marginally well off. Unable to take much profit from his shop, he paid for the journeys by acting as a guide to first-time pilgrims. This year, for instance, he had three women, a trio of rich sisters, lined up as clients. He was still arranging their plane tickets when we met. The first week after Ramadan, I found him filling out visa applications, which he posted the next day to Rabat. The following week he proudly showed me a return-mail packet of beribboned papers. I naturally took an interest in all this, having as yet no visa of my own.

I also took an interest in his video collection. Home movies were one of Abd al-Hadi's sidelines. A cork board hung on a nail inside the door, to which were tacked a dozen or so invitations. Abd al-Hadi shot footage of family occasions all over the city. He sold copies of the cassettes to participants and charged a cover fee. He specialized in marriages, it seemed. The day his paperwork arrived, a cassette was playing on a VCR connected to a small screen on the counter. The camera work was jumpy. The audio tracks were good.

The material looked rich enough for a doctoral dissertation. The celebratory sequences were stunning. Balanced on the shoulders of three brothers, the bride bobbed around the room on a legless throne to the shrill blast of three split-reed *raita*s, local oboes. She wore a samite kaftan glittering with gold and silver threads. While the brothers swayed her palanquin and sang, the bride stared ahead with folded arms, her eyes impassive. She wore a two-foot gilded crown, and occasionally the headgear grazed the ceiling. Finally, the music paused, and the bride was lifted down. Then the groom took a turn, riding the raised throne around the *sala*.

I asked Abd al-Hadi about his Mecca clients.

"Very old," he said. "One is blind. None of them has even a living brother. They want to go to Mecca before they die, and I have been there. *Alors*, they bought me a ticket. As their escort."

Like most religious journeys, the hadj has been bound up with trade since it began. I wondered if he would do a little business.

"*Bien sûr*. The oil economy makes equipment cheap there. I'll bring back a couple of cameras, a TV."

I tried to picture Abd al-Hadi leading his trio through the heat waves, shouldering a twenty-one-inch screen. He wrote on a card the name of his hotel in downtown Mecca. I said, *Insha' Allah*, I would look them up.

*   *   *

Abd al-Qadir performed his hadj in 1985. He was a tall, lanky man about my age, with a hangdog face, and he spoke fair English. His skin was a few shades lighter than Swiss chocolate. His immaculate white *gandoura* set this off.

Abd al-Qadir's large bazaar was positioned in the best block of the wide rue Semarine. Here instead of tourist junk he offered Berber carpets and fine jewelry, but it was not his wares that stopped me. It was the music—a solo performance by one canary pouring out its heart from the shop's door. Any good canary can be pleasing; a very good one may inspire awe. This one trilled as precisely as a flute and showed great passion. I paused long enough to admire his song and was soon being led inside for a closer look.

The bamboo cage hung by a chain above a counter. As we approached, Abd al-Qadir cooed. The moment the bird heard this, it fell silent. For a minute or two we stood below and tried to coax it back to singing. Nothing worked.

We backed out of the shop and returned to the doorway. Abd al-Qadir produced a second stool.

I asked where he had come by the canary.

"From a man in the bazaars, not far from here."

"It's a very fine one."

"Yes," he sighed. "I paid too little."

A waiter passed through the crowds with a silver tray. Abd al-Qadir waved him over and ordered coffee. It arrived in tall glasses perfumed with jasmine.

"You are an American?" he asked.

"Yes."

"I've watched you passing here for weeks. You never buy anything. Finally I asked someone about it. They say you are Muslim. I don't think you have come to town to shop."

"No," I said. "I'm staying with friends. I'm on my way to Mecca."

"*Hamdullah!* How long will you stay in Mecca?"

"Three or four weeks," I said.

"Three weeks in Mecca? *No, no, no.*" He tapped a long finger on my wrist. "You stay a few days, you visit the Grand Mosque, then you leave town. The best place to make the hadj from is Madinah."

"Madinah?"

"Yes. When the Meccans ran Muhammad out, the people of Madinah took him in. Muhammad drew up the blueprints for Islam among the Madinans. They are more . . . gentle. If you get the wrong guide in Mecca, he will overcharge you for a glass of water. If you're two blocks from the mosque, he'll put you into a cab just for the money."

"Did it happen to you?"

"No, not to me. I had no *mutawwif.*"

The *mutawwif*s are traditional guides charged with the task of taking care of pilgrims. They are supposed to find you lodgings, provide your food, and lead you through the complicated rites. Their performance is often thought of as desultory. Ibn Battutah and Sir Richard Burton, whose journeys to Mecca were five hundred years apart, complained in similar terms about these guides. Today, Abd al-Qadir said, they were outnumbered. From a few hundred thousand pilgrims in 1940, hadjis now numbered in the millions. The days of one family–one guide were gone forever. In theory, every pilgrim is assigned one. In fact, the guides could not keep up.

I said I thought the guides were there to help.

"Once they were guides," he said. "Now they are institutions, just pieces of paper. Do you know how many Muslims were in Mecca last July?"

I had heard around three million.

Abd al-Qadir shook his head. "More."

Every pilgrim had an opinion about the guides. Some Moroccans praised them and wrote them letters every year, enclosing gifts. Others, like Abd al-Qadir, expressed real malice.

"How did you manage?" I asked.

"I went alone. When I had somewhere to go, I took a taxi."

His basset face looked remarkably calm. His independence impressed me, and I said so.

"But, why? Every pilgrim who makes the hadj is just one person. No law says you have to band together. I had a good hotel room. I had some extra money. *Safi.*"

Safi means "enough." Moroccans use the word to end strong statements.

Having offered this advice, Abd al-Qadir began to outline my itinerary, ticking off stops along the pilgrim's way. He laid them out calmly in their proper order, starting with Mecca, going on to Mina Valley, the Plain of Arafat, then Muzdalifah. It was a route I knew by heart from books and maps.

While we talked, gusts of wind began working their way beneath the lattice covers of the market, rattling the half-tacked-down bamboo. These giant gasps from the Atlases presaged hard rain. They ripped over the covered lane like flames licking dry brush. When big drops began banging on the lattice, the lath broke up the water and drained it off. From the back of the shop the canary started singing.

Abd al-Qadir kept talking, fitting the tone of his words to the rain. "The important thing," he counseled, "is to make your base Madinah. The main rites of the hadj only take five days. You can bus down to Mecca the night before and get out a day or two after. It may mean more driving, but the people of Madinah are very sweet. Do you have a piece of paper?"

He meant written proof that I was Muslim.

"Yes."

"Good. And don't worry about the crowds. Things will be elbow to elbow, but that's how one makes friends. Even Mecca is peaceful. The hadj diminishes people's self-importance. It shrinks their egos to peanuts. You will see."

There were hadjis who could afford a jaunt to Mecca, and next door men who did not have a dime. Elias Canetti's charge to "consider all beggars," for "God will bless you for every beggar you give to," could mean a lot of blessings in Marrakesh. In almost any corner of town you passed a few people holding out their hands. Others reclined or sat on a strip of cardboard if they had it, nursing a child, eyes turned to the sky. They did not beg for coins to buy a drink. They did not drink or joke or work in numbers. The camaraderie among street people in the West seemed foreign to them. Except for the blind contingents they worked alone.

There were the halt, the armless, the legless (who moved about on wheeled boards), the senile, the disfigured, the fake and the truly afflicted: the child bent double, the widow weeping, the toothless crone with caved-in jaws. I had been in parts of the world where souls like these would chase you for a handout. Here you had to concentrate to catch a word. The usual chant was "Alms for the love of Allah, and forgive my parents who could not provide." The donor replied, *"Bismillah"* ("in Allah's name") as he gave. Islam made a rite of even this transaction, conferring piety on the upper hand and dignity on the lower. A small coin called a *guirsh* insured their bread.

The *guirsh* is the smallest division of the dirham. Deflation has created these brass coins of token value, which even poor people can afford to give away. And give they did, it seemed to me, in rivers. One of the commonest sights in the souk was a man bent down, fishing coins from his pocket. The action was swift, the donations offhand, selective. Not much was lost or gained in any one transaction, but the system worked. The conscience responded; the touch was gentle.

Islamic law requires the hadj of those who can afford it. Its rewards act as a goad to the middle classes. All over Morocco men work hard, sometimes for years, acquiring the economic edge to leave their shops for a spell and go to Mecca. Prior to airplanes, when the journey was more daunting, requiring months and sometimes years of travel, the pilgrim returned with elevated status. Nowadays the rewards are more personal. One's neighbors still pay attention when the suitcases come out, but a fiftyfold increase in hadjis has made the trip less impressive. These days one goes to fulfill a major obligation, to round out one's life, to renew one's spirit, often dampened like Sharif's in the swamps of commerce. Some mourn the passing of older, slower ways. Most feel it is better. Moroccans are family-oriented people. The airplane reduces the trek to a three-week absence, and more pilgrims with less money can undertake it. They go to complete a set of rites and to see the place they have bowed toward for a lifetime. They come home with a title in front of their names: al-Hadj.

The hadj is the fifth pillar of Islam. No one I encountered planned to miss it. Even sophisticated city dwellers viewed the rite as transformative: your life could be changed by it forever. Elias Canetti had got it right in his book *Crowds and Power:* in the minds of most contemporary Muslims you hadn't really lived till you'd made the hadj.

Among Moroccans too poor to afford the trip, there were stories of miraculous transportations, astral projections, and magic-carpet rides to the holy shrine. These tales grow more plentiful the farther one lives from Mecca. Edward Westermarck's three-volume *Ritual and Belief in Morocco* retails dozens:

> One of [Sidi Hmed Buqudja's] followers expressed a wish to go to Mecca. The saint told him to go to the sea and throw himself in the water. He went there but could not persuade himself to follow the saint's advice. . . . A man came riding on horseback, and asked him what he was doing. On hearing that . . . he would reach Mecca if he threw himself into the sea, the horseman fearlessly rode into the water. The saint, who was hidden in the sea, at once took the horse with the rider on his shoulders and carried them to Mecca.

In other stories the shrine is brought to you:

> Mulai M'sish once told some of his followers to go with him to the top of the mountain . . . because he wanted to show them from there the Great Mosque in Mecca; and so he did. . . .
>
> Sidi l-Hadj l'Arbi of Wazzan caused the Ka'ba to come to Wazzan and walk around him seven times, just as the pilgrims walk around the Ka'ba in Mecca.

Originally instructive devices rather like Zen koans, stories like these were first invented to internalize a spiritual message. Later they became a part of local folklore and were accepted at face value or as hagiography.

I had been hearing about an exquisite shrine, the Kouba el Baroudiyn, tucked away a few blocks from Ben Yusef's. A café sat nearby with a covered

terrace that cut the sun and allowed for reading. Full of resolve, I settled
here one morning with my guidebook. By now many more travelers were
in town; perhaps the germ of tourism was catching. For the last week I'd
been intending to devote a day to Rogerson's tips on the monuments of
the city—to provide a hint of direction to my research. Generally these
projects left me cold. Now I was determined.

The waiter brought coffee to my table and set a glass of water near the
cup. I read with interest—and did not notice a scarecrow figure weaving
toward me. Probably I thought it was a shadow. When the shadow fell on
my pages, I looked up. A local beggar stood a yard away, squinting at me
in a filthy T-shirt. His face was dark with sweat and charcoal, and when our
eyes met he cringed, then tossed me a searching glance and stared at my
water, ready for the worst. I saw what he wanted, and nodded. He raised
the glass to his lips and began to drink.

The water passed the man's Adam's apple in smooth glugs. Before it
was gone, all hell broke loose at the end of the terrace. The waiter bore
down on my table, cursing, lost in his anger, although the water had cost
him nothing, and the day was already hot. Did he hope to improve his tip,
I wondered, by defending a tourist? His shouting only upset the clientele.
At the next table three Moroccans raised their voices.

"*Ça va!*"

"*Malesh!*"

"*It's nothing!*"

One man stood as if to cross the terrace. "*Shu'ma!*" He wagged his
finger, accusing the waiter of forgetting his Islam. This stopped the waiter
in his tracks. For an instant he stood motionless before us—one hand on
my table to protect me, the other leveled at a man in rags.

The beggar looked down at the hand thrust toward him. His position
in the world appeared reversed for just an instant. The open palm was
turned, this time, toward him. Gradually his expression changed; a half-
insolent smile crossed his lips. Then in slow motion he gently balanced the
glass on the waiter's palm, backing away as he bowed, not batting an
eyelash.

This brief, dreamlike disruption passed down the terrace like wind over
the plumage of a bird. Then the waiter shrugged and turned away to take

an order. Other customers began arriving. Bit by bit the day resumed its
flatness. I drank my coffee. I went back to reading.

According to Barnaby Rogerson, the small saint's shrine called Kouba el
Baroudiyn was all that remained of the twelfth-century city. About the size
of an inflated gazebo, its two-story walls and pea-cap dome were said to
express the best of Moorish art. In fact, the *kouba* was a time capsule. While
the grace of Moroccan architecture declined over the centuries, the shrine
slowly sank beneath the sands. When finally unearthed in 1948, what
emerged was unique and perfectly preserved. The major themes of North
African architecture were stated here more clearly than in any surviving
building in the region. Most scholars say it has no equal.

I had to see it. Even Mostopha said so. Only my aversion to sightseeing postponed the visit. Finally at breakfast he brought it up again and
this time provided me directions. I found the *kouba* eight blocks from his
house.

It stood south of the mosque behind a long wall, the plaster of which
was cracked in a dozen places. I knocked at a wooden door with metal
strappings. Above the lintel hung a board with the *kouba*'s name. The
whitewashed sign was cobwebbed. There were no awnings. This lack of
official fanfare reassured me.

I knocked again. A wrinkled guide in a pale shift led me into a
courtyard with a fountain. A few robed men sat washing at a pool. At first
glance the shrine was unassuming. It stood near the water, like a bathhouse.
The plan was simple: a pale, white stone rectangle pierced by facing pairs
of ground-floor doors with horseshoe arches, repeated higher up on all four
sides by rows of scalloped windows joined at the top to a turban dome. The
harsh light on the white walls made it difficult to see into the building. The
flat, black doors and windows gave up nothing. You had to get inside the
structure to feel its force.

It was all in the dome, as far as I could see: the intricate interlacing
arches, the vine-leaf carving, the shell palmettes and corner squinches that
grace every shrine and palace in Morocco. The difference here lay in the
boldness of execution—like seeing the actual canvas of Picasso's *Les Demoi-*

selles d'Avignon after suffering through fifty reproductions. The *kouba* contained the template of a millennium-long tradition. This was art.

✧　✧　✧　✧

*T*he building led back to the book again, an inevitable connection in a city where the walls of public buildings resemble chiseled pages, enlarging on the words of the Qur'an. Lines of sacred verse incised in moldings scroll through mosques and meeting halls and schools. They buttress the infrastructure of the city. They run like footnotes through the town.

The word *qur'an* means "recitation." Leafing through my copy after lunch, I came across a host of synonyms, expressing different attributes of the revelation. The book defined its pages as the Guidance (al-Huda), the Mercy (al-Rahmah), the Reminder (al-Tadhkira), the Distinguisher (al-Furqan), the Maintainer (al-Qayyim), the Guardian (al-Muhaimin), the Spirit of Life (al-Ruh), the Light (al-Nur). The merchants I was meeting quoted it daily. This literacy among people who often could not read testified to the vitality of their culture. It made me remember the book of Proverbs:

> *Where you walk it shall lead;*
> *when you lie down it shall watch over you;*
> *and when you awake, it shall talk to you.*

Because I could not read the Arabic, some Moroccans did not believe the Qur'an could speak to me. Its revelations, they argued, were welded to its language, and translation required human intervention; this alone reduced my copy to a commentary. Publicly I was in no position to argue. Privately I could only disagree. The bass notes of the Qur'an ring clear in any language. The "perspicuous message" lays out a two-fold proposition: that universal laws, however veiled, govern the actions of the world and that contrary aspects of existence—death and suffering, for instance—have causes and a place in the scheme of things.

As for understanding, the Qur'an proposes a universe of signs, then counsels reasoned curiosity as the best way to "read" it. Ignorance has no place here. "Seek knowledge, even into China," Muhammad said. As with the Greeks, the proper consequence of awe is study. This was faith and science joined. This was Isaac Newton, who looked upon the universe as a riddle, a code that could be deciphered by examining logical evidence for clues. Islam does not submit to your usual Western division of objective and subjective, of science and religion. The Qur'an contains nothing to contradict the scientific method. It proceeds along Newton's lines, and Einstein's, depicting creation as a system of signs in the shape of a test, as a test in the shape of emblems. Its impulse toward inquiry fuels the same engine that drives most modern thought.

Islam called itself *din al-hanif,* "the primordial religion." It confirms and renews the original views of Moses and bears an essential likeness to Judaism. Both are fiercely opposed to polytheism, have no saints or priesthood, and adhere to sacred books of written law.

The Qur'an brought the myths of Genesis into line with modern science, employing a cosmogonic model astonishingly like our big bang theory. In this book plants are no longer created before the stars, creation *includes* time and is continuous, God does not rest on the seventh day, and original sin has been done away with. No Muslim bears the failings of another; one's own wrongs and atonement are enough. Every child is born as God's vice-regent, equipped with *al-fitra:* "an innate disposition toward virtue." Dietary law is simplified. Women acquire property rights. Child slavery and infanticide are forbidden.

Arabian Jews of the period dismissed these innovations as heretical, but Islam diverged even more from the Christian mold. Although the Qur'an upholds the virgin birth, accepting Jesus as a world prophet, it rejects the worship of a man as Allah's son. Muslims also view as extreme the monastic asceticism of the desert fathers. Whereas early Christians took a path of worldly abstention, Muhammad and his followers drew no lines. Church and state were one thing to the Prophet. Body and soul were partners, too. He addressed sex frankly, warmly, and in detail. Saint Paul's disaffected "better to marry than to burn" held no meaning for him. Nor did withdrawal from the world.

CHAPTER EIGHT

About the House

*I*n the last few weeks Mostopha's business had not been doing well, owing to a bad investment he'd made toward the end of Ramadan.

The fast had boosted sales in the souks. Its grinding rounds of abstinence, with no one eating until sunset, led to extravagant meals after dark. Prime cuts of meat, the finest fruits and dates appeared on even average dinner tables. People bought the best with no thought of tomorrow. It went beyond groceries. At night, as families strolled about the markets, one form of compensation led to others. Even small shops did a booming trade. At the start of the fast Mostopha invested heavily in bright ceramic serving plates and bowls, then proceeded to sell large numbers of both items to housewives wanting to brighten up their kitchens. Bolts of cloth for new djellabas sold well, too, as did school clothes and sandals. What with gift giving at the end, the small shops on the feeder lane earned a quarter of the year's profits in a month. Once the new moon appeared, the frenzy slackened.

A few days before it was over, Mostopha's ceramic stocks were running low. Predicting a final flurry, he reinvested his earnings in fresh wares. I arrived at the shop one morning and could not get through the door. Stacks of platters and serving dishes swamped the entry. The scale of the purchase was a calculated gamble. Three weeks later the stock remained unsold.

Warm weather was not producing the expected flood of tourists. Usually by early May the New Town hotels were well booked. This year the planes from France were arriving half empty. Day after day Brahim and Sharif sat parked on their stools, lamenting every angle of the recession. When a rare clutch of tourists did pass by, the overly avid merchants sprang to their feet and started shouting. Good prospects were driven off by hard sells. A partial paralysis descended on the souks. Torpor took over, broken by small sales and disappointments.

One Thursday a three-month electric bill came due. That night Qadisha's pressure cooker cracked, and Mostopha did not mention a replacement. I lent him the money to pay the power company. A few days later he repaid me, but by that time the dirham had been devalued. At dinner we ate more rice, more pasta.

Marrakeshi merchants were not the only people short of cash that spring. One night on the *sala* television, we watched Mikhail Gorbachev address the U.S. Congress. Now that the cold war had ended, the Soviet leader was seeking investment money from the West. The Iron Curtain had come unhinged, his union stood on the brink of bankruptcy, and a rage for secession was sweeping Eastern Europe. Already the Berlin Wall had been pulled down—and was being sold through the mail to collectors. In the darker republics dictators of thirty years withdrew. Stasi spies and Bulgarian informers were being routed. Overnight in Bucharest a party card changed from a ticket to ride to a death warrant. The great game appeared to be over. Gorbachev was speaking of venture capital. In the next twelve months he would dissolve the Warsaw Pact, trash Lenin in the Soviet assembly, and manage to win a Nobel Prize.

While the Kremlin purged itself of Karl Marx, Western powers gloated. Following Gorbachev's speech French cable news aired footage of breadlines in Moscow. Poor Mother Russia! Mostopha shook his head.

"Don't a lot of Muslims live there?" he asked.

Nearly half the Soviets were Muslim. I spoke of mosques in my grandfather's village in Byelorussia.

"You're kidding."

"No. My father knew the call to prayer."

"Was he a Muslim?"

"No. He picked up the words from his father, I guess, the way your kids learn songs from the radio."

Mostopha pointed to the screen. The camera now panned Prague's Wenceslas Square, where a hundred thousand happy Czechs stood cheering Vaclav Havel. "This," he said, "is very, very good. These countries have always been poor. Now things may change. Some Arab leaders must be getting nervous. They won't want their people to see this and start thinking."

"But people are seeing it."

"Yes."

The screen was now awash with the blood of the dictator Nicolae Ceausescu's Christmas execution in Romania. Mostopha pursed his lips. At the end he grinned.

"What?"

"I was thinking: this is going to change the pilgrimage."

Watching the world news through Moroccan eyes often surprised me. I hadn't considered the Soviet breakup from this angle. It was true. For seventy years state-mandated aetheism had suppressed the Soviet hadj while racist visa restrictions reduced it to nothing. I asked Mostopha what he thought it meant.

"You're going to see Russians in Mecca this summer."

During rough times in the past Mostopha had made ends meet by raising canaries. He had bred them at home and sold them in wicker cages to store owners, who believed the music attracted business. An average male sold for three or four dollars. One with a very fine voice cost ten times more. The songbird market was never large, but even during hard times it persisted. The bird in Abd al-Qadir's bazaar, for example, had been purchased from Mostopha around tax time.

In addition to canaries, Mostopha had specialized in homing pigeons. A dovecote above a trapdoor on the roof still extended down past the windows of the blue room. Today the loft lay empty; eleven years before I had seen it filled with carriers, tumblers, and fantails. Mostopha had trained pigeons with a passion. Some nights they were all he talked about.

Teaching a pigeon to home takes time and patience. The instinct has to be developed in short stages. Training begins a few blocks from the loft. It continues as the more mature birds are carried one, then four, then seven miles away. Much depends on these carefully spaced releases. As Mostopha could not afford to neglect his shop, the traveling end of the training fell to Qadisha. I still recalled the day when, as his guest, I had volunteered to walk Qadisha and her cages to the bus station. In all she had with her about a dozen birds. After some confusion over buses she had boarded one for Benguérir, fifty miles away. I returned to the house and waited for the birds.

Once you release a pigeon, the bird climbs quickly, orients itself at a height of several hundred feet, then heads directly for the loft. It is a thrilling sight to watch them vanish, and very unsettling, too, when the birds are yours. They vanish quickly, achieving speeds of a mile and a half per minute in level flight. From Benguérir the bus would take twice as long to return as the pigeons. Mostopha had said to expect them around noon. I went home as instructed. At one o'clock I began to worry. At two o'clock I ran down to his shop. We hurried back. We raced upstairs to find the birds beating at the windows, but Qadisha did not return until late that night. The bus had not stopped in Benguérir at all. We'd bought the wrong ticket, for a bus bound for Settat, another ninety miles down the highway.

The birds were remarkable but hard to sell. Whereas France and Belgium enjoyed a booming trade, with *sociétés colombophiles* and cash-prize races from Paris to Liège, the Moroccan market was small and uninformed. Once in a while this worked in Mostopha's favor. One day he had snatched up a rare escaped *palonia* in the souk for seven dirhams, from an ironsmith who did not know his birds, and sold it a few days later for three thousand to a Belgian in Rabat. There were also occasions when Mostopha used his birds to transport stamp-size packets of semiprecious amber from Essaouira, where it cost less. But these events were windfalls. As a pigeoneer his only steady income came from appearances at weddings and celebrations of the hadj. A returning pilgrim's family was always pleased to watch the birds explode out of their cages. The birds, people said, were like hadjis. They headed home. Clients clapped and looked thrilled, but they did not pay much. The canaries made money. The pigeons he raised for love.

A copy of *Pigeons Standards* still lay in the *sala*. Once I came across the tiny purse a pigeon wears strapped to its breast to carry a message. The birds themselves had been gone for about a year.

I questioned Mostopha about it. He said, "A bird in a cage keeps a man imprisoned. We couldn't go anywhere, even overnight. The feedings, the cleaning, the babies: I swore for years to quit raising them."

It was the king who convinced him to give it up.

One day a soldier had come to Mostopha's shop. It was that time of year when the king came to visit the city, and the army was planning a parade. A cavalcade from the airport would deliver the king at noon to the Aguedal palace. The officer wanted to hire Mostopha to release his birds at the gates as the cars arrived. Mostopha showed up at nine with three dozen pigeons. A cold wind was blowing off the mountains, and Qadisha had made mufflers for each cage. Mostopha set the birds down by the wall and watched the festivities. Performers from the *djema* filled the road: stilt walkers, jugglers, a Genowa troupe, Guedra dancers in kaftans and silver jewelry. They all froze for nothing. The king had been called away to an Arab summit meeting in Tunisia. Mostopha found this out as the sun was setting. Hauling his cages back home through the crowds, he became so angry that in the *djema* he set them down, pulled up the doors, and let the pigeons go. Of course, they reached the house before Mostopha; it wasn't the end of them. But the end was near.

The more profitable canaries had drawbacks, too. Some refused to sing; others woke you at sunrise. Their breeding and feeding tied the family to a schedule and put summer vacations out of reach. This part particularly soured Qadisha. On August nights in Marrakesh temperatures could hover above a hundred degrees Fahrenheit. She hadn't been to the beach in seven years.

That fall Mostopha sold the canaries. The pigeons were given in pairs to Qadisha's family in Amizmiz. Mostopha had had to leave the loft in place, because now and then an escaped bird returned to his rooftop. The only permanent resident now was the yellow male living in the blue room. A few days later Mostopha sold him, too.

After a 10-percent drop in the value of the dirham some Moroccans feared the country was heading for collapse. More than one man in the last few weeks had asked me to help him find work in the States, but when Mostopha raised the subject, his wife opposed it. Qadisha did not want her husband to fly to America. The gold there was buried, she said, too hard to find. Nor did she want to start raising more canaries. Mostopha worked hard enough already.

"Life is short," she would say. "Nobody knows the day it will end. People who try too hard make their time here hell."

If she seemed cavalier about money, there were reasons. Her family, Mostopha said, were all religious, and no one more than her favorite uncle, Omar, whose life affected hers in many ways.

I had already heard something about this uncle. Now I learned more. As a young man Omar Adnas had earned a living selling charms to local families. Omar specialized in medicinal charms for children, but once in a while he also worked with treasure. Several large fortunes had been buried around Amizmiz in the 1920s, by tribal headmen fleeing from the French. According to Mostopha, the location of the gold was known, but the caches were sealed with a curse. Faith and superstition run together in Morocco. Even decades later rightful heirs were frightened by these hexes. Naturally those who knew of Omar's skill employed him to defuse the whammies. The payments were handsome, in keeping with the risks. Before he was thirty, Omar owned two houses.

One day a nephew of Thami el-Glaoui showed up at Omar's door.

"You know about this man?" Mostopha asked.

I nodded.

The name Glaoui is synonymous in Morocco with wealth and corruption on a princely scale. Thami, who golfed in Europe and helped the

French depose his king, had governed Marrakesh into the fifties. Ruthless, grand, and venal, he raked in a pasha's share of every concession in the city, from tea to tin to prostitution rings. Thami died in 1956. As a youth he had buried gold in the mountains, too. Its location was not in question. The nephew wanted Omar to help him recover it.

Omar questioned the old people in the region. His research was distressing. Thami's cache was protected by an especially grizzly curse. Two men (some said the owners of the gold) had been slain on the site and thrown into the diggings. Their bodies represented one half of a formula. The hex they sealed could only be reversed by murdering two more males of the same family. This much Omar willingly revealed, hoping to dissuade the greedy nephew. He refused further help, but none was needed. Fresh throats were cut, the gold was hoisted up and shared. Omar declined his part, but the damage was done, the judgment rendered. A few weeks later his legs began mysteriously to stiffen. Soon he was being borne through town on a wagon. The legs withered. Omar never worked with gold again. He restricted his practice to curing children, but nothing helped. When Qadisha was born, he had been crippled for five years.

I never knew what to make of tales like this one. Mostopha had offered it up one night to explain his wife's indifference to money. Apparently she had been chastened by Omar's fate. The assertion itself seemed logical: every child is influenced by elders. Only the terms—magic hexes, buried gold—seemed fantastic. It made me think of Miranda and Prospero. And what a fate! After a night of such stories I would fall asleep in a room flooded with moonlight. By morning the place looked real enough again, but it made me wonder. *Did* Omar's legs have something to do with his favorite niece's objection to raising canaries? Everything that counts goes on in the darkness. We can never know another's inside story.

A few days after Mostopha sold his last canary, tourists began appearing in the town. Every day more showed up, in polished cotton jumpsuits and sun hats, joining the steady flow of local shoppers. They never seemed to travel on their own. They arrived in groups, with guides, for a walk on the wild side. They rarely brought the kids, which seemed a shame. The circuslike souks would have been a good education. Adults with shopping on the brain saw the bazaars as an economic center. It was equally a region of the spirit. The few teenagers I passed were always wide-eyed.

Merchants regarded tourists as a part of nature. They waited on these seasonal returns. They went to lengths to cultivate rapport. They barked out prices in half a dozen languages. They offered free looks, free tea, loss leader items. On a usual day I passed knots of Germans, British, Italians, Swiss, a few Danes, and many French, as well as vacationing Moroccans. I saw them in the markets and I saw them in the *djema* after dinner, crowded around the sword-swallowers and monkeys. Juice vendors draped their booths with strings of colored lights to attract night business. The city overflowed with new arrivals. They added themselves to the lines at the PTT, where I went to make phone calls. Taxis were harder to come by. Rates increased.

Merchants on the feeder lane were preoccupied with their business, and I saw less of Mostopha at this time. His narrow shop was toe to heel with tourists. From 10:00 A.M. until dinnertime the whole *medina* brimmed with action. The presence of new prospects whipped parts of the market into a frenzy. Tour groups got the bulk of the attention. A single person passed almost unnoticed. In certain stretches I walked quickly for no reason. Other times I drifted with the crowds, loafed, eavesdropped, soaked up sights. A couple of hours of this was enough to sate me. Then I might pass by Mostopha's shop.

One day I found him wrapping up a sale of glassware to three Italians. The man looked anxious to leave. The ladies lingered, chatting with Mostopha. Each one held a large package wrapped in newsprint. Mostopha held a folded wad of bills.

It was never easy to tell from his expression how well or poorly he'd made out. None of his goods were packed away in boxes—a customer could stare at them all day, but because they had no price tags at their corners, no one but Mostopha knew their worth. When the bargaining began, the first price quoted was often an enigma. You knew it was more than you should pay; but how much more? His face said nothing. The tourist who countered with half the initial figure received the same smile as one bidding less or more. The smile was worldly, amused, and noncommittal. You could read sociability in it but also reserve, as if the price were engraved on his mind, and it was the buyer's business to divine it. This look of enlightened disinterest was mostly a pose. In fact, no price in the store was fixed in stone. It could change with the time, with the number of items you wanted, even with how long you had been in town. In any case, it was not a cause for disinterest. The same small silver box inlaid with turquoise might bring a hundred dirhams right now from a Spaniard or a thousand from a German later on. Mostopha had only a little better notion than a buyer of the object's going price. He knew what he'd paid for it wholesale. What it might bring depended on many factors. I'd often seen him price a first item at almost nothing, to lure a buyer inside the shop. This had been the case with the Italians. The man had been drawn in by the price on a miniature chess set. The glassware went to the women, later on.

One day after a week of steady sales he took me into the back of the shop and counted out two hundred dirhams. He was ready to replace Qadisha's broken pressure cooker. He wanted me to make the purchase for him.

The cost of the cooker would be about forty dollars, and I insisted on going in halves with him. As a guest I had benefited more than I could express from Qadisha's cooking. The kettle would make a perfect house gift.

"OK, but it has to be an SEB. The other brands cost less, but they're pot metal, they crack. Or they're made of aluminum. Poison."

I wrote down the trademark. Mostopha drew me a map of the shortest route to the hardware stores. As usual his cartography confused me. I handed back half the money and was just leaving the shop when Brahim pulled up on his motor scooter. Mostopha arranged with Brahim to drive me to the souk and help buy the cooker.

"Otherwise you'll be overcharged," he said.

That night Qadisha served chicken from the new SEB. The meat lay in a light sauce beneath a mound of couscous. It was preceded by a cascade of appetizers and two salads. Now that the tourists had arrived, we could again afford hors d'oeuvres.

As the meal was ending, I complimented Qadisha's cooking. She in turn attributed the sweetness of the chicken to my half of the new cooker.

Mostopha laughed. "It takes more than a pot from Spain to cook like Qadisha."

In his opinion the credit was due to the French couple who had raised her. "The woman's name was Miriam," he said. "She'd been a chef's assistant in Lyons before they married. The husband worked for a French-Moroccan bank. They couldn't bear children, you know; they'd tried and tried. When Qadisha came into their home, they were overjoyed. Voilà, a Muslim farm kid brought them back together! Miriam treated her like a real daughter. She taught Qadisha everything she knew. For example, most Moroccan women know a dozen herbs and spices. My wife knows fifty. She showed Qadisha the herbs that cure, too, and how to cook fish. Some Berbers die at a hundred without tasting good fish. Miriam thought the world of Qadisha. So did her husband. When Qadisha and I were married, it broke their hearts."

This little revelation came out quickly, adding a new wrinkle to their courtship, a dark passage I had not expected.

Mostopha sighed. "But what did they suppose? That a Muslim girl would not grow up and marry? They wanted to kill me when we went to Amizmiz! We talked with her father. And that was *more* trouble, because I came from Casablanca. It took three weeks."

"Does she ever visit the French couple?"

Mostopha looked irritated. Then he shrugged. "They moved back to Lyons after she left them. They couldn't stand it."

CHAPTER NINE

Winding Roads

I had planned to cover a lot of ground at the start of the journey, to cross
Morocco in April and May, before the scheduled pilgrimage began.
Marking up maps at home, I had found it possible to confuse Islam with
a country, to imagine myself in pursuit of its shape, riding grain trucks,
buses, cycles, rapid trains, exploring a faith as if it were a landscape, tasting,
comparing, taking its measure, lining up clear views like a surveyor. Instead
I had found what I wanted in one city, within a circuit of several dozen
blocks. Moreover, I was living, not merely observing. My plans had failed.
Things were going fine.

In this way a journey becomes a wall against which the traveler dashes
expectations. You are supposed to be taking a trip; instead, it takes you. You
think you will discover the hidden faces of the sites you visit, and so you
may—it is a workable conceit. But no matter how deep you delve, you will
never unveil the inner workings of the journey.

It was three or four weeks after Ramadan when I first felt the hadj season taking over. There was nothing very abrupt about its arrival. It crept over the city by increments, in undefinable stages, the way a tide inches up on a man sleeping on a beach. I could not put a date on it, but one of the earliest signs that things had changed came with a visit to Abd al-Hadi's repair shop.

The goods in the window looked the same, the glass panes still lay layered in dust, but inside, back of the counter, things were different. Usually Abd al-Hadi worked alone. Today two assistants sat behind him on low stools, bent over chassis and consoles. They wore blue smocks and eye loupes. Each one held an electric soldering gun. A few weak bulbs hung overhead on strings, and when anyone pressed a trigger, the room glowed under the pressure like a sweatshop. Pungent whisps of sulfur laced the air.

I peered across the desk at Abd al-Hadi. His fingers, twisting and snipping, never stopped. His baby face looked sallow in the half-light, like a peach that would not ripen. A couple of weeks had passed since our last meeting. I'd dropped by now to catch up on his plans. When I mentioned the women he was supposed to be taking to Mecca, he sighed and raised his eyes from a nest of wires.

"My pilgrims want to leave town now," he said. "My customers want their equipment. Wearing two hats, it gives a man a headache."

I replied that the hadj was still five weeks away.

"It's not much time. The sisters want a week in advance in Madinah; all this must be done before I leave." He waved a hand at the work stacked up behind him. "Have you your visa?"

"Not yet."

He tightened down the back of an amplifier. "Take care, *ami*. These arrangements aren't made in a weekend. Did you cross the ocean just to fall into a well?" And he actually leveled his screwdriver at me.

For thirteen hundred years more men and women than all the wires in this shop had made the hadj. They had done it simply by showing up in the right month at one of several stations outside Mecca and engaging a local guide to take them in. Those coming from a distance attached themselves to an annual caravan, paid its leader something for food and protection, and proceeded overland as time allowed. Ibn Battutah, whose book begins with such a journey, left Tangier in June 1325 and crossed the Rif mountain region on horseback. Arriving at Tunis in October, he joined a camel train that carried him through Libya to Egypt. This trip of three thousand miles took eleven months. After another year spent touring the Middle East, he set out for Mecca from Damascus. The last leg of the journey took two months. In 1876 the English traveler Charles M. Doughty left Damascus with a similar caravan. The march to Mecca still took fifty days. Five hundred years had passed since Ibn Battutah. The pace of the pilgrimage had hardly changed.

In the next fifty years it changed forever. Men who crossed the Hejaz by camel in 1920 reported numerous sightings of cars and trucks. By 1924, a paved road ran from Iran to Mecca, trimming the overland journey to five days. At first few took it. By 1930, half the Iranian pilgrims came by bus.

Motorized transport led the way. Greater forces followed. By 1960, the airplane, petrodollars, and a forty-hour week had stripped away forever the medieval trappings of the hadj. The rites prescribed by Muhammad remained unchanged, but gone for good were the camels, the overland marches, the caravanserai. In their place lay a paper trail of regulations and arrangements, of bureaus and agents, of procedures and vouchers that varied from country to country, about which I did not know much at all.

My ignorance peeved Abd al-Hadi. Why hadn't I arranged these things before leaving? I said I had tried.

In March I had turned up a California agent whose office advertised a pilgrim tour. His flier, on a billboard at the mosque in San Jose, described "a first-class three-week guided hadj" departing in mid-June from L.A. Airport. The price of three thousand dollars included airfare, meals, and hotels. We hit a snag at the beginning. Before the man could sign me on, he said, I would have to produce a Saudi Arabian visa. To get the visa, the Saudis wanted proof of a round-trip fare. Did I want to pay down half without a visa? In that case, he would issue me a voucher.

I preferred, I said, to meet the tour in Mecca. He nodded profusely. He said, "I will have to check."

I left the office mildly depressed. The date and point of departure conflicted with my plans; and perhaps because of my citizenship, the man later refused to help me with the visa. I called several other agents, without luck, then filled in the visa form myself and mailed it off to the Saudis, without the voucher. A few weeks later, to my surprise, a man named Khalil al-Khalil phoned from the Saudi embassy in Washington. Sheikh Khalil was pleasant and attentive. The visas were not yet available. They would not arrive until after Ramadan.

"I'll be in Morocco by then," I told him.

He took my name and said to call back, collect, when the fast had ended. "Don't worry. I will see to this," he said.

On paper my hadj came to a standstill. Determined to pass Ramadan in Morocco, I caught a plane in the nick of time, leaving behind the insoluble issue of visas. I still felt the decision was a good one. Now Abd al-Hadi warned me to wake up.

"Even at home," he said, "these things take time. Everything goes in stages."

"What are the stages?"

"Well, a Moroccan begins by making a deposit with an agent. The agent reserves your passage—on a plane, a bus, a boat—and mails the passport to a *département* in Rabat. The *département* confirms the passage and sends your passport to the Saudi embassy. The Saudis issue the visa and send it back. The *département* then issues a travel permit, in care of the agent. You pay what is owed and get your papers. Once that is done, the agent arranges for lodgings in Mecca. Or the hadji may do that himself. Moroccans with money leave it to an agent."

"How long does all this take?"

"Two or three weeks, *insha' Allah. Mais, pour vous?*" he shrugged. "You're not Moroccan."

A customer stepped through the door to pick up a turntable. Abd al-Hadi stopped working to write up the bill. Before capping the pen, he scribbled a phone number onto a scrap of paper and passed it to me.

"Go to Rabat on the next train," he advised. "You can call the Department of Hadj Affairs. You can see your ambassador. You can see the Saudis. But you better phone first. The Saudis never answer."

"What about Tangier?" I asked. "I have friends there. I don't know anyone in Rabat."

More customers arrived. One that came in for a tape deck went away happy. Two others were going to have to wait all day. Abd al-Hadi wrote them fresh tickets and smoothed things over. The men went out. I turned to leave.

"Wait," he cried. "I'm still thinking."

He took up a tape recorder, worked off a bolt, and gave advice to a workman.

"Tangier might be all right," he finally said. "It has consulates and agents. The best way, though, would be to go back home."

"But I'm here, in Morocco! I'm going to Mecca!" I nearly forgot to add the required *insha' Allah*.

The room became quiet. Finally, from behind a puff of solder, one of the workmen mumbled a few words. It was gibberish to me but oddly rhythmic and final sounding. I squinted at the man, then at Abd al-Hadi.

"Treeq s-slama alu darat," he repeated. "One of our proverbs: 'Take the safe road, even though it winds.' "

I could not tell where the safe road lay or whether the choice he advised me to make existed. That night at dinner Mostopha agreed with Abd al-Hadi. It was time to move.

A story, he said, had been going around the market. A few days before this a Saudi prince had arrived in Casablanca from Riyadh. This man was like an alarm clock, Mostopha said. He arrived every year just before the hadj with a suitcase full of tickets, rented a floor at the best hotel in Anfa, then went down into the streets and passed them out. The tickets went to people the prince bumped into: a teacher bending down to tie his shoe, a watch repairman stepping off a tram, a waiter at dinner. The person's material station did not matter. The prince simply asked a few questions, confined to religion, of people who happened across the royal path, and five minutes later, bingo—they were pilgrims, with round-trip flights to Mecca in their hands.

Tired of considering plans, I slipped across the hallway after dinner. With the disappearance of the last canary, a mattress had been moved into the blue room. While the kids watched TV, I lay down for a breather, spread my files on the bed, and vanished into the travels of Ibn Battutah.

Ibn Battutah set out from Tangier on the fourteenth of June in 1325. He was twenty-one, the son of a judge, and something of a mystic. Swayed, he wrote, by a deep desire to see the Prophet's birthplace, he quit his friends and tore himself from his family, obedient to an overmastering impulse.

He traveled alone through the Rif region to Tlemcen, a trek over wild land, of which he says nothing. Apparently, on the way he contracted malaria. At Tlemcen, in modern-day Algeria, he met two ambassadors to the court of the sultan at Tunis. He traveled with their party to Algiers, crossed the Jurjura Mountains, went on to Bougie. East of Constantine he was ill again. To keep from falling in his weakened state, he lashed himself to his saddle with a turban and did not dismount until the group reached Tunis. Here, after some weeks' rest, a pilgrim train setting out for Cairo elected him its leader. The caravan left in November, moved south through Susa and Qabes, then east to Tripoli. In Libya it was joined for several stages by a large detachment of archers, who protected it from thieves.

In April, ten months after leaving home, Ibn Battutah reached Alexandria. "A noble city," the traveler writes, "well guarded, well built, with a magnificent harbor." In Egypt his paragraphs grow more leisurely. He visits the Pharos lighthouse, beginning to crumble, and Pompey's pillar. He calls upon some local leading lights, including the *qadi* of the city, whose voluminous turban the Moroccan mocks:

> I saw him one day sitting in the forepart of a prayer niche, and his turban was not far short of filling it up.

A few days later the tone of the narrative changes again. Ibn Battutah hears of a holy man, Abdallah al-Murshidi, who

> lived a life of devotion in retirement from the world, and bestowed gifts from the Divine Store, for he was one of the great saints who enjoy the vision of the unseen.

Learning the whereabouts of al-Murshidi's hermitage, the pilgrim goes there. At nightfall the sheikh invites him to sleep on the roof, to avoid the heat. Ibn Battutah demurs. The sheikh insists. Something extraordinary happens:

That night as I was sleeping on the roof of the cell, I dreamed that I was on the wing of a huge bird which flew with me in the direction of Mecca. The bird then made towards Yemen, then east, then south, and finally made a long flight towards the east, alighted in a dark and greenish country, and left me.

In the morning the sheikh takes his guest aside and asks what he dreamed the previous evening. Ibn Battutah relates the dream; the sheikh explains its meaning:

"You shall make the Hadj and visit the Prophet's tomb at Madina. You shall travel through the lands of Yemen and Iraq, the land of the Turks and the land of India. You will stay a long time."

The sheikh gives him cakes and silver coins. Ibn Battutah continues up the Nile.

Soon after this meeting he announces what will become his master passion: "to travel across the earth." By the time he leaves Mecca, he has made it a rule "never to cover a second time" any road he has traveled.

Exceeding the flight of the bird in his dream, Ibn Battutah made good the sheikh's projections. He had crossed, before he was finished, 90 percent of the Islamic world. He traveled to China. He crossed the Sahara. He died an old man near his birthplace in Tangier . . .

Highwaymen, fever, unbearable heat locked in a written capsule older than Chaucer—reading Ibn Battutah's volume calmed me. It seemed to dispel the uniqueness of my troubles.

Mostopha adjusted quickly to my imminent departure. He suggested three things I should do before leaving town: I must buy the right clothes, say proper good-byes to my friends here, and draw up a list of presents to bring back from Mecca. For his part he offered to bind my Qur'an in leather and to see me to the airport when I left.

I had a telephone call to Washington to make before we got started. These days a trip to the New Town took an hour. The tourist season was in full swing, and the broad rue Semarine ran thick with shoppers. Mother of all the feeder lanes, this stretch of cobbled boulevard, straight as an arrow, wide as a four-lane road, lay lined on either side with good bazaars. I had not imagined commerce could ensnare so many bodies. At any crossroads the crush was staggering. Every back stood packed against two sternums. Elbows butted, kneecaps ground, children scurried by like running water: all for a hat or blouse to drag back to Paris. My leisurely stroll to the square was compressed to a claustrophobic mince. Touts pursued everyone. Guides hissed, "Hey, m'sew! Hey, Merikani! Wanna see markets?" A roar rolled over the bazaars.

I taxied to the New Town. At a switchboard I gave an operator my name and a Washington phone number, and took a seat on a marble bench with half a dozen others. The plywood booths across the way were filled with callers. Through one I could hear a Moroccan woman wailing. It was a family matter, and people on the benches looked away. When my call went through, the operator disconnected the woman. No one looked disappointed. I crossed the floor and opened the booth. A short figure in a black *hayeek* rolled out, pressing a scarf to her neck as if she were wounded. I avoided her stare and stepped into the booth. I raised the receiver.

"Salaam aleikoum."

"Aleikoum salaam," I said. "Sheikh Khalil?" The connection was good. We did not have to shout.

Sheikh Khalil, aide-de-camp to Saudi Arabia's cultural ambassador, was a quiet-spoken man and still the only Arabian I knew. For a number of years in the 1980s he had studied literature in the United States. His English was fluent. He had translated Persian poetry into Arabic. He took a lively interest in English verse.

The cherry blossoms were gone, he said. The visas had arrived in Washington.

The visa was the sine qua non of any hadj arrangement, and it relieved me to hear that he had it. Visas to Mecca came in two versions: business and pilgrim. The hadj visa entailed strict controls; with the ever-increasing numbers there were quotas. I hoped I was not too late. Sheikh Khalil did not foresee a problem. "When you're ready to leave," he said, "come to Washington."

Flying the wrong way around the globe for a piece of paper strained all logic.

"Surely I could get the visa here."

"Insha' Allah."

"Yes?"

"But you would merely have a visa. If you come here, perhaps we can help with your arrangements. It's just a suggestion."

I said I would call him when I reached Tangier.

"Insha' Allah."

I had met a handful of ardent people in Marrakesh that spring. Strikingly different, each in his way had offered me hospitality and insight. When it came time to leave, I wanted to do something for them.

Mostopha suggested I bring them gifts from Mecca, but that was standard behavior for a pilgrim. I wanted to do more than shop for them. Accordingly I developed a plan to take their prayers to Mecca. In the next few days I would visit each one and record his words on my tape deck, then play back the tape at the high point of the hadj. Even a proxy prayer counted for more there.

Medhi thought the idea was good. I met him outside his shop one afternoon. The crowds had thinned out, it was midsiesta, almost June, and hot. He gave over the barking of goods to a boy in blue jeans, and we seated ourselves on stools outside. A waiter emerged from the crowd with glasses of lemonade. We sat in the doorway and sucked the ice and sweated.

A trace of smoke curled by. I sniffed the air.

"Frankincense," Medhi said.

I said that American churches burned it at Christmas.

"Do you have many Christian friends?" he asked.

"Most of my friends in America are Christians."

Medhi looked grave. "And you?"

"My mother was a Christian."

"And your father?"

"A Jew."

"Hamdullah!" he cried. "You're everything!"

I explained that for years I'd been nothing. That in me two great religions had petered out. The problem did not lie with Moses or with Jesus. My life had simply overshot their limits. I hadn't known this was so, I said, until I'd begun to perform the prayer positions.

"The *salat* led you to Mecca? That is good!"

I said, "I'm not there yet."

He said, "You will be."

"Insha' Allah."

My visa problems amplified my worries. My moods suffered swings. My plans were insubstantial. I began to fear the Saudis would find some way to bar me from Mecca. Or they might mistake me for an impostor.

"Nonsense," said Medhi. "Go to Tangier. Go to Washington. Go to Cairo! Allah is giving you more chances than you need. Don't you see, it's a test."

"Of what?"

"Of your strength as a hadji. *Mon ami,* do you think the hadj begins in Mecca? No, no. It starts the moment you decide to go. Forget itineraries! The only itinerary is *al-sirat."*

Sirat means "the path." "The favored road." "The route that follows the way life is laid out." From Latin, *strata.*

"Let the hadj be your *al-hud,"* Medhi went on. "A guidance."

This came quickly, as most things did with Medhi. *Al-hud,* I knew, is a qualifying noun sometimes applied to the Qur'an. A divine lamp in a dark place is its essence. Appropriate, certainly, but I had not heard it used in terms of the hadj. Did Medhi mean the journey contained its own directions? Finally, I nodded.

"You just have to watch out for *Shaytan."*

A smile creased the corners of his mouth.

"Don't think, if I mention the devil, I'm not à la mode. Europeans never talk about him." He chuckled. "Maybe Satan has blended in, in France! Do you think they've got rid of him? *Moi, je ne sais rien du nord.* He's alive and well down here, though. Do you know what he looks like?"

I shook my head.

He pointed to his chest: "A soft spot. Not big at all. Right *here.* That's why a Muslim says *bismillah* at every meal."

Bismallah, "In the name of God," is the first word of the Fatihah and is often used as a blessing and protection. Mostopha would say *"Bismillah"* when opening a door, stepping into a car, and so on.

Medhi asked me, "Do you know the story of the two Shaytans?"

I nodded.

"Tell me."

Moroccans often cast Satan in a parasitic role. In the tale I'd heard, two satanic agents meet in a roadhouse. One Shaytan is as big as a mosque; his companion has wasted away to nothing. As they sit drinking tea, the starving Shaytan asks the fat one how he grew so large. "I inhabit a man who never says *'Bismillah.'* Thus, whenever he eats, I get all the food. When he drinks, I get the buttermilk. He's as skinny as you," says the fat one. "I think he's dying." The starved Shaytan has a pious host, and the opposite situation.

Medhi shook his head when I finished. "It's always different. Buttermilk," he sighed. "But you left out the ending."

"I did?"

He nodded. "The fat Shaytan takes the skinny one home to dinner."

Medhi tape-recorded the Fatihah and asked me to bring him a scarf or a string of beads. Sharif wanted a liter of Zamzam water. I found him reading a book at the back of his shop.

The Zamzam well in the mosque at Mecca had been famous in the days of Abraham. It is mentioned in the Psalms:

> *Blessed the man whose strength is in thee:*
> *in whose heart are the ways of those that,*
> *passing through the valley of Mecca,*
> *make it a well.*

In both the Torah and Qur'an the angel Gabriel reveals this well to Hagar and Ishmail in the desert.* Whatever else a pilgrim carries home, he

---

*Ishmail is the progenitor of the Arabs ("Ishmaelites").

must bring water. The smallest jars are saved for years, doled out sparingly in times of illness, daubed on the forehead when a Muslim dies.

Initially Sharif asked for a gallon. We settled on much less due to the weight. I wrote down the order and glanced at the book he was reading. Brahim, across the way, had lent it to him—a volume of the sayings of the Prophet and his companions, al-Bukhari's *hadith*.

Among thousands of comments collected in the first years of Islam, Bukhari's are considered among the most reliable. I had searched in vain for years for a set in English.

"Does it say anything about the hadj?" I asked.

Sharif skimmed the table of contents and turned up a chapter. He passed a finger down the page from right to left. He stopped, then looked confused. "It says something about . . . jihad. Wait here a minute." And he stepped across the way to consult Brahim.

Jihad has a superficial currency among Western journalists, who use the word to designate a patriotic war waged by fanatics. In Arabic it means "struggle and perseverance," a portmanteau concept with many applications. Later I would discover a complex literature on this subject. At the time I could not connect it to the hadj, and I suspected Sharif had hit on the wrong chapter. He returned a minute later with Brahim. Brahim put on a pair of glasses.

He perused the passage and said, "Sharif is right. 'Umar, one of the Prophet's companions, is likening hadj to a jihad here. Is something the matter?"

"I thought it meant 'war.' "

"Not necessarily. There are two jihads. One is the fight in defense of Islam. The other, we call it the greater jihad, is your own war against ego."

"Ego?" It sounded academic in the *medina*.

"Your greed. Your laziness. Shaytan."

"How does one know the difference?"

"If you don't know the difference, you shouldn't be talking about it. A child could tell."

"Yes. Of course."

"Pilgrimage is a jihad because when you travel, you face hardship. You have to control your desires and cleanse your heart." Brahim leafed forward a few pages, shut the book, and shrugged. "Somewhere in here the Prophet says that the best jihad begins at dawn with no intention of harming anybody." He kissed the book and gave it to Sharif.

When Sharif explained my plan to record their prayers, Brahim declined. His objection to furthering faith through electric gadgets seemed genuine. I did not press him. Naturally this did not stop Sharif.

When the recording session was over, Brahim asked about the specifics of my trip. When would I leave? Would I fly or go overland? When would I return to Marrakesh? Having no concrete plan, I gave him several. My anxiety on the subject lay near the surface. Soon both men were counseling the merits of trusting Allah. Sharif proved especially eloquent on the subject. He knew what it was to feel rushed, he said. He had wasted years of his life and was still catching up. But the hadj was different. One had to let a pilgrimage unfold. Visas are easy to come by, he said. If I did not have one yet, there must be reasons.

Brahim said, "Perhaps it's a blessing."

"Exactly! What looks like a curse may not be," Sharif said.

*T*he next day Mostopha presented my new Qur'an. In place of paper covers it now wore calfskin boards with raised bands and gold foil on the spine. Issued at Princeton in 1986, it looked like a Reformation first edition. The work reminded me for the hundredth time that traditions endangered throughout the Muslim world were being kept alive by Moroccan craftsmen. Twenty years before this Sarah Hobson had combed Persian Isfahan in search of leather items and found in the stalls not a single hand-bound book. The work on my Qur'an had cost eight dollars.

I took the book into the Djema el Fna. I had left some valuables locked in a hotel safe there. After a coffee I stopped by to pick them up.

A twenty-year-old Moroccan in a T-shirt leaned at the counter. Smiling through poor teeth, he greeted me in garbled French, spotted the Qur'an, and asked to see it. I passed him the book and watched him flip through it backward, stopping at the chapter he had memorized in school. A flush came over his face as he began reading the original, haltingly at first, then with more fluency, until he was moving smoothly through the verse.

He read perhaps twenty lines, then stopped. "Do you understand it?"

I said I could not read the Arabic.

"It means Allah made you," he said. "And he can take your life, then give it back to you. He can do anything. He makes everything. Who created the clay that Adam came from? Allah made it, Allah had it shaped. Men make nothing." Inspired briefly, he pointed to a sofa near the doorway. "A man thinks he made that chair? It came from a tree; it's covered in cowhide. It comes from nature. Everything comes from nature. Man makes nothing. He's from nature, too. Allah made all of it."

Gradually the clerk trailed off and began to look embarrassed. "I should not preach," he said. "I'm not a good Muslim. Once, perhaps. Not now. Not for many years. But no one remembers Allah all the time. Everyone forgets. The book reminds us."

After a silence I asked to see the manager.

" 'Ali will be back this afternoon. He went into town for a newspaper."

I said I would come back then to collect my things. I wrote 'Ali a note, and the boy pigeonholed it. The Qur'an lay open on the counter.

"May I keep it till then?" he asked. "It's the first one I've seen with the English."

I left it with him.

Brahim and I had arranged to meet in the *djema* in order to say good-bye to Si Mallek. I had thought he would bring the old man along again, but Hadj Mallek was at work in the *medina*. His tailor's cubby lay near Mostopha's shop.

Si Mallek was not a retail vendor. In his shop he had no products to display, therefore no shelves, no desk or counter, no furniture at all. The stall was about the size of a walk-in closet. Here his clients brought djellabas, kaftans, suit coats, shirts, and slacks, which Si Mallek altered, darned, or seamed. In proportion to the space, it saw a steady flow of business. Piecework lay in piles against the back wall. Finished items on hangers filled the doorway. A rack had to be moved to let us in.

Si Mallek's piety and learning were widely acknowledged in the souk. Dropping by his stall two weeks before, I'd found him engaged in a tête à tête with the chief imam of the Mouassin mosque. Mostopha had expressed surprise that the old man remembered me. In fact, Si Mallek was a man with time to spare. He greeted me warmly whenever I passed there.

We stooped at the door and went in and sat on rugs. The floor was deeply spread with Berber carpets, one an exquisite small kilim from the tribe of Bou Sbaa. The name Allah, stitched in gold on a card of green felt, hung framed in the entry. Otherwise the walls were bare.

Hadj Malek often extolled my late conversion. Whereas everyone he knew had been born to Islam, I had come to it by a rational decision. I met this reaction again and again in Mecca and gradually developed a response. Perhaps it was only politeness. Today it unnerved me. I had come to Morocco to learn more about Islam; to be treated as somehow superior put me off. When Si Mallek took this tack, I objected.

I said, "I'm just a little Muslim."

Brahim put my words into Arabic. At first the tailor shook his head. As I continued to emphasize my novice status, he seized my wrist, looked me in the eye, and began squeezing harder, until his thumbnail bit into the skin. The strength in his hand surprised me. I stared back as if he were crazy. Si Mallek laughed.

"No one is a small Muslim," he said. "There is no such thing! You have learned a lot here: the meaning of prayer, the ways of the mosque, how to shake hands. If you still feel small, perhaps you haven't used what you've been given. Look at the world around you. Look at the *argan*."

The *argan* is a wild, stubby thorn tree well equipped to survive in Morocco's south. Its limbs are gnarled, its bark immune to insects, and it barely needs water. Like the olive, it produces a hard, green fruit. The *argan* fruit, however, is inedibly bitter to every living creature except goats, who climb into the trees every spring to eat them. The *argan* provides fodder and something more. Once the goats have excreted the pits, men rake them up and wash and press them. This process produces an orangish liquid, which people use for lamp oil in the south.

Si Mallek said, "Do you know about this oil?"

I nodded.

"Good. You have learned many things here. Now forget something. Forget yourself. It's not our job to measure between Muslims. We're all alike in that respect, like pits in the gut of a she goat. Hold your worth whatever happens. You'll soon be used."

Si Mallek's homilies were always brief. He did not so much preach as reduce a problem to basics. He had done so in a literal sense with the prayer positions, compressing them into the letters in Adam's name. Today he placed my humility on par with goat droppings. It was over in a minute.

Brahim explained my plan to tape his prayers. The tailor grinned. He composed himself, clipped the mike to his gown, and recited the Fatihah, followed by a short prayer for the dead. His face glowed at the finish. Brahim, who took a dim view of these recordings, showed no sign of disapproval. It did not seem to occur to him to confuse Si Mallek's conduct with his own.

That night I played back the tape for Mostopha. My tiny recorder sat on the table between us. It contained a cassette the size of a matchbox, good for an hour at half speed. Nothing on so miniature a scale was available that year in Morocco. Mostopha's fascination was apparent. Half kidding, he tried to talk me out of it.

"Don't take this to Mecca," he advised. "If the Saudis see it, they'll think you're spying."

"If they stop me at customs," I said, "I'll play them the prayers."

"Espionage," he chuckled. "Like your father."

My father, he knew, had been a private detective. And while it was true that the job had affected my youth, it did so in different ways than Mostopha supposed. Along with packets of baseball cards, I had possessed from a very early age a collection of FBI wanted-persons fliers. I could work a lie detector, too. I knew words like *operative*. Now and then as I was growing up, my father took me along to shadow suspects. Sometimes he worked cases in Brazil. These exposures to crime left a certain impression on me, but I did not dream of entering the business. I wasn't encouraged. My father described his work mostly to dismiss it, as the going over of other people's laundry. Before I was sixteen, he gave it up.

Undoubtedly I had my father's curiosity. Finding grounds for espionage, however, said more about Mostopha's youth than mine. He had grown up on George Raft thrillers in Casablanca.

Probably that was why he wanted the machine. When I said I would need it to play back the prayers at Mecca, he asked whether he might buy it when I returned. The item cost thirty-five dollars at a thrift store in California. I said I would give it to him as a present.

I went on to Abd al-Qadir's in the morning, stopping for half an hour to tape his prayers. From there I dropped by Abd al-Hadi's repair shop.

Knowing by now that he planned to stop first in Madinah, I wanted to have the name of his hotel. The shop's screen door stood open when I reached it, but one of his assistant's manned the desk. Abd al-Hadi had gone home to pack, he said. His flight to Saudi Arabia was leaving at midnight.

That night, lying awake in bed, I heard an airplane rise over the town. As it rumbled by, I remembered Abd al-Hadi and his clients. Their smooth departure unnerved me. Anchored here by a lack of plans, I felt tied to the anxious end of a flagrant gamble. My wrist still burned where Si Mallek had grabbed it. His seemingly angry outburst had disturbed me. Now the meaning of his words hit home. I was not a novice. Then why behave like one? Obviously the hadj did not start in Mecca. I had been on the pilgrim trail all along. The hadj was not a brass ring to seize or miss or be denied by officialdom. It was a process, a right, an obligation:

> *Tell the people to make the Hadj.*
> *Let them come on foot through steep ravines,*
> *Or ride lean camels*
> *To reach the advantageous place*
> *Speaking God's name on the appointed days.*

The most difficult part of Islam for me was not the fast or daily prayers or *wudu'*. It was the concept of *insha' Allah*—a rider attached a hundred times a day to every mention of the future. Any Muslim's promise, hope, or plan carries the phrase "God willing" or sounds preposterous. This deep *provisionality* of Islam challenged my most ingrained Western reflex: to look ahead, to cover my back, to live with one foot in the future. It was the conflict between these views that kept me pinned here, debating whether to move or to be moved.

Listening to myself, I heard two voices. "If you don't have bad luck, the chances are good you will get there," said the first voice. Like racetrack patter, it made an even blend of hope and despair, treating the hadj as a wager with the cosmos. By and large I heard this voice when I was by myself. Among Marrakeshis even a mild projection was always counter-weighted with "God willing." Chance, luck, fortune good or bad had nothing to do with it. They were not active concepts in the *medina*. Nor did people use subjunctives. The future tense was footnoted with *insha' Allah* or omitted altogether. Different from leaving an outcome to chance, not at all like letting go, *insha' Allah* added a grain of faith to adrenal impatience, a saving trace of doubt to the best-laid plans. This coexistence of belief and doubt, one feeding the other, seemed paradoxical. I didn't know what to make of it moment by moment.

The hadj, meanwhile, was building up around me. Its sounds came through the walls at night. It ran like a river on Mostopha's television. I could close my eyes in bed and follow its course across the mountains, into Libya and Egypt, crossing the Red Sea, knocking at Mecca's door. As for the Ka'ba, the shrine itself, I could see that too: in a circle of pilgrims a veiled cube of granite—magnetic, glowing in the dark.

I waited until the next day to pick up my valuables. It was Sunday. The souks were less crowded on Sundays at this time of year. In wintertime Morocco, the Christian Sabbath meant nothing. As summer came on, the influx of Europeans imposed a second day of rest.

Saturday night acquired new meaning, too, chiefly related to alcohol. By this time the rooftop cafés on the square were serving beer and wine. The night before at the CTM two men had apparently toppled over a railing. The square looked less lively this afternoon. Near the walls of the Club Mediterranean I passed a hung-over Moroccan collapsed in a door-way, wearing a French waiter's uniform.

The desk boy slumped at the counter as I came in. His shirt had been ripped, I noticed, and a nasty gash across his nose exceeded the ends of its bandage.

"*Un accident?*"

"*Oui, du verre.*"

A broken glass in the bar upstairs had just missed gouging out his eye. I assumed he'd been part of the rooftop brawl, but the wound went unexplained, and I dropped the subject. I asked whether he had finished reading my Qur'an. Of course, he had forgotten all about it. Rooting through papers, throwing open drawers, he apologized profusely. The book finally turned up on a shelf under the desk. He touched the spine to his lips as he handed it over. He also retrieved my papers from the safe.

I took a slow taxi to the New Town. Above the park on rue Gueliz a travel agent offered me a seat on a morning flight to Tangier for sixty dollars. The heady perfume of blossoming orange trees in the courtyard made me hesitate. I had thought to stay in town a few more days, to say longer good-byes and pack my bags, but later flights were booked into the next weekend. I bought the ticket. I stopped at Mostopha's shop to show it to him, then went home to pack.

I did not enjoy these reunions with my luggage. My object back in April had been to settle, to acclimate quickly, to become a part of life here. My bags denied such things were possible. They forced me to face my excesses, too. A lot of my gear lay in storage in Tangier, yet here were socks and shirts I'd had no use for, alongside a couple of hefty unread hardbacks vying for space with Moroccan objets d'art. Who did not dream of traveling once in his lifetime with just a passport and a pair of gloves? I stuffed, unzipped, rearranged, sweating, cursing, thinking back to a parrot I had owned once—a normally even-tempered African gray, who went into shrieking fits at the sight of a suitcase. The bird knew what these things stood for: confusion, desertion, broken faith.

That night Qadisha served rolls and honeyed milk while we watched TV. All week the local stations had been airing special segments on the hadj. Tonight we watched footage from the Casablanca airport. The first flights were loading up for Mecca. Most of the passengers wore long white robes.

Well-wishers surrounded every pilgrim. Later they flocked the runways to wave good-bye.

We watched in silence. When I glanced at Nishwa, she began to cry.

"*Triste,*" Qadisha sighed. "She's been sad all day. One can do nothing with her. She doesn't want Abd al-Majeed to go." Nishwa turned her face to me and pouted.

"Maybe she wants to go with him," Mostopha said. "Eh, Nishwa? Do you want to see Mecca with Uncle Majeed and help him bring back your gift?"

Nishwa's tear-streaked features lighted up briefly.

There were problems with the gift list.

Ibrahim and Raschid wanted jogging shoes. Qadisha requested pots and pans. Mostopha suggested a clock or a ghetto blaster.

Every returning pilgrim brought back gifts. Coming from Mecca, they possessed an aura. I did not want to disappoint my hosts. On the other hand, there was my luggage, already bursting at the seams across the hall. At the risk of being tactless, I made a short speech. Everybody saw my point of view and adjusted accordingly. We settled on a pound of *kamari* incense, a sari for Qadisha, *thobe* gowns and sandals for the boys.

"And for Nishwa?"

Mostopha shook his head. "She wants a robot."

Nishwa pronounced the word without its *t*, as the French do. The "robot" she wanted was the latest in toy soldiers: a battery-powered enforcer figure molded in plastic, equipped for outer space with bone-crushing limbs and spark-emitting eyes. It came in various dimensions, from palm-size to stupendous, according to the war you wished to wage. Nishwa, I suspected, was feeling surrounded by her three brothers. Her request, on the verge of tears, was not a whim. Of course, the robot could not be purchased in Morocco. She had seen it advertised on French TV.

"*El-kebir,*" she whispered.

"She wants the big one," Mostopha said, measuring the height against his knee.

The room became quiet. I capitulated.

We watched Moroccan soccer before turning in. I kept hoping the game would be interrupted by a live program from Mecca, but the game ground on. Casablanca was losing.

At halftime Mostopha left the room. He came back carrying his best *gandoura*.

"I want you to take this to Mecca for me," he said, handing me the garment. "And before you leave, take it to the Zamzam well and wash it."

Qadisha glanced at me.

I had read about this custom. Once returned, the gown would be put away and not worn again until he died, when it would become his shroud. I folded the garment, left the room, and set it with my bags.

Nishwa began crying.

I took her on my lap and unwrapped a piece of blue candy.

"She wants to go with you," Qadisha said.

"To be sure you bring back the right robot," said Mostopha.

CHAPTER TEN

A House on Loan

"We wanted something thoroughly and uncompromisingly foreign—foreign from top to bottom—foreign from center to circumference—foreign inside and outside and all around—nothing anywhere about it to dilute its foreign-ness—nothing to remind us of any other people or any other land under the sun. And, lo! In Tangier we have found it."

Mark Twain, The Innocents Abroad

*M*ore than a century has passed since Mark Twain visited Tangier. He arrived on the steamer *Quaker City* with 150 New Yorkers for a five-month tour of Europe and the Christian Holy Land. Tangier was a minor anomaly for the Americans, an unscheduled stop on an otherwise Protestant itinerary. It was also Twain's first glimpse of a Muslim city. Few of the ticket holders could have liked it. Twain was mesmerized. The tile floors, Delacroix arches, chairless rooms, biblical dress, and a ruined bridge built by Caesar—"a crowded city of snowy tombs," he writes—outstripped Twain's definition of the strange. For the next ten pages his bombast trails off, chastened, almost, by the raw and timeless city.

Tangier in 1867 was already the least Moroccan of Morocco's cities. For several centuries the royal court had drawn a protective ring around the town. No sultan ever called there. Tangier was preserved as a diplomatic hive, a sop to Europe, a means of keeping strangers at arm's length. Its tribes were too heterodox, its embassies largely Christian. Royal cartographers sometimes dropped it from their maps. For Europeans, on the other hand, Tangier held promise. Its harbor near Gibraltar offered control of the strait and entry to an interior rich in trade. Twain compared it with Baghdad. For the sultan it was Sodom and Gomorrah. In 1780 he offered it to Spain for a hundred thousand dollars, but the deal fell through.

Tangier is a seaside city set on hills. On my first visit here during Ramadan I hadn't taken much notice of its beauties. Today from the back of a cab driving into town the place looked green and pleasant, its streets swept clean for a visit that day by Portugal's President Soares. Phone poles on the parade route streamed with banners. Portraits of the king hung nailed to trees. The heat laid a layer of oppression on the festivities. The checkpoints were wrapped in crepe, but the soldier's faces looked complacent—the faces of men who had seen these things before.

In the heart of town my driver dismissed Soares with a raised finger. Portugal had ruled Tangier off and on for about a century, then passed it on to Britain in 1661, as part of a dowry. Moroccans, and especially Tangawis, had already seen enough of foreigners to inoculate them forever against vain hopes. On the other hand, they liked a good parade. Schoolgirls lined the sidewalks singing anthems. Soares's plane was still an hour away.

The cab crept down avenue Mohammed V, past military cordons and a bandstand, then turned up a little mountain called the Sharf. Rodrigo Rey Rosa's house, where my extra bags were stored, lay up this road.

The driver dropped my luggage at a pair of iron gates. The grounds looked deserted. Rodrigo was still in Paris, working. I found the hidden key and went inside. The house, new, barely lived in, was built on a one-floor plan with six white rooms. An enormous, half-tiled bathroom gave off a faint lime smell of new cement. Because the rooms contained no furniture or carpets, they echoed like a foundry when the door banged. With so few contents, it was easy to set up housekeeping.

A mattress lay on reed mats in a bedroom. In the kitchen I found a one-ring camp stove, sugar and coffee in the larder, two pots, two pans, a bread knife on a board, running water, gas, electric lights. Off the kitchen lay a terrace with a clear view of the strait and a home below. Radio music played between the houses, but a bougainvillea trellis blurred the view. I'd seen laundry hung there to dry on my way in. When I looked again, the line was empty. I did not expect to meet my neighbors on the Sharf.

A double row of orange trees formed a tiny orchard beside the house. Their limbs threw warm shade and bitter fruit. I stretched out beneath them. The grass felt lush and cool, perfumed with citrus. A bumble bee breezed past.

Shreds of parade music woke me, from the bandstand down the road. Uphill the minaret of a mosque poked through the trees. The cabbie had said I would find a shop up there, to buy my groceries. I went inside to wash and change. I was setting out for the store with a woven basket when the call to *'asr* prayer came down the hill.

I went inside and put on a djellaba.

The walk took about ten minutes. The one-lane road curved steeply going up, lined with viny walls and overhanging houses. I mounted in spirals. The minaret at the top turned round and round. It was slimmer than those in Marrakesh. Instead of bare, reddish stone, its sides were brightly patterned in Spanish tiles.

A few involutions below the mosque I came to the food shop, a bare bones version of an Andalusian *tienda:* unpainted shelves behind a wooden counter, milk stacked up in paper tricorns, lengths of white bread end-up in a bin. There were yogurt cups, la Vache Qui Rit for cheese, and a sweating mound of butter near the soft drinks. I bought amounts of all these, a honeycomb chunk, and a kilo of bananas, worked them into the basket, and paid the bill.

Outside a puff of cloud ran over the mountain. At the top the street opened on a square. Other roads converged here, too, and a few Moroccans straggled up them, moving in twos and threes toward the mosque. Its doorless arches opened on the plaza. While I waited, two men tied a burro to a hitching post at the entry. I walked with them into the courtyard of the mosque.

I left my basket and sandals at the door and joined a few dozen people in the prayer hall. The floor was covered in reed mats. Ten or twelve women sat on the west wall; a few men were baby-sitting sons. Everyone knelt or sat cross-legged, waiting. Some told beads, some whispered, and then a man stood up and faced in the direction of Mecca. We filled in and straightened our rows. *Salat* began.

'Asr is one of the unvoiced, daylight prayers. Only the rustle of cloth disturbed the quiet. We performed the first *rak'ah*s in unison. After that the

pace began to vary, the older men going more slowly while others added extra prayers. At the last salaam, when the heads turn right then left, I looked into the face of a man beside me. On his brow lay the dark, round bruise—a mark of piety—that Moroccans call the raisin, from pressing the forehead often to the ground.

Later we drifted back across the courtyard. I picked up my basket and stepped into the square.

*A*t the house I put my impressions in a notebook. For about twenty years I had been coming to Morocco as a non-Muslim. In that time I naturally assumed that race and culture created unalterable lines of cleavage between peoples. Now the lens I had looked through appeared to be shifting. Perhaps it was even dissolving before my eyes. Two months ago I'd been frightened to enter a mosque here. Tangier had not changed. The change was in *me*.

I addressed a few postcards home and took a nap. A red towel hung drying on the terrace. A hummingbird buzzed the towel as I dozed off. When a knock hit the door, the sound bounced through the empty house like buckshot. I got up to see what was the matter and found a young woman standing on the porch. Her black hair hung in double braids. She wore a satin blue djellaba. Her name was Sa'ida.

"We live next door," she said, pointing up the drive. "Rodrigo told us you'd be coming, months ago. Have you seen my husband?"

I had not seen her husband.

"Strange. He was in the orchard. He sent me to find you. We saw your light last night."

I followed her gaze into the trees. She laughed like a bell, then looked worried.

"You've seen nobody?"

"No."

"Will you help me find him?"

We set off up the drive. Spears of sunlight slanted through the foliage, and as we walked along she questioned me. Where had I been since April?

Was I married? Where was my wife? Did I miss her? Would I ever go home again?

The hill was steep. We walked slowly. She led me into a house through the front door. In the foyer she called out, "Hamza! Hamza!" No one answered. She seemed amused.

She parted a beaded curtain, and we stepped into a sunlit sitting room. The chairs and tables were European, nondescript. The house felt freshly inhabited. Newlyweds, I thought. In a corner off the kitchen door, an upright piano and an organ formed a wedge.

"My husband's," she said. "He had them shipped from France. Do you play, monsieur?"

I had played as a boy. Not now.

"Not at all, monsieur? Not even a little?"

She stepped into the kitchen, where a maid in skirts was leaning on a mop. Sa'ida introduced me.

Hamza Kropf appeared at my door the next morning with a wicker basket of pears, goat cheese, and bread. We made breakfast in the kitchen, then sat on the counters, talking. Hamza was a lanky, quiet man in his early thirties. He wore a curly beard and spoke Swiss French.

Yesterday's missed meeting went unmentioned. The important thing, he said, was that my arrival in Tangier had coincided with a meeting at his teacher's house.

Hamza was European and a Muslim. He belonged to a local branch of well-known Sufis, the 'Alawis. His parents had been 'Alawis, too. The order's principal shrine was in Mostaganem, Algeria, but smaller centers were scattered throughout Morocco. Their regional leader would be a guest of honor at the meeting. Hamza wanted me to come along.

I had heard of the 'Alawis and their legendary sheikh, Ahmad al-'Alawi. Martin Lings at the University of London had written a book about him, *A Sufi Saint of the Twentieth Century*. A French physician, Marcel Carnet, had left an affecting account of the sheikh and their friendship. Al-'Alawi died in 1934, leaving thousands of students here and in Europe and a dozen published works in verse and prose. In his time he had been a celebrated mystic. It surprised me to hear that the order was still vital.

Hamza and I agreed to meet at six o'clock the next day.

After breakfast I walked into town. The city looked prosperous. I passed new residential sections on the outskirts, many more mosques than a decade before, and fewer foreigners. Banners still lined avenue Mohammed V, but the festivities had ended. The crowds were back to normal for a weekday. The sky was cloudless. Overlooking the port at every cross street, views of the strait stretched all the way to Spain. I turned downhill into the market. At a newsstand I stopped to ask directions. I was looking for Yusef Menari's small café.

Yusef and I had been friends twenty years before. He had started out with a shop the size of Mostopha's, then changed hats and become an official guide. These days he ran deluxe bus tours for Pullman all over the country. Like many successful Moroccans, he found that owning his own café provided a respite. I had heard about his success in the travel industry. I hoped he could advise me on getting to Mecca, but no one seemed to have heard of his café. The lanes at the back of the souk turned to culs-de-sac.

*T*hat afternoon I went to see Paul Bowles, taking a cab past the big Kuwaiti mosque, then down a lane past the boarded-up U.S. consulate. His apartment faced this building, across the road.

Years before, as a publisher, I had brought out two small books of Mohammed Mrabet's stories in Bowles's translations. I had liked the work and wanted to do something for Moroccan authors. On my previous trips I had always found Bowles helpful. For me his salon was a mental clearing-house. I could wash up there after weeks or months of travel and find a bright, genteel man who spoke my language. He had lived here for forty years. He knew the country.

I never knew what to expect when I went to see Paul. You could not telephone ahead. He had no telephone. Today the hall outside his flat was stacked with film equipment. Camera cases lay piled by the stairs. Plugs bristled from outlets. Extension cords ran under the front door.

A technical assistant let me in. Entering the study, he waved a light meter at the windows. I followed him through the door, past a Bolex camera. Paul was seated at a cluttered desk. Another technician stood wrestling with a reflector. To Paul's right sat Claude Thomas.

"Paul's become famous," she laughed.

"Again?"

Claude had translated several of Bowles's books into French for Gallimard. She nodded. "Now he's doing TV interviews."

Paul squinted at the camera, looking startled, a birdlike figure caught in a long lens. That year the filmmaker Bernardo Bertolucci had turned one of his novels into a movie. Its Hollywood budget had stirred the media.

A makeup man withdrew. The camera rolled, but there were problems with the lighting. Between takes Paul passed me a book he had been saving, *Sandstorms*, by Peter Theroux. I took the book. I said I would come back later.

The whole apartment seemed given over to capturing literary reflection. Mohammed Mrabet, the Moroccan author, sat on a couch in the living room while a sound man crouched at his feet, adjusting dials.

"School makes a man's mind a zero," Mrabet was saying. "Books drain the brains of people through their shoes. The Qur'an is the only book I ever read."

"But you are an author," the man objected.

"I've published a dozen books," Mrabet laughed. "What have they brought me? I have three lives. My life with Europeans, in which I feel very Muslim. My life with Moroccans, who treat me like a foreigner. And life by myself, when I dream up stories."

"What do you want?" the man asked.

"A life with money."

"Why?"

"It would be something new."

When the interview stopped, I asked Mrabet the way to Yusef's café. He looked surprised that I knew Yusef. They had played together as children, he said. "Yusef's the one rich man I know who doesn't waste time making all his friends feel like failures. When you're with Yusef, you are with Yusef. He's the same for everybody."

He drew me a map to the café.

Delacroix had made sketches in Tangier in the 1830s. Matisse, a regular visitor, had become addicted to its light. Kerouac called the city Rimbaud's Other. For Europeans and even for Americans, particularly those who endured McCarthyism, Tangier was a logical place for an artist's laboratory. The markets are clean, the flats are inexpensive, the climate is more agreeable than Europe's, and anything can happen, in three or four languages. For example, you can rent a hotel room for twenty dollars where William Burroughs wrote *Naked Lunch*. Jean Genet had lived and worked here. Francis Bacon. Tennessee Williams. Samuel Beckett.

Near the flat where Djuna Barnes wrote *Nightwood*, a boy stepped out of the shadows leading a goat.

"Café Zizwa?"

He pointed to a pair of granite stairs. Beside the door sat a man with a tray of matches.

"Yusef Menari?"

The man motioned behind him.

I stepped up into a long, narrow train car of a room. A wooden bench and tables lined one wall. A handful of men sat quietly sipping coffee. I mentioned Yusef's name to a sad-eyed waiter. He shut down the espresso maker and led me to a doorway strung with beads. He snapped on a light switch, and the square room twinkled. Its walls were studded with hundreds of pink and purple geodes the size of grapefruits. Their crystal centers flickered in the light. A granite shelf circled the room. Painted panels ran up to the ceiling: Day-Glo seascapes, an Arab skyline, a harbor. Lacking windows, the room looked something like a submarine.

Yusef lay on his back on a bench in the corner. I thought he must be asleep, but he was ill. Last week in Fez he had taken a busload of Spaniards to a museum. They had wanted to see how a Muslim performed *wudu'*. Yusef had found some water in a pool and made the ablutions. The tourists seemed pleased, but the water had had something in it.

"An occupational hazard. How did you find me?"

I showed him Mrabet's map.

"Do you know Mrabet?"

We talked about my stay in Marrakesh.

"Are you keeping a record?" he asked.

"I try."

"Try harder! And don't think like a child. If you want to know what things mean, ask yourself questions. Even the hadj is pointless without that. You can tell a child, 'Be good and you'll go to heaven.' But once he's an adult, he has to think beyond that. Does Paradise have dimensions? Does Allah have a face? Does he have to behave like a man for men to believe in him?" Yusef sighed. "God is the way things are, but people are lazy. Even religion requires imagination! Instead, you get ventriloquists and dummies, a few men with something to say and the rest repeating it. Be careful! Orthodox minds are the most primitive."

I remembered why I had always liked Yusef and why I had come to see him. "I'll be careful," I said. I brought up my visa problems. I asked if he knew a good guide.

"The only one worth a *guirsh* is al-Hadj Nasir."

He called to the waiter, who called to the match vendor, who called to the boy with the goat across the street. While Nasir was being sent for, Yusef praised him.

Nasir took pilgrims to Mecca every year, arranging every aspect of the journey. Other guides did the same, but Nasir was different. He was honest, for one thing, and he had a younger brother in Mecca who was a *mutawwif.* The two worked together.

"If I wanted to send my own grandmother on the hadj, I would send her with Nasir. He treats pilgrims like babies," Yusef said.

The boy came back without the guide. Nasir had gone to Rabat to arrange for visas. He would not return until Monday.

Yusef looked relieved. "I thought he had left for Mecca."

It was decided that we would meet Nasir on Tuesday. I gave Yusef my address.

"If anything changes, I will send the boy. What about medicine?"

"Medicine?"

"What do you have with you?"

I told him. He looked disappointed.

"It's not enough. You need Cipro for the stomach. You need sulfa and a pill to help you sleep. Don't underestimate Mecca in July. It's a hundred and thirty degrees at noon, and a million people are camping on the street. You're going to need a hotel room, air-conditioned. I will have the pills here on Tuesday."

He raised himself from the bench. His skin looked pallid. "Be careful what you drink there, too," he said.

The next day I laid a mat on the terrace and spread out my journals. They were soft, palm-size notebooks containing a patchy record of my months here. They bore no relation to a book. I had always hoped to write about this journey, but Marrakesh did not offer much time. Life in the *medina* proved too eventful to permit more than the keeping of a diary.

Tangier was different. Living alone, with no family around me, I found the days quieter and more oblique. Tangier was a profoundly Moroccan town, but unlike Marrakesh, it did not look it. Proximity to Europe cast a familiar scrim on everything. Most Tangawis dressed in Western clothes. The modern quarter was larger than the *medina*. There were even Christian church spires on the hill. The Western scenery often made me squint at the odd effects obscured behind French backdrops.

The first surprise was my meeting with the Sufis.

Hamza met me as arranged, at six o'clock. The sky ran marble pink over the harbor. We drove to an outlying quarter I'd never seen. As the car slipped through the hills, my thoughts were churning. I could hardly believe my luck, to be crossing paths with the 'Alawis, and yet the final mile made me nervous.

Sufism is the mystical dimension of Islam, a means of seeking divine awareness and love through the subtler aspects of faith and detached abandon. Its goal is concrete but ineffable: to implant within the adept a physical awareness of spiritual existence, rooted in direct experience. The Sufis called this remembering. Of all the Muslim sects and schools, Sufism aims most squarely at an I-Thou relation based on love. I found the proposal attractive but daunting. Its practice was based on the inner meaning of rites I had barely learned. I wondered if I was not going too fast. I described the feeling to Hamza as spiritual ground rush.

He stared out over the car hood and said that a man could not go too fast in certain matters.

"Besides," he smiled, "Islam is not a rocket. It's more like finding a perfect slice of orange. The question is, Once you see it, what will you do? You can write a book on the beauty of its skin, you can praise its perfection, but that may only make a person shy. When *I* see the orange, I want to put it in my mouth. The kind of thinking you're doing stalls the process."

Hamza's face had flushed now; we were on his favorite topic. Sometimes his head shook in midsentence, as if speech could not convey all he had to tell. "I'm a computer programmer," he said. "I have a good brain. But I don't try to eat with it. I chew with my mouth, *tu vois?* Of course, the brain would like to do it all. The brain is an incessant volunteer. I admire its versatility, but it wasn't designed to do everything. You can't drink soup with a fork, *par exemple.* To eat the orange, you need a straight path to it. Passing through the brain is just a detour."

He brought the car through a lazy curve and pulled up at a large suburban house. The path to the door was lined with rose beds. On a red-brick porch I was introduced to our host, a burly man in his fifties named Hassan. Hassan was the leader of the local 'Alawi *foqra*. With my hand in his meaty one he exuded the easy force of a retired wrestler. His striped shirt lay open at the collar. He brought us up into a banquet hall.

The second-story room was large, rectangular, and airy. Low couches lined the walls on all four sides. I counted eighty men seated in groups on low couches, chatting lightly over tea and dates. Some reclined as they conversed, giving the place an air of Plato's *Symposium*. There were tropical fish tanks built into a pillar and tall china cabinets on one wall. We were shown to a banquette. A boy set a tray of pastries on our table, then poured water from a ewer on our hands.

We were sipping tea when distant chanting came in at the windows. Down the road I heard the tramp of marching feet. This was not another state parade. It was the *foqra*, advancing like an army up the street.

"What are they singing?"

"A poem of Sheikh al-'Alawi's," Hamza whispered.

The feet stamped up the walk between the rose beds, entered Hassan's house, and marched upstairs. The stone steps boomed and echoed. Two men pinned back the double doors, and a stream of white-robed adepts swept through the entry. Half or more were in their early twenties, sixty men caught up in a joyful noise, arms swinging, faces gleaming as they passed us, forming ranks at the center of the *sala*, dropping to the carpet in neat rows.

Deportment in the banquet hall was formal. The students faced a wall of couches lined with elders. Robed and grave, the mentors sat straight backed, hands folded on their laps like a benchload of mandarins. The burly Hassan had slipped into a djellaba. Squeezed beside him, appearing somewhat lost, sat a round, lightly balding red-haired man of forty in a three-piece business suit. Because of his dress and height, about five feet two, I did not pick him out as the guest of honor.

The *foqra* began to sing to him selected trios and duets from the *diwan* of Sheikh al-'Alawi. There were no instruments, no drums. The mood was sweet, like a serenade. A chorus added refrains between the stanzas.

> *The blows of love play tricks on men*
> *And destroy them stage by stage.*

> *I asked: am I acceptable?*
> *The elders said, Make yourself empty.*

> *I know what you mean,*
> *I replied*

> *But consider my state*
> *And show me some compassion,*

> *Sadness is only the start*
> *Of the weight I carry.*

The short strophes ran together into fifteen-minute blocks, each song in its own hypnotic scale. Now and then one of the elders read from the Qur'an. Occasionally the red-haired man made a comment.

The choir had great reserves. The hall was crowded. As the singing continued, a light steam filmed the windows. The room grew warm. My couch ran perpendicular to the *foqra* in their rows. One student, jammed in near me on the floor, by leaning back could rest his spine against my kneecaps. Behind him sat another in his teens. When that one sang, his right foot brushed my toes.

The recital reached a high point with a different sort of piece. It consisted of variations on one word repeated up and down a lilting scale. The word was Allah. It started out simply enough—I sang along—voices rising in the heated air until bit by bit the middle *ll*'s dropped from the word like the body of an airplane and the song changed into aspirated breathing: *Ah—UH! Ah—UH!* At the back of the room a voice cried *Allah,* and the beat redoubled, the wings took off, the entire hall sucking in drafts of air at the solar plexus, which were held a moment, then shunted out in light explosions. Multiplied a hundred times, the sound was stunning. My eyes began to dart.

By this time the man whose foot brushed mine was leaning slightly forward. He rocked up and back, keeping time to the music. At first I thought nothing of it. Gradually, as the beat increased, the man seemed to lose control, until his rocking developed aspects of a seizure. I assumed the elders would come to his aid in any real emergency, but when his whole frame stiffened, I began to wonder. I could see that the music had induced a kind of ecstasy, but why in only this particular student? I hadn't planned to be so near the action. When his forehead unexpectedly became pinned to my left foot, I nearly panicked. By now he was foaming lightly on my sock while his legs swept open and shut like a pair of scissors. No one moved to change the situation. I sang to keep my courage up. Near the end of the song he lay stretched out, rolling from side to side; then his body went rigid. A sigh like a wisp of steam escaped his lips.

A moment later two companions came behind him, hoisted his body onto their backs, and lumbered away with it. The chanting continued. It had never stopped.

*   *   *

A softer psalm closed out the evening. When it was done, tablecloths appeared, and a meal of several courses was served: rounds of pigeon pie two feet across followed by bread, steamed vegetables, and joints of mutton.

Moroccans do not converse much while they eat. By the time I felt able to bring up the fainting student, the room was calm. Hamza whispered answers to my questions. The event, while new to me, was not very praiseworthy. These things happened often, Hamza said, especially among the younger students. He compared the man to a soldier who after a long day's march had come to a river without a bridge and gone on marching right down into the water. Hamza's tone implied that had he been paying attention, the man might have ridden out the wave, not been swamped by it. In other orders trance states were sought out. I had seen them among the Genowa. I had seen them at Baptist revivals, too: the swooning limbs of a choir member followed by *rigor ecstasis,* the gaze on a face that a minute before had looked human.

The river, which seemed like unconsciousness to me, is described by those who step into it as purgation. In Morocco, among less sophisticated orders (the Hamadsha, the Jilala), the trance is linked to the actions of local saints. In the south the saint "rides" you. In the north he "visits." A Jilali once described it to me this way: "You leave your body as though you were leaving a house. But you leave the door open. And while you are out, the saint comes in and cleans it. Then the saint leaves and leads you back through to the door." People compared the results to walking on air.

Two men stopped me, going down the stairway. One, named Moulay, asked how I'd liked the singing. The last song, he said, was quite special. Had I noticed the way it reduced God's name to breathing? "You see," he said, "some men reach God by repeating his name. We get there by forgetting it." Other than that I'd seen nothing special this evening. "You must come to Algeria. There you will see something special."

The second man had the same first name as mine. His face looked familiar. Moulay said this was because I'd been staring all night at a portrait of the man's brother. The photograph hung above the elders' couch, between Hassan and the red-haired man: a young-looking face, considering his station, the acting sheikh, I was told, of the *tariqa*, the inheritor of Sheikh al-'Alawi's chair.

The man said, "I'm leaving for Mostaganem this evening. Would you like to come with me?"

Algeria lay a two-day drive to the east over rugged mountains. I said I might manage a visit after the hadj. He produced a pen and wrote down an address and a phone number. "Go to the consulate and get a visa. You can take a bus to the border at Oran. Just tell them you're a tourist and get into the first cab. You don't really need an address. All the cabbies know the way."

As the red-headed man approached, I turned to Moulay.

"And your guest tonight?" I asked. "What is his function?"

"Sa'id is a Sufi, just like us. But he's also *le responsable des responsables.* He travels all over Morocco bringing order to the centers. That's his job."

Sa'id stood at my elbow now. His forehead reached my shoulder. He asked if we were discussing politics.

I said, "I don't think so."

"Good. It's a waste of time. In Algeria we have too much of that. The Socialists fill the streets one day; the Muslims march the next. Then it's the Democrats! They wear out their shoes, and none of it puts bread in the poor man's pocket. Sufis have a different politic. The body and the soul are not the same. The soul has no border, no *douane.*"

"How many 'Alawis are there?"

The order had a good following, he said. Thirty thousand or so, here and in Europe. Of course, they were in the minority, he added. The motor of the world was always like that. Artists, thinkers, Sufis were always the few. The majority made nothing real happen. It was the other 10 percent that drove the world.

I had mentioned to Hamza the book I was thinking of writing. He brought it up now.

"A book, about what?" Sa'id looked doubtful.

"The hadj."

"Ah, well, thank God! I thought you were writing a textbook on Islam. Impossible subject! Where does one find it? Islam is a word with fifty different meanings. And it's all mixed up with politics these days. You have one Islam in Pakistan and another in Saudi Arabia. You have Saddam Hussein and his cannon for God. The Kuwaitis who worship oil. The Iranians begging God to destroy them both. Where is Islam?"

"Don't ask the Americans," I said. "Most Americans don't know Islam from a tomato."

"Maybe your book will help change that."

"Most of my people believe the TV," I said.

He nodded. "The Muslims have not faired well on your television."

"No one has faired well," I said. "The average American student can't find Georgia on a map."

Sa'id chuckled. "Be sure you have a map when you get to Algeria. Mostaganem is a very small city."

We shook hands. I went downstairs.

❖   ❖   ❖   ❖

During the next few days I organized my notebooks every morning, laundered clothes, and dried them in the sun. After lunch I napped or read. In the afternoon I climbed to the hilltop grocer's, or strolled into town for provisions. I saw Paul every other day. I dined several times with Hamza and Sa'id. Nights, I listened to the BBC.

The Sharf was otherworldly with quiet. Downhill, traffic throbbed in a golden haze, and freighters blasted bass notes in the harbor. At night there were foghorns. Some evenings I strolled around the kasbah walls. The town was divided, like Marrakesh, between a New Town and an old quarter. In Tangier everyone seemed to live in both places simultaneously. That was part of its genius as a city—to offer life's essentials on two planes. As the town was split, so were the people I knew here. Paul Bowles had not been home in thirty years. Mrabet led three lives. Rodrigo wrote of his homeland, Guatemala, as hauntingly as if it were the moon. In Tangier, if anywhere, exile lent enchantment to the view.

*   *   *

When I played a tape of 'Alawi songs for Paul, he squinted at the sound and finally nodded. "It's the real thing," he confirmed. "But what does that mean?"

In the 1950s Paul had collected indigenous music here, for the Library of Congress. As a writer his attraction to Morocco seemed rooted in the irrational vitality of its people. Of their music and dance he had written:

> How much we could learn from them about man's relationship to the cosmos, about his conscious connection to the soul. Instead of which we talk about raising their standard of living! Where we could learn *why*, we try to teach them our all-important *how*, so that they may become as rootless and futile and materialistic as we are.

Certainly this applied to the 'Alawi music, but the Genowa's ritual choreography interested him more. "Did you happen to see them in Marrakesh?" he asked.

He drew back a cabinet door and exposed several shelves of the music on cassettes. "You never can get enough of it," he said.

"Are there Genowa in Tangier?" I wondered.

"Of course."

Driving through town with Mrabet the next day, I saw them. We had turned onto rue Mexique, a perfectly European-looking side street, and were coming downhill to an intersection when three men dressed in cream-colored robes and saffron skullcaps crossed the road. Mrabet slowed to let them pass. One bore a drum on his shoulder, covered with sequins.

I asked Mrabet about the 'Alawis in Tangier.

"They have a school in Emsellah," he said. "I've never been in it." My interest in the 'Alawis seemed to exasperate him. "If you're going to be a Muslim," he said, "stick with Allah. Go to the mosque and don't listen to anybody."

Mrabet was always advising me to be careful. His passport had once been rescinded on account of his stories, and the government had changed his legal name. He had published a dozen books in Bowles's translations and earned himself a following abroad, but at home he was circumspect. He had a wife and children. He advised me to watch out.

*   *   *

That night three dogs slipped under the gate into the courtyard and set up a chorus baying at the moon. My roof lay level with the driveway. As their howls reached a peak, the dogs skittered down the drive onto the rooftop. I chased them off, returned to bed, and tuned in the BBC.

News Desk was doing another piece on the Iraqi supergun.

That spring, the story ran, an order from Baghdad had been placed with a foundry in Britain, for fifty-four lengths of hollow steel pipe. Each piece of pipe was 132 feet long. Officially they were for an oil plant in Basra. The forty-inch bores were finely rifled, however. Fitted together, they seemed to form the barrel of a cannon large enough to lob shells into neighboring Israel. Because this represented a weapon five times larger than NATO's biggest gun, British authorities had seized the shipment.

This was the "cannon for God" that Sa'id had mentioned. Although its existence could not be confirmed, the rumor cast a cloud on the Middle East that summer. Saddam Hussein was a bellicose neighbor, for Arabs as well as for Israelis. He commanded the world's fourth-largest army.

When Tuesday morning rolled around, I walked into town for my meeting at Yusef's. Down in the harbor sunlight mottled the skins of two white freighters. I wondered whether they were pilgrim ships. In 1867 Mark Twain had written that

> hundreds of Moors come to Tangier every year and embark for Mecca. They go part of the way in English steamers, and the ten or twelve dollars they pay for passage is about all the trip costs. They take with them a quantity of food, and when the commissary department fails they "skirmish."

I had always preferred ships to airplanes. I made a note to ask Yusef's guide about it.

Passing the post office, I dropped in to telephone Khalil. The call went through the first time—a miracle by Marrakeshi standards. Khalil gave me instructions and the number of a flight to Saudi Arabia. "You'll meet a man at the airport," he said.

"Which airport?"

"The hadj airport, at Jidda."

"What's the man's name?"

"I'm not sure yet. He will find you."

Khalil sounded rushed. A Muslim high school in Washington had telephoned, he said, asking for a graduation anthem. "They want it this week," he sighed. "And it has to be in English."

I'd had some experience with the English ballad. In view of his help it seemed like a fair exchange. I offered to write the song.

"It ought to rhyme," he said shyly.

"I'll wire it to you."

I walked toward Yusef's, thinking about the anthem.

On a stone-benched pavilion overlooking the port at the top of the road I stopped to examine more closely the freighters in the harbor. From here I could see they were aging steel-hulled vessels streaked with oxides. Joseph Conrad had written of ships like these—"old as the hills, lean like a greyhound, eaten up with rust." The white shapes I'd taken for pilgrims on deck were only painted barrels of petroleum. I could make out their flags now. The ships were British.

Yusef sat on the café steps, conversing with the match vendor. His health looked improved. He wore a puckish grin.

"I have something for you."

We went inside and sat down in the submarine room. On a bench lay a carton stamped with a green crescent. It contained bottled medicines. Yusef opened the carton, raised each bottle to the light, and read out the dosage. There were painkillers, sulfa, antibiotics, and a water purifier. I thanked him. The pills were a present. The prices on all the labels had been rubbed out.

Yusef dispatched the goat boy to find Nasir. Meanwhile the sad-eyed waiter brought us tea. Today Yusef warned me again not to think simply.

"You hear people talk about heaven," he began. "They say it's a place." (He pointed to the doorway.) "They think it's over there somewhere. They live that way and they die that way, insistent. 'Heaven's a garden. Hell is a furnace. Allah has a throne.' "

He looked at me slyly.

"Does he have a face, too, do you think?"

This suggestion would make any Muslim recoil. Polytheism, totem worship, comparing Allah to anything are anathema in Islam. Even the male pronoun is just a convenience.

> *No vision can grasp Him.*
> *He encompasses every view.*
> *He is unfathomable,*
> *Entirely aware.*

I answered no.

"Of course not. And yet the Qur'an says,

> *Don't dismiss those men*
> *Who call on him morning and evening,*
> *Seeking his face.*

"Somebody once asked Omar Khayyám the question, What would a man who looked into God's face see? Omar answered that he would see every face he knew, every place he had ever been, the face of the earth, the moon, and the face of heaven. Like looking into the sky at night, the stars, and the night behind them. God's face would be bigger than that," Yusef said.

The boy came back with a message just then. "Nasir is very busy," Yusef sighed. "He's taking three hundred pilgrims to Mecca this summer. He's rented a building; he's leased two airplanes. The boy brings you Nasir's apologies. You are not the only hadji having problems. He was called down to Rabat, early today."

The boy handed Yusef a yellow slip of paper.

"It's the address of Nasir's brother in Mecca," he said. "Nasir wants you to have it."

I put the slip into my passport. I had wanted to talk to Nasir about ships.

Yusef sighed. "These days, eighty percent of the pilgrims go by airplane. A ship takes forever. People have jobs to get back to, people have families. They have no time, and so the ships are few. The last one left Tangier a week ago."

When the boy was gone, I mentioned my phone call to Washington.

"It's your choice," Yusef said. "Nasir returns on Saturday. He invites you to lunch with him."

✧   ✧   ✧   ✧

*T*hat night the dogs wakened me again, roughhousing on the roof. I chased them off and threw back the shutters. A half-moon hung by its tips over the mountain. I switched on a lamp, boiled water for tea, and worked at Khalil's anthem for an hour. The song went smoothly. As I finished, the call to prayer came down the hill.

An extra verse distinguishes the predawn call from the four that follow it. The additional words are *Assalatu kairum minanaum:* "Prayer is better than sleep." I showered and dressed and stepped through the gates, up the hillside. The cobbles grew wet as I climbed. The moon slipped down.

In the mosque on the hill I performed the *fajr* prayer with a dozen men and two schoolboys. It was 4:30 A.M. Half-asleep, I had left the house in a plain white shirt and slacks. The light was poor. We formed a single row facing the niche and were busy straightening our line when I happened to notice that everyone else had a robe on. No one except myself looked remotely Western. Suddenly I felt very wide awake.

The bowing began. We performed *salat,* sat back for a while, then stood and crossed the yard. By the fountain two elders stopped to greet me. If they wondered where I was from, they did not ask.

In one sense nothing unusual had happened. We had performed a *fajr* prayer. I'd attended a lot of them with Mostopha at Ben Yusef, but this was different. Today I had come on my own in Western clothes to a mosque in a city close to Europe. Cultural lines were firmly drawn here; the laws of survival discouraged crossing them. I had not intended to test these waters. I had only forgotten to hide inside a djellaba. Waiting to start the *salat,* I prepared for the worst: rage, expulsion. Instead, a few old men had glanced my way and seen another man starting his morning.

Si Mallek had said to forget myself. Yusef had warned against thinking like a baby. Hamza counseled me not to think at all. Before I reached the house, I had made my decision. I would take the most immediate route to Mecca. I would not wait five more days for al-Hadj Nasir. I was going to set myself in motion. I wouldn't hire a guide to do it for me.

I drew up a list of errands. When the stores began to open, I walked to town.

I began at the Minzah, Tangier's best hotel. Although prey now to tour buses and a floor show, its lobby still retained the charm of a former palace. The reception desk boasted a fax machine. I tipped the desk man, handed him my song, and watched him feed it through the rollers.

Next I went to the Saudi Arabian consulate. It was only a small bureau, two flights up, behind a door with a crossed-swords seal. A man took my passport. He suggested I come back in three hours.

Paul Bowles lived a few blocks away. I went up to his flat to report my plan and return the book he had lent me. I had read quite a bit of it. Peter Theroux's *Sandstorms* was a lively account in English of his apprenticeship as a journalist in the Middle East. The author was light on his feet, unimpressed by sham, and engaging about individual Arabs. He spoke Arabic; he read Arabic fiction. These last two factors alone distinguished his book from many others. When I handed it back to Paul, he noticed my page marker.

"If you haven't finished reading it, take it with you."

"I'd better not," I said.

"Not the sort of thing a pilgrim should be reading," Paul surmised. "Still, you have a day or two. Keep it. You can leave it at Rodrigo's."

I took back the book with the same mixed emotions Theroux himself expresses about the genre:

I tended to read these books with mounting resentment, because they could not help but be glib, and yet who could do a better job? Saudi Arabia in particular was a poser. A travel writer could record his thoughts about the high walls, empty streets, and pitiless heat. He would meet almost no one, certainly no Saudi, who would confide in him. Describing the difference between this alien culture and our own would be easy, but what was the point? Making people understand other people would have been to stress similarities, to see them from the inside.

Sandstorms wouldn't be much help where I was going.

Paul said, "Send me a letter if you think of it. I've never received one from Mecca."

"Insha' Allah," I said. "Assuming I'm let in."

"Oh, I shouldn't worry. People call it the House of Friendship, don't they?"

"What?"

"The Ka'ba. The House of Friendship."

I wasn't thinking about the Ka'ba then. I was thinking about the customs booth at Jidda. Paul sat back and lit a cigarette. I surveyed the room: the mantelpiece with its African figures, the huge rhododendron on the terrace. I'd been coming here for twenty years, I reflected, and in all that time I had never heard Paul tell anyone not to worry.

It made me nervous.

Part Two

❖❖❖❖❖❖❖❖❖❖

CHAPTER ELEVEN

The House of Friendship

I had chosen Morocco as my starting point because it was familiar territory. Previous visits over the years had accustomed me to its widely varied landscapes, its delicate peasant foods, and its ancient mores. I was able to bargain in the local language and count in dirhams in my sleep. I knew the alleys of the major cities. I had friends there.

In Saudi Arabia I knew nobody. I had never even been inside the country. I was only going now to perform a demanding set of rites whose complexities already made me nervous. I did not intend to add to this the task of measuring deserts or assessing its people. I would not be traveling, in any case. I would be almost exclusively in Mecca, Muhammad's birthplace and the least representative of Saudi cities. In light of Theroux's remarks about Saudi reserve, I could not expect to find very many friends there. Whatever waited at the far end of the runway would be very different and more impersonal.

As the airplane took off I steeled myself a little. Tedious hours aloft were relieved now and then by brief stops to change flights in Casablanca, in Tunis. That afternoon, for the last leg of the trip, I boarded a jumbo jet at the Cairo airport. The flight had originated in New York the day before, and its several hundred passengers looked bedraggled. Most were sleeping. Taking the last free seat beside a window, I glanced around only enough to see that nearly everyone wore pilgrim clothes. It was a short ride and oddly quiet. Scattered here and there across the aisles were the makings of a group of men with whom I was going to spend the next month in Mecca. But I did not know that yet. The sun rolled down behind us, tinting the Red Sea a violent orange. Nobody spoke.

We landed about 8:00 P.M. at the hadj airport in Jidda and I followed a planeload of pilgrims down the ramps. The women among us were scarved and wore white kaftans. Every man had on the white *ihram*, two regulation lengths of seamless terry cloth that males approaching Mecca always wear. The lower wrap fell from my waist to my shins. The top half hung loosely off the shoulders. This sacramental dress, ancient and pastoral, is a common motif on Sumerian statuary dating to 2000 B.C.E. Against the airport's high-tech background we looked like shepherds emerging from a steam bath. The muggy Red Sea heat is legendary. I broke into a sweat leaving the plane.

We entered a stadium-size concourse full of hadjis. I stopped in my towels to gawk at the wing-spread roofs. Tented on all sides, they gave the effect of a Bedouin encampment. In overall area this is the world's biggest airport, containing a dozen enormous terminals. This year, in a period of six weeks, a million pilgrims were going to set down here, a jumbo jet every five minutes, four thousand hadjis every hour. It was also the world's only "annual" airport, its systems too specialized to handle normal traffic. At the end of the season, a few weeks hence, the whole complex would close until next year.

Our group divided and subdivided, moving down the mall. I passed through customs, then joined a knot of three dozen pilgrims in a hallway. A Lebanese man with a curved stick took the lead. I had seen him on the airplane, wearing loafers and a Western business suit. His staff was a saw on a pole, for pruning trees. His name was Mohamad Mardini. Offhand, cherubic, in his thirties, he seemed to know more than the others where we were going. The saw, he said, was a gift for a friend in the city. Its blade was covered by a cardboard scabbard. Walking, I kept my eye on him in the crowds. If we fell behind, he raised the saw to direct us.

I fell behind twice. Once to take a drink of water, once to inspect a room that led off the hall. The size of a college gymnasium, brightly lit with shiny marble floors, the room was jammed with package-tour pilgrims, Malaysians in canvas slippers, turbaned Afghans, a few thousand white-clad Pakistanis. I had not expected to see so many women—young wives, sisters, daughters, matrons, crones—nor was I prepared for the dozens of languages. When I stepped back into the hall, my group had vanished.

I found them outside in a car lot, piling into vans with sliding doors. The sky was dark, but heat still welled up off the asphalt. A driver strapped my luggage to the roof. He wore a checkered head scarf and a *thobe,* the long white choir robe that Saudis favor. When the bags were secure, he jumped inside and revved the engine.

We moved into the foothills of the Hejaz. The name, meaning Barrier, pretty well described the escarpment we were climbing. Its western face walled off Mecca from the sea. Above lay the Tihama Plain. This road is called the Corridor of Dedication. Millions of hadjis have traveled it, trekking back into the peaks where Islam was conceived.

The night was moonless. Freeway lighting curtained off the land. Where it died away, I saw high desert dotted with scrubby thorn bushes and steppe grass. The road curved up through switchbacks, flattened to a plain, then climbed again. Isolated peaks poked up like islands. Now and then in fields beside the road we passed small herds of camels. Oddly formal looking in the headlights, they raised their heads from grazing as we passed.

As we rode along, the men began chanting the talbiya:

> *I am here to serve you, Allah. Here I am!*
> *I am here because nothing compares to you.*
> *Here I am!*
> *Praise, blessings, and the kingdom are yours.*
> *Nothing compares to you.*

These lines are the hadj's hallmark, as much as the *ihram.* I heard them repeated day and night for weeks. The fifth line, echoing the second, wrapped back on the first line like an English round. The Arabic is chanted:

Labbayk, allahumah, labbayk!
Labbayk, la shareeka laka,
Labbayk!
Innal-hamda, wa n-ni 'mata, laka walmulk.
La shareeka lak.

Talbiya means "to wait, in a ready state, for an order or direction." One of its functions is to clear the mind, to prepare you for anything. In the van it began the moment we left the airport. Before long I would hear it in my dreams.

The *ihram* had a powerful impact on me, too. For one thing, it put an end to my months of arrangements. In a way it put an end to me as well. The uniform cloth defeats class distinctions and cultural fashion. Rich and poor are lumped together in it, looking like penitents in a Bosch painting. The *ihram* is as democratic as a death shroud. This, I learned later, is intentional.

Mecca lies fifty miles east of the Red Sea. It is a modern city of one-half million people, splashing up the rim of a granite bowl a thousand feet above sea level. Barren peaks surround it on every side, but there are passes: one leading north toward Syria; one south to Yemen; one west to the coast. A fourth, a ring road, runs east to Taif. By day the hills form a volcanic monotony. At night they blend into the sky and disappear.

The first thing I discovered about Mecca was that I'd been spelling the name wrong. West of town we passed a fluorescent sign with glowing arrows and six letters sparkling in the headlights: MAKKAH. The orthography threw me. With its two hard *c*'s, Mecca is the most loaded Arabic word in the English language. Without them, what is it? No one here said MEH-ka. They said *ma-KAH*. The accent took getting used to, but English-speaking Makkans insisted on it. "Do you spell Manhattan *men-HET-en?*" one of them asked me.

A title was linked to Makkah on every road sign: al-Mukarramah, "the Ennobled." With its special laws of sanctuary, with its status as the birthplace of Islam, the city was sacred ground, however you spelled it. It was also strictly off-limits to nonbelievers. Another sign, at a freeway exit, read

STOP FOR INSPECTION
ENTRY PROHIBITED TO NON MUSLIMS.

The van rolled to a stop beneath the sign. Two soldiers stepped out of a booth and played their flashlights through the cab. Visas were checked. The hadjis continued chanting. A few looked nervous.

Some Westerners think of Makkah as forbidden to foreigners. In fact, it exists to receive them and is largely composed of them. Most of the populace descends through thirteen centuries of migrant pilgrims who settled here after their hadj and did not go home. The result is a cosmopolitan city, where every nation and race has taken root. Naturally it is completely Muslim. Only a Muslim has any business being here.

The officers brought back our passports in a basket. We left the checkpoint and continued on. Hejazi landscapes are studies in barren grimness. It was hard to imagine a sanctuary among these mangled limbs of mother nature. Bare hills rose in the headlights—treeless ridges reminiscent of Death Valley. The skyline looked straight out of Stephen Crane:

> *On the horizon*
> *The peaks assembled;*
> *And as I looked,*
> *The march of the mountains began.*
> *And as they marched, they sang,*
> *"Ay, we come! we come!"*

At the top of a final ridge the road swept east and joined a freeway. The asphalt here was lit up like an airfield. Luminescence bathed the rubbled hills; then, at blinding speed, the van shot under a giant concrete book. I swung around in disbelief, staring back through the windows. There it stood: a sculpture the size of an overpass, an Oldenburg mirage of huge arched crossbeams supporting a forty-ton Qur'an. *Did you see that?* Then we came over the lip of a canyon. The lights of Makkah lay fanned out in a bowl.

* * *

We stopped at the Hotel al-Waha, on a street lined with modern-looking buildings. A sign on the hill read UMM AL-QURA ROAD. I left the van and waited at the curb to see what would happen. Glad to be standing, I busied myself helping the driver untie luggage. Before we finished, the other men were inside the hotel. Our shepherd, Mardini, stood in the doorway, waving me forward. "We're going to stay here for a while," he said.

I went into the lobby and lined up at the counter for my room key. The desk clerk, a fair-skinned Arab in a goatee, insisted on calling me Roy Thomas. I shook my head.

A man behind me laughed. "He thinks because you're from California, you must be Roy. I'm from California. This is not Roy Thomas. I know Roy Thomas."

"Who," I asked, "is Roy Thomas?"

"My professor." He was a boyish-looking man in wire-rimmed glasses. We exchanged a few words. His name was Mohamed Fayez, a graduate-student engineer from U.C. Berkeley, by way of Tunis. Fayez was slight with a quizzical brow reminiscent of Woody Allen's. We stood beside our bags, taking in the action.

Forty men in terry cloth filled the lobby, chatting, sitting on couches, watching TV. Bolivia, Brazil, Guyana, Chile, Argentina, and Peru were well represented. Of the rest a third were African-Americans. Others, like Mardini and Fayez, had roots in North Africa or the Middle East: an Algerian from Denver, a Ghanaian from Detroit, a Palestinian from Culver City. Together we formed a gallery of Islam's diaspora. We had the Western Hemisphere in common.

I said, "Which one is Roy Thomas?"

Roy Thomas was not here. A year ago, Fayez said, Thomas had formed a committee to welcome Nelson Mandela the South African freedom fighter to the Berkeley campus. Now that Mandela had finally been let out of prison and was coming to Berkeley, Thomas felt obliged to make good his word. A big reception was scheduled for tomorrow.

"It was supposed to have happened a month ago," Fayez said. "Now he's missed the hadj."

I said, "It's a pretty good reason."

"Allah decides everything," he said.

As the elevators began to work, a wave of exhaustion closed over me. The hands on my wristwatch were set for a different time zone. I jiggled my key, excused myself, and went upstairs.

I showered first, then turned on the TV. A constant stream of pilgrims passed under the windows. It was almost midnight and the streets were filled. The excitement was palpable. Touching my fingers together, they seemed to vibrate with a migratory throb. I slipped a belt around my waist to secure the *ihram,* folding two inches of cloth over the strap. I could now move freely and bend over.

A map of Iran filled the television screen, and an announcer in a *thobe* read from a clipboard. There had been a massive earthquake in Iran, in the mountains of Zanjan. Damage assessments were still coming in. Already a hundred villages lay in ruins. Aftershocks were being recorded, too, the nearest one six hundred miles from Makkah.

The telephone rang.

I stubbed my thumb reaching for the receiver. It was the desk clerk. "Mr. Thomas?"

I went downstairs.

*T*wenty minutes later we were climbing with the crowds up Umm al-Qura Road. Happily this part of Makkah was set on bedrock. The buildings appeared to be carved into the hills, with a solid, quake-proof look about them.

At the top of the rise, where the street was closed to cars, a throng of five thousand people moved up the pavement. Reaching the crest, I came up on my toes. Everyone knew what was down there, glowing at the bottom of the valley: the largest open-air temple in the world.

I fell in behind Mardini as we climbed. Soon I was being introduced to a Saudi guide named Sheikh Ibrahim, a professor of *hadith* at the local university. I asked him what the Prophet had said about the mosque.

"Plenty," he chuckled.

Ibrahim was a gentle man, the most taciturn of the four guides attached to our party. A few blocks farther on I asked again.

He said, "Just remember: the Ka'ba is a sacred building. But not so sacred as the people who surround it," and pointing to the ground, he made a circle with his finger. "Whatever you do here, don't hurt anyone, not even accidentally. We are going to perform the *'umrah* now. We will greet the mosque, circle the shrine, walk seven times between the hills, like Hagar. Think of it as a pilgrim's dress rehearsal. Don't rush, don't push. Take it easy. Get out of the way if anyone acts wild. If you harm someone, your performance might not be acceptable. You might do it for nothing."

Sheikh Ibrahim's explanation of the *'umrah*—a pilgrimage of a more individual nature, the lesser, or minor, pilgrimage carried out at any time— was the longest single speech I would hear him make in the next four weeks. The view from the brow of the hill cut off further discussion. Behind a concrete overpass rose the biggest minaret I'd ever seen.

Down below, a mosque in the shape of a mammoth door key completely filled the hollow. Lit from above, roofless at the center, it seemed to enclose the valley bowl it covered. The proportions of this eccentric structure were staggering. The head of the key alone comprised a corral of several acres. In addition, attached to the east wall, the shaft of a two-story concourse ran on another quarter mile. For so much stone the effect at night, beneath banks of floods, was airy, glowing, tentlike. Seven minarets pegged down the sides.

This was the recent surrounding mosque that encapsulates a much older Ottoman courtyard. Ibrahim called it Haram al-Sharif, "the Noble Sanctuary." Its 160,000 yards of floor provided room, on a crowded day, for 1.2 million pilgrims. Galleries lit up the second story. Parapets ran right around the roof. From the crest of the hill the minarets looked canted. I could not begin to guess the building's height. Its outer walls were faced in polished slabs of blue-gray marble, and the marine shades differed stone to stone. The veins shooting through them looked like ruffled surf. The minarets were spotlit. On every side the valley glowed.

I had never seen such a beguiling temple complex. Saint Peter's Basilica in Rome is roofed and open to tourists. Palenque covers more ground, but no one uses it. My aversion to sightseeing vanished before this pool of light and stone. All the must-see points were in one building.

We followed the road downhill beneath a bridge. Chunks of the mosque heaved into view as we went down, here a gallery, there a tower, shifting behind facades and concrete rooftops. Then the street curved sharply and the building disappeared.

A hot breeze swept down the hillside. Behind, the hum of traffic died away. The lots, where cars and buses parked at quieter times of the year, were occupied tonight by camping pilgrims. Fires burned low between the groups. Bedrolls lay open under bridgeheads. At the edge of the road we came upon a circle of Ghanaians reciting the Qur'an around a lamp. Most of the encampment was asleep now.

We entered a canyon lined with bazaars and food stalls. Where it leveled out, the mosque came into view. Its second floor had a Colosseum-like curve to the upper galleries. Across the road we stopped before a gate, forming a huddle. Ibrahim addressed us.

In the next few hours we were going to pay our respects to Islam's main shrines. The visit would have three parts. We would greet the mosque and circle the Ka'ba. We would drink from the Zamzam well. We would imitate Hagar's run between two hills in search of water. There were fine points concerning these procedures. Questions followed. Ibrahim or another guide replied. When everything was settled, we waded into the crowds around the mosque.

Most hadjis arriving at Makkah enter the *haram* through Bab al-Salaam, "the Gate of Peace." Ibn Battutah went in by this gate; so did Ibn Jubayr, his predecessor, who left a well-known account of his pilgrimage in 1184 C.E. Tonight crowds on the stairs kept us from fulfilling this tradition.

Mardini shrugged. We continued around the mosque to another gate, Bab al-Malik. A shallow flight of steps led up to a foyer. We deposited our sandals at the door and stepped across the threshold, right foot first.

Inside we offered the formulaic greeting:

> *This is your sanctuary.*
> *This is your city.*
> *I am your servant.*
> *Peace is yours.*

You are salvation.
Grant us salvation,
And guide us
Through the gates of paradise.

Crossing the foyer, we entered a series of pillared, curving halls. In surrounding naves lit by chandeliers, fields of pilgrim families sat on carpets, reclining, conversing, reading the Qur'an. Their numbers increased as we moved deeper into the building. Books on waist-high shelves divided quiet colonnades. Brass fixtures overhead were interspersed with fans lazily turning. We continued down an aisle through the crowds. The Ka'ba, Islam's devotional epicenter, stood in an open courtyard dead ahead, but we could not see it. There were three hundred thousand pilgrims in the complex. Our walk from the outer gate took fifteen minutes.

The colonnades enclosed an oval floor of about four acres. The oldest columns in the mosque flanked the perimeter, columns that Burckhardt, Burton, el-Fasy, and Qutb al-Din all felt compelled to count and could never agree on.* On the east wing they stood in quadruple rows; elsewhere they ran three deep into the building, making a courtyard portico.

I had read about this building and glimpsed it on Moroccan television, but taking its measure now was out of the question. Its proportions could not compete with its population, or with the emotional state of those I saw. To begin with the aisles and carpets held an astounding racial microcosm: Berbers, Indians, Sudanese, Yemenis, Malaysians, and Pakistanis overlapped Nigerians, Indonesians, Baluchis, Bangladeshis, Turks, Iraqis, and Kurds. It was a calm crowd with almost no pushing. Our numbers did not result in agitation. The rush to reach Makkah was finished. The hadjis had arrived. Now the laws of sanctuary took over. This was the peace we had petitioned in the foyer. Everyone felt it.

Across the way a vigorous-looking Afghan in his eighties, six feet tall

---

*Qutb al-Din counted 555 pillars; El-Fasy, 589; Burckhardt, 450 to 500; Burton, 554. The pillars stand twenty feet high, with varying diameters to about two feet. Most are carved from the local granite; half a dozen others look clearly Attic. Tradition claims they were brought from Panopolis, Egypt.

with burnished skin, stood praying into his open hands while big tears dropped onto his palms. A deep exhilaration knocked at my rib cage. Counting up columns in this became absurd.

As we walked, the aisles were subtly descending, conforming to the valley floor. We passed out of the covered portico and stepped down into the marble courtyard. This was the head of the key, the building's hub.

Moroccan mosques, to which I was accustomed, were all arranged in figures of four sides. The core of the mosque at Makkah is on the round, an open, roofless forum overlooked by tiered arcades. The marble floor is 560 feet on the long sides, 350 feet wide, and polished to the whiteness of an ice rink. At the center of this hub stands the Ka'ba, a four-story cube of rough granite covered in a black embroidered veil.

This monolith is Islam's most sacred shrine. Thomas Carlyle, the Scottish historian, called it an authentic fragment of the oldest past. It was already ancient when Muhammad's grandfather restored it in 580 C.E. Its severe simplicity and black reflection lend the mass an upward rhythm. Tonight a light breeze ruffled its cover, and the slabs felt strangely cool beneath my feet. After acres of ceilings it was soothing to look up and see some stars.

We were fifty or sixty yards from the Ka'ba, moving around the outskirts of the forum. Knots of hadjis, stopped in their tracks, stood everywhere around. The first sight of the shrine was literally stunning. Men wept and muttered verses where they stood. Women leaned against columns, crying the rarest sort of tears—of safe arrival, answered prayers, gratified desire. I shared these emotions. I also felt an urge to escape my skin, to swoop through the crowd like lines in a Whitman poem, looking out of every pilgrim's eyeballs. I heard Fayez call out as he hurried past, "We made it! We made it!"

A doughnut ring of pilgrims ten rows deep circled the shrine, forming a revolving band of several thousand people. We kept to the edge of them, skirting the cube, and faced its eastern corner. Here a black stone in a silver bezel had been set into an angle of the building. This was its oldest relic, the lodestone of popular Islam. We faced the stone and stated our intention:

> *Allah, I plan to circle your sacred house.*
> *Make it easy for me,*
> *And accept*
> *My seven circuits in your name.*

Each hadji began at the black stone and circled the Ka'ba counter-clockwise. This ritual is called turning, or *tawaf.** At a distance the wheeling pilgrims obscured its base, so that for a moment the block appeared to be revolving on its axis. As we came nearer, the shrine increased dramatically in size. On the edge of the ring we adjusted our *ihrams* and raised our hands to salute the stone. Then we joined the circle.

Keeping the shrine on our left, we began to turn. Ibrahim and Mardini went ahead, calling words over their shoulders as we followed. There were special supplications for every angle of the building, but not many pilgrims had them memorized. Now and then we passed someone reading set prayers from a handbook, but most people were speaking from the heart. I caught up to Mardini and asked him what was proper. The invocations all but drowned us out. "One God, many tongues!" he shouted. "Say what you want, or repeat what you hear. Or just say, 'God is great.' " I dropped back into the wheel and did all three.

The first three circuits of *tawaf* were performed at a brisk pace called *ramal,* or "moving the shoulders as if walking in sand." Richard Burton likened the step to the *pas gymnastique.* I had not imagined the hadj would be so athletic. Each time a circuit returned to the stone, it was all I could do to remember to raise my palms and shout, *"Allahu akbar."* It was not the pace or the distance but the crowd that was distracting. On the perimeter of the ring I noticed wooden litters passing, on which pilgrims weakened by age or illness were being borne around. These pallets marked the circle's outer edges.

Coming around the northwest wall, we included in each circuit a half circle of floor marked by a rail. Inside the rail lay two slabs of green stone said to mark the graves of Hagar and Ishmail. Directly above, a delicate

---

*The first obligatory rite of the hadj and *'umrah, tawaf al-qudum,* "the turning of arrival," is expected of every visitor to Makkah.

golden rainspout protruded from the roof of the Ka'ba. The prayer at this spot alluded to the rainspout:

> *On that day*
> *When the only shade is yours,*
> *Take me into your shadow, Lord,*
> *and let me drink*
> *From the Prophet's trough*
> *To quench my thirst forever.*

The liturgy and the place were of a piece here.

We performed the quicker circuits near the Ka'ba, on the inside rim of the doughnut. When they were done, Mardini began taking side steps, distancing himself from the shrine as we moved along. I followed suit, working my way to the outer edge of the circle, where we performed our last four rounds at a leisurely walk.

As the pace fell off, space opened around us. I could see the black drape rustle on a breeze. It hung down the Ka'ba on all sides, covering the cube in heavy silk. Its name is *al-kiswa*. I later heard it called the shrine's *ihram*.

One had to perform the *tawaf* to comprehend it. Its choreographic message, with God's house at the center, only came clear to me in the final rounds. Orbiting shoulder to shoulder with so many others induced in the end an open heart and a mobile point of view.

The final circuit brought us back to the eastern corner. We saluted the black stone as we swept past, then washed up on an outer bank of marble, behind a copper enclosure the size of a phone booth. This was called the station of Abraham. Prayers offered here acquired special grace. We faced the Ka'ba and performed two *rak'ahs* together.

Our rite of *tawaf* was complete now, but the evening was not over. Next we descended a flight of steps to a cavernous room containing the Zamzam well. Cool air flooded the stairwell, cutting the night's heat as we went down.

In Ibn Battutah's day the Zamzam well was housed aboveground in a large pavilion. Today the floor has been cleared of these installations. The water drawers and leather buckets have vanished, too, and the profiteers who placed exorbitant fees on the concession. Even the well has been relocated, to a wedge-shaped amphitheater underground.

The air was deliciously damp the first night I went down there. The slanting stone floors ran with surplus water. Hadjis not content merely to drink dumped buckets of the liquid on their bodies, and strangers toweled off each other's backs. The atmosphere was like a friendly bathhouse. Here and there, on a dry patch, lay a solitary sleeper.

Rows of aluminum washbasins were arranged around the room. I took a sip from a public cup chained to a sink and was stepping aside to give Fayez room when a tremor ran through the basement. Beads of condensation shivered in the rafters. The *tawaf?* I thought, and then the vibration stopped. Fayez looked startled.

Makkah's most watchful Western chronicler, John Lewis Burckhardt, wrote this about the well in 1814:

> The Turks consider it a miracle that the water of this well never
> diminishes, not withstanding the continual draught from it. . . . Upon
> inquiry, I learned from one of the persons who had descended in the
> time of the Wahabys to repair the masonry, that the water was *flowing*
> at the bottom, and that the well is therefore supplied by a subterraneous
> rivulet.

Makkah would not exist without this well. Its appearance in the bone-dry Hejaz is a fundamental wonder: the first condition of desert urban life. For thousands of years it supplied the whole town for drinking and ablutions. Seeing it, I understood why Muhammad had linked water to prayer and installed a purifying rite at the heart of his practice. Even in pre-Islamic times the well was sacramental. Today pilgrims drink from it to fulfill tradition. Minerals render it heavy, but I found the taste of Zamzam water sweet, not brackish, and very, very cold (its having passed through a cooling system in the basement).

The legend of Hagar's arrival in this valley is related in the book of Genesis:

> The angel of God called to Hagar out of heaven, and said unto her, "What ails you, Hagar? Fear not; for God has heard the voice of the boy where he is. Arise, lift up the boy, and hold him in your hand; for I will make him a great nation." And God opened her eyes, and she saw a well of water; and she went, and filled the bottle with water, and gave the boy a drink. And God was with the lad; and he grew, and dwelt in the wilderness, and became an archer.

The Bible casts Hagar in a passive role. Weeping, lost in a wilderness, she sits with eyes averted, unable to watch her child's death. Muslim legend describes a more active agent. In these stories Hagar runs between two hills, passionately seeking water in a desert. Her drive is emotional, physical, existential. At stake are faith and her family's survival.

The course of Hagar's quest is still, I now discovered, in active use within the building. Our last labor of the night was a ritual jog between the hills. The rite, called *sa'y,* takes place in the concourse on the long side of the key. To reach it, we crossed the Ka'ba floor, saluted the stone, then walked out of the courtyard, heading south.

A series of arches led through cloisters to a gate. Here the head of the mosque and its shaft were joined, forming a marble lane called *al-mas'a.* Later I heard one hadji refer to it as the racecourse. I was unprepared for the length of this passage: a quarter-mile stretch of covered mall, split in two lanes for pilgrims coming and going.

The course began at the top of a hill called al-Safa, jutting from the base of Mount Qubays. It ended at the second hill, al-Marwa, in the north of the building. I had never seen hillocks housed inside a building; domes had been set in the ceilings to accommodate their crowns. A complete lap covered about eight hundred yards. Here, as around the Ka'ba, old age and illness were shown consideration. Down the center of the *mas'a,* on a median strip dividing the two lanes, frail pilgrims were being wheeled in rented chairs.

Saluting the shrine at the top of each relay, we completed seven lengths, or about two miles. My legs began to throb in the third round. The contrast between the mystical *tawaf* and this linear, headlong rush could not have been greater. Wandering loosely between fixed points, doubling back on itself around the hills, the rite expressed persistence and survival. The *sa'y* was not a circle dance. Its intent seemed to be to instill compassion for the victimized and the exiled. This was the mall of necessitous desire.

We finished our run and stepped down onto a ramp beside al-Marwa. By now our *ihram* towels were streaked with dirt and sweat. We had come through the *'umrah*. We were *muta 'ammirin*. As we stood shaking hands (Mohamed Fayez high-fived me), two self-appointed barbers stepped from the wings, offering their services. In order to put aside the *ihram* clothes, a pilgrim who plans to return to them for the hadj is supposed to have a desacralizing haircut. Generally this means a token snip of three or four neck hairs. When it was done, we returned to Bab al-Malik for our sandals.

✧   ✧   ✧   ✧

*I*n the dark on the hill going back to the hotel, I noticed two or three men from the group trying to give Ibrahim money. Each time he refused.

This starkly contradicted the slanderous talk I had heard about the guides here. Abd al-Qadir in Marrakesh had warned me off these people like the plague. Their extortionate rates were a set piece in the oldest commentaries. Time after time pilgrims strapped for money, tried by exhaustion, cholera, and thieves, arrived at the site of their aspirations only to be fleeced by their *mutawwif*. Eldon Rutter, who made the pilgrimage in 1925, accused them of never missing an unearned tip and of eternally evolving new ways to get them. Ahmad Kamal wrote in 1961:

> All pilgrim guides belong to closed Makkan guilds. Each guild is organized to cater only to pilgrims of a particular nation or area, whose languages or dialects the guild members speak, and with whose peculiarities they are familiar. Such knowledge is a two-edge blade, bleeding the unwary as often as it protects them. . . . Dwelling in close proximity to the Holy Ka'ba has not turned them into angels.

"We sow no corn," the saying went; "the hadjis are our crop."

I caught up to Mardini and asked him about it. The pilgrim guides were much maligned, he said. In the past they had deserved it. Today their activities are regulated. Some remained rapacious in their greed, but the majority performed a service fairly. They worked hard. Their earning periods were brief.

Ibrahim and his fellow sheikhs were different. They had day jobs to begin with, and PhDs. They were professors on vacation picking up a second wage, not cicerones. They worked in the hire of the Islamic Affairs Department, guiding official guests and delegations.

I said I had not known we were an official delegation.

"In a distant way," Mardini said, "we are guests of the king."

Mardini's view of the guides opened my eyes. I wondered where our group would be without them. We had stepped off a bus and been plunged into a labyrinth of rites. It was the same for every hadji. Regardless of status, you reached Makkah exhausted and in a state of exultation and were required to perform on the first night. A good guide was indispensable, it seemed. It was not, as in Rome or at the Taj Mahal, a matter of missing the artwork. The correctness of your hadj was at stake. For a vast majority of pilgrims this was a once-in-a-lifetime event. They would not have the money or the chance to try again next year. Everyone needed to get it right the first time.

Mardini knew a lot about these things because he had made nine pilgrimages. He had attended university in Makkah and later worked for the pilgrimage banking system. He knew the routes the money took at Makkah; he knew the rites of the pilgrimage so well that Ibrahim had picked him as an assistant. Gradually I began to see that Sheikh Khalil, back in Washington, had attached me to a formal delegation and, within that delegation, to Mardini, its most capable member. Khalil had said a man would meet me at the airport. I had not been able to guess what that would mean.

I was just catching on when Mohamed Fayez rushed up to congratulate me. As we walked, his elation gave way to a case of nerves.

"Did you feel it?" His voice was high, reedy.

"Feel what?" Mardini asked.

"The aftershock! The earthquake! Just like California."

"Where did you feel it?"

Fayez said, "In the well." His eyes were rolling.

I said I had felt the roof shake, too, but dismissed it as people circling the shrine. I glanced back at the mosque, then up to the mountains.

Mardini laughed and stamped the road. "Makkah is on bedrock! Solid Granite! The Zanjan region is a thousand miles away."

Fayez remained unconvinced. We climbed the hill past the locked bazaars, discussing a recent San Francisco earthquake.

CHAPTER TWELVE

Erasable Names

*U*pstairs I fell asleep for a couple of hours. I could not be sure how long Fayez had been knocking. When I opened the door, he stood smiling in the hall beside his roommate, a tall youth of about twenty named Ahmad.

Apparently I had slept through the *adhan*. The predawn prayer was due to begin, they said. When I groaned, Fayez added that one prayer at Makkah equalled twenty-five thousand prayers elsewhere—missing a chance like this was out of the question. I commended his fervor.

Ahmad, who towered above us, disagreed. "The value of any prayer is up to God," he said. "Don't intimidate the man, Mohamed."

Fayez consulted his wristwatch. "We can sleep when we get home," he said.

While I showered and dressed, they sat in a couple of armchairs by the window. The heat was such that the air-conditioned room had not cooled off. Fayez mopped his brow on the arm of his gown. Ahmad produced an ice-cold water bottle. I had placed a thermometer outside on the sill, to try to keep track of temperatures at Makkah, and when I showed Ahmad the mercury, he whistled. At 3:00 A.M. it was ninety-nine degrees Fahrenheit.

"Worse than Kuwait," he said.

Ahmad was amiable and Palestinian, an exile with a philosophical view. His father had moved the family from Gaza to Kuwait after the 1967 Six-Day War. Ahmad was born there. Kuwait, he said, was best for the Kuwaitis. Outsiders, like his father, were able to find work and raise their families, but even if they stayed for a hundred years, they would never be treated as first-class citizens. Real Kuwaitis had the largest per capita income in the Gulf. Their population was minuscule, but they were not about to share this happy fate with four hundred thousand guests from the occupied territories. The Kuwaitis hired and paid foreigners well, to sweep the streets and man the storefronts. But if the wrong man should awake at dawn and feel like getting rid of a guest worker, you could find yourself on the border that afternoon.

I wondered how often this happened.

"Too often," he said. Recently a traffic law had been published in the city of Kuwait, stating that any "nonresident" caught speeding more than twice could be sent home. "Home," Ahmad mused. "As if we had one."

"Twice in one year?" Fayez asked.

"Twice in one lifetime."

Otherwise Kuwait was not so bad. The pay was the best in the Gulf, and he had many friends. He would be going back after the hadj, to attend his sister's wedding. If I wanted to see how it was, I should come along.

Fayez said, "Let's get him down the street first."

I laid a *gandoura* across the bed and slipped into my best pair of *serwals*—the Moroccan version of Bermuda shorts. On the landing I remembered the air-conditioning; I had locked the door and left it on full blast. Ahmad took my room key and hurried back. The controls were near the ceiling, he said. He could reach them.

Having by now performed the rites of *'umrah,* I saw, coming down the hill again, that the d shape of the mosque was far from eccentric. This design

had been been purposely devised to enclose two ritual arenas: the boule-
vardlike *mas'a* and the rink of the Ka'ba. Both areas had been laid down in
prerecorded time along the lines they occupy today. These lines show
purpose. The *sacra via* runs on an east-west axis; the four-cornered cube
still marks the compass points. Clearly, the lay of the mosque has been
aligned by cosmographic logic, like Stonehenge or the sun temple at
Thebes.

I could also appreciate its enlarged proportions. In the hadj month of
1939, one hundred thousand pilgrims had come to Makkah. This month
about the same number arrived each day. The mosque complex had been
expanded in every direction to accommodate them. A lot of rock had been
moved to make more room.

It was 3:45 in the morning, but that meant nothing. The canonical
hours replaced the clock at Makkah. To reach the mosque in time, we
would have to rush.

Where Malik and Bab al-'Umrah streets converged, the dense crowds
threatened to divide us. Fayez, much shorter, bobbed around Ahmad's
shoulders. A group decision was next to impossible. Luckily Ahmad had
been here as a boy. He led us around the mosque to an eastern gate.
Although the press thinned out near the *mas'a,* we still could not get in.
The ground-floor cloisters were packed, and hundreds of pilgrims were
forming rows on the outside stairs. Ahmad continued to another entry. It
led through a hall at a tangent to the Ka'ba. An escalator carried us past the
second floor to the top of the complex. We left our sandals on a ramp there
and walked onto a roof under the stars.

The marble felt cool here, a hundred feet above the floor. A light
breeze blew. We crossed the terrace to a rail and looked down. The shrine
was surrounded by ranks of seated pilgrims awaiting the prayer. Their
curving rows radiated outward, like ripples from a rock dropped in a pool.

Over the rail, across the way, I had a clear view into the second floor
galleries. Lit orange globes depended from the pillars like fruit in an orchard. Here and there on a patch of open rug a few men and women sat
reading the Qur'an. The level roof was sparsely settled, too. Fayez laid out
a prayer mat near the railing, a couple of dozen others sat around, but 90
percent of the balcony was empty.

The first stars were beginning to wink off now, and the *tawaf* had stopped completely. When loudspeakers ruffled in the towers, everyone rose. At any other mosque on earth people prepared for this moment by forming straight lines and facing Makkah. At Makkah the prayer is circular. Any way you face, you face the shrine. I scanned the crowds to locate the imam. He stood near the Ka'ba door, a pale speck with a microphone beside him. He leaned on a stick. He wore a white scarf called a *kaffiyeh*.

When he tapped the mike, a group of porters came wading out of the wings in crimson head scarves. They made their way down an aisle through the crowds, bearing four pallets on their shoulders. The pallets looked like the rented litters that carry old people around the shrine, but the litters jostled oddly at each step. There were bodies on them, shrouded in coverlets.

I turned to a stranger beside me to confirm this, but by then the biers were resting on the ground. Positioned near the feet of the imam, they seemed like couches reserved for weary dignitaries. The man said, "Those people? They look asleep."

Today's imam appeared frail, but his voice was not. It sailed out over the mosque and rang back clear as a bell off the granite hills. The clarity of the Makkan *adhan* is famous. The stony hollow acts as a sound dish, and the callers are among the world's best. Even the sky cooperated, acquiring a pastel skin, adding shades, then deleting them, shimmering slightly, a desert northern lights.

The sky and the call to prayer got all the attention. I left the rail and joined Ahmad and Fayez. Our row stood only a few yards back. I could still look down directly into the courtyard. When the crowd whispered a unison *ameen*, the sound swelled up from the mosque and filled the valley.

After the last salaam, we came to our feet. This time the imam faced the shrouded bodies on the biers and repeated a four-part prayer for the dead. We replied with four sets of *Allahu akbars*. Mathematically it was reasonable in a gathering this size for at least three hundred people to die daily. Later on I became philosophical when faced with this ceremony. Muslims are raised to treat death with dispatch—"Death is the brother of sleep" is a popular maxim. And the heat, after all, demanded quick interment. But some days had to pass before I was used to it.

Janaza, the prayers for the dead, are brief, but that did not rule out displays of feeling. As the bearers marched out with their burdens, I caught sight of the man I had talked with earlier. He was standing a row in front of me now, at an angle that gave me a side view of his face. The man was crying. Dozens of others stood similarly reminded, hands at their sides, tears streaming down their cheeks. When the *tawaf* started up in the courtyard, my two companions sank down to the carpet. I sat between them, thinking of Iran.

A few hours later I woke in bed for the second time that day. The bed across the room had not been lain on. The covers were rolled down, but the pillow looked spotless. Mardini, my roommate, apparently never slept.

I stumbled out of bed to the window and drew back the curtains. The panes were hot to the touch. The sunlight looked copperish. Two flights down, in Umm al-Qura Road, a crowd of men in *thobe*s covered the sidewalks. The women, mostly in kaftans, walked erectly. Many people had on their Friday best.

I unpacked a new *gandoura*, one I had found in the rue Semarine and got at a bargain. The pocket was double stitched and the cloth had sheen. Unlike a Saudi *thobe*, the *gandoura* is sleeveless. Also it leaves the ankles bare. I wondered if I would stand out in this at Makkah. Though it was badly wrinkled, I put it on and went downstairs.

The stairs led to a dining room on the hotel mezzanine. I passed Fayez in the doorway. I complained of exhaustion. He consulted his wristwatch again.

"If you can't make it here, you can't make it anyplace," he said cheerily. *"Jum'a* prayer is very soon. Don't miss breakfast."

In his hand he held a sheet of thin blue paper. It was a telegram from his family in Tunis, to say that his grandmother was coming to Makkah. He hadn't expected her.

"But that's amazing," I said. *"Al-Hamdulillah.* Praise God."

"Yes! But how will I find her?" He showed me the telegram. The message, in French, had been garbled in transmission. The type trailed off at the name of her hotel.

Fayez rushed off to the lobby to telephone Tunis. I went into the dining room. Ahmad was there, having breakfast with five or six others.

I sat down across from an African-American man named Abd al-Qadir, who ran a prisoner rehabilitation program in the Hudson Valley. He discussed his work as we ate.

Islam, he said, had been doing good works in the jails for years. Normal life came to a stop in jail, he said, and a man had time to ask questions. It was not all bad. He passed out some photographs of a concrete room in what looked like a basement. It was a prison mosque. At first, he said, attendance had been low. Now, a few years later, two hundred men a day came for *salat* and counseling.

Mardini looked at the photographs and nodded. "We have mosques like this in Michigan," he said. "I go there sometimes." Mardini was a state chaplain in Dearborn.

"How long have you lived there?" I asked him.

"For about five years."

"And before that?"

"I was a student here, in Makkah. I was born and raised in Lebanon."

Everyone at the table, it seemed, worked in some capacity for Islam. Besides Abd al-Qadir, the jailhouse imam, there were Usama, a Chilean merchant, one of the elders in this group; Rafeeq Manifa, an economist and exiled Libyan whose father had been an adviser to King Idris; Abd ar-Rahman, a publisher who ran a Muslim bookshop in Chicago; and Abd al-Mu'id, an Algerian computer engineer from Colorado. Usama raised funds to build mosques in Santiago; Abd al-Mu'id wrote Quranic software.

"That's more or less it," Mardini said. "We're the Western delegation."

I must have looked puzzled.

"Don't worry about it," Ahmad said. "We're just a bunch of Muslims."

Abd al-Qadir's roommate, John Muhammad, was a cheerful, self-effacing man from Atlanta. When we left the table, he had trouble standing up. He winced, set a hand on his chair, and gripped the small of his back to hold himself steady. I recognized the symptoms of a problem that had laid me up in bed once for three months. John had sciatica.

Ahmad stopped me going out the door. "Come to my room," he said, pointing to my gown. "I'll lend you a pressed one."

✧   ✧   ✧   ✧

I came back down to the lobby in cotton pants and a Saudi *thobe*.

The *thobe* is a classic and forgiving garment. It puts the best shape on any body and has the maneuvered simplicity of a toga. The garment Ahmad lent me was well made. The cloth shone like silk and felt cool on the skin. The *kaffiyeh* confused me. A red-checked muslin square, it looked and behaved like a shrunken tablecloth. I could not find a way to keep it on. Piled on my head, draped over the shoulders, however it was disposed, the folds kept slipping.

Ahmad arrived, flipped on the TV, and led me to a mirror. Making a few quick passes above my eyes, he arranged the scarf the way Makkans wear it, giving the cloth a twist where it bordered my forehead. "Real Saudis pinch it here," he said.

We sat down to watch the last few minutes of an NBA play-off, and Mardini joined us. The intermissions were mostly religious. When a time-out was called with twenty seconds remaining, the taped game segued into a *hadith*. Elegant script scrolled down the screen:

> *A Muslim is the one*
> *who avoids harming people*
> *with his hands or tongue.*

The game resumed, ending 112 to 98 in favor of the Celtics.

Ahmad turned off the set, and I looked out the window. Crowds swept by on the sidewalk, a steady stream. When Abd al-Qadir finally arrived, assisting a limping John Muhammad through the lobby, we followed them out onto the road.

*   *   *

Malik Street, going down to the mosque, was lined with stucco storefronts. Balconied apartments leaned above us. A handful of hotels topped the skyline at ten stories. Rarely did we pass by any building older than a century or two. Already in Ibn Battutah's day Makkah was a modern city, updated by each new caliphate and subject between times to ruinous flash floods. In 1814, Burckhardt called the Ka'ba its only ancient structure. It still is.

The mosque made a slow dissolve behind a bridge and came back into view as we reached the square. The heat blasting off the pavement felt architectural. It marched up the road at us, tossing phantom ripples. Today being Friday, the plazas around the mosque were overfilled. Hadjis sat on the walks facing the building. The approaching crowds were dense. We formed a protective flank behind John Muhammad, trying to guard his back, and waded in.

"He could get hurt here," I called to Mardini.

As a wall of shoulders closed around us, Abd al-Qadir's eyes began to roll. With a nervous wave he commenced steering John to the edge of the plaza. Ahmad went behind to protect their rear. They bobbed away like a raft going over a rapid.

I followed Mardini to the nearest gate, where rows of hadjis stood, backed down the staircase. After five or ten minutes of dogged inching forward Mardini relented, and laying out his head scarf we sat down. We were twenty yards shy of entering the building. Others filled in rapidly behind us until we had a foot of room between the rows.

Back up Malik Street for as far as I could see, the mosque was surrounded in a tide of cotton. When the loudspeakers clicked on, a hush lapped the city. You could hear a truck's brakes squeak ten blocks away.

After *salat* we stood again, and the prayers for the dead were recited. This event, which had so surprised me at first, occurred five times a day. Perhaps that explained why the stories I heard about death here were so so well honed.

Death put on a legendary face at Makkah. People said that the angel Israfil came down to earth with a book on the day you died. To some he appeared as a monster; for others he wore white. His book contained a list of "erasable names" that was always changing. To someone pretending not to recognize him, he said, "Don't you know me? I am your prayers." Or your name was inscribed on a leaf from a tree near God's throne. In either case, when the angel arrived, you knew right away what he wanted. If you resisted, he offered an apple from paradise with the word *bismillah* written on its skin. When a man saw the apple or smelled it, he gave in.

After the Janaza prayer we left the mosque and waded back uphill. As the sun blazed down, the incline seemed to double. Now I began to appreciate Ahmad's *thobe*. Its sleeves kept my skin from burning. Its whiteness re-flected heat. When it belled around the feet, it made little breezes. Com-bined with a *kaffiyeh*, it was the nearest thing to portable air-conditioning.

You went through two or three *thobe*s a day in June. Mine, on loan, was soaked through the back and arms after one outing. Mardini suggested I purchase five or six. At the crest of the hill we passed a line of bazaars set up off a sidewalk. Mardini selected a shop and we went in.

The Kurdish owner, a man in his eighties, reclined on a pile of rugs, smoking a narghile. His twelve-year-old great-grandson showed us around. The boy had bright, round cheeks. The man was blind. Mardini chatted between them while I made a selection. Then a price was quoted.

Rather than argue the figure down too soon, Mardini said, "But we want a half dozen." I had seen this done at Mostopha's many times.

The boy climbed up to a shelf and brought down the boxes. Mardini added a prayer rug to the pile, a canteen, then three *kaffiyeh*s. Arabic began flying, and the price of each item fell as the pile rose. In the end the outfits came to fifty dollars.

I gave the boy the riyals. He passed the bills to the blind man, who put them into a box and handed back a small packet of Kleenex. I fingered the tissues.

"He owes you a half riyal," the boy explained. "But we don't use coins here."

"Where?"

"In Makkah. Coins make noise in the mosque. And the *ihram* towels don't have pockets. It's a nuisance."

We put the items into sacks and carried them through the crowds to the hotel.

I went upstairs to shower and change and came back down to the desk with a bag of laundry. I handed it over the counter to the desk clerk. He wrote up a ticket.

"You look like perfectly Saudi now," he said. I had changed into one of the newly purchased *thobes*. He reached up and pinched my scarf into position. I noticed a lot of fresh luggage piled by the stairs. New arrivals were still pouring into Makkah.

"You wait!" the clerk said. "Next week one hundred thousand more come every day."

"To this hotel?"

He looked stricken. "Allah protect us! To the city!"

I said something about that meaning a lot of Kleenex.

I crossed the room and sat down on a couch to wait for Abd al-Qadir. I had seen him last at the back of the mosque, supporting John Muhammad on his arm. I passed the time counting pilgrims out the window. I soon gave up counting.

Everything about the hadj involved big numbers. The airports had cost billions. The mosques covered millions of square feet. The head counts were huge and subjectively impressive. I almost never saw the same face twice. So sudden an influx in such a small city gave the hadj an astronomical appearance. Normally about five hundred thousand people lived here. Now that many and more arrived each week. I thought of Fayez attempting to track down his grandmother.

I had come across a copy of Joseph Conrad's *Lord Jim* on a paperback rack at the Casablanca airport. Here in the lobby I began to read. Published first in 1900, *Lord Jim* was still the only work of English fiction whose moral action revolved around the hadj. I read to a point where the pilgrim ship, the *Patna*, was being boarded:

> They streamed aboard over three gangways, they streamed in urged by
> faith and the hope of paradise, they streamed in with a continuous
> tramp and shuffle of bare feet, without a word, a murmur, or a look

back; and when clear of confining rails spread on all sides over the deck, flowed forward and aft, overflowed down the yawning hatchways, filled the inner recesses of the ship—like water filling a cistern, like water flowing into crevices and crannies, like water rising silently even with the rim. Eight hundred men and women with faith and hopes, with affections and memories, they had collected there, coming from north and south and from the outskirts of the East, after treading the jungle paths, descending the rivers, coasting in praus along the shallows, crossing in small canoes from island to island, passing through suffering, meeting strange sights, beset by strange fears, upheld by one desire. They came from solitary huts in the wilderness, from populous campongs, from villages by the sea. At the call of an idea they had left their forests, their clearings, the protection of their rules, their prosperity, their poverty, the surroundings of their youth and the graves of their fathers.

When it seemed certain Abd al-Qadir would not come, I decided to slip upstairs for a nap before *'asr*. Crossing the lobby, I glanced at my laundry stub. The clerk had made out the ticket to Sheikh Thomas.

✧   ✧   ✧   ✧

John Muhammad did not show up that night for dinner. Fayez and several of the others were missing, too. After the meal I went up to John's room. I found him lying on his back in bed, his legs propped on pillows.

Things had gone badly at the mosque today. In a hallway, leaving after *jum'a* prayer, a crowd of Turks had swept him out of Abd al-Qadr's grip. John had made his way alone toward a staircase, then the ranks behind him swelled, and something twisted. He had managed somehow to return to the hotel, where Sheikh Ibrahim had called an ambulance. Now John could barely walk, and his left foot tingled.

"It feels like ice water's pouring down my leg."

"It's not your leg," I said. "It's the nerve in your back."

The doctors had said the same thing.

"You've got sciatica," I said.

"A prolapsed disk in the lower lumbar region," John quoted the doctor. "I'm supposed to stay prone until the hadj."

"What did they prescribe for you?"

He showed me a vial of Tylenol and codeine.

I went down to the kitchen and convinced a cook to send John's meals upstairs. Then I went to my room to get Yusef's medicines.

"Take one of these every four hours to kill the pain," I told him. "And one of these to reduce the inflammation. And one of these to relax the spasm. You've got a spasm in your back and its pinching a nerve. Tylenol can't touch it."

John Mohammad laughed. "You talk like a doctor."

"I've had the same thing," I said. "I was flat on my back for months with this. Be careful."

"What about the hadj? What about *salat?*"

"*Salat* is good exercise," I said.

I left him some reading materials and went downstairs.

Fayez lay collapsed on a couch, watching television. Beside him sat a man with a sun-blistered head. They're dropping like flies, I thought to myself. Fayez's eyes looked rheumy. He had stayed in the mosque all day, reading the Qur'an. In Fayez's view the *haram* was a spiritual bank where one could lay up profits by righteous action. To read the entire Qur'an there, for example, was said to convey an *'umrah*'s worth of grace.

"How long would that take?" I asked him.

"*Insha' Allah,* I can do it in eight days." The effort was taking a toll on him, however.

Tonight the TV was filled with public announcements. When a show came on about heat prostration, the man with the blistered head perked up and watched.

Fayez had managed to track down his grandmother. He had not actually seen her yet, he said, but one of the sheikhs, through a housing office, had managed to locate her hotel. Fayez was supposed to go over in the morning.

"Get some rest," I told him. "I'll wake you up."

At 9:00 P.M. I went to the mosque and remained there until 11:00, mostly watching. I returned to the room to find a note from Mardini. He had gone to visit friends across the city. The curtains were drawn. The pruning saw was gone. I got into bed and read a few pages of Burckhardt's *Travels in Arabia*. A little after midnight I fell asleep.

CHAPTER THIRTEEN

A Likeness for Yourselves

*J*ohn Lewis Burckhardt arrived in Jidda beset by economic difficulty. His entire purse that day consisted of two dollars and some sequins sewn into a leather amulet. He arrived in July 1814, when the heat is at its worst. Coming ashore in the rags of a beggar, he would have looked like one more impoverished Sudanese pilgrim. Burckhardt was Swiss and a graduate of Cambridge.

Napoleonic politics prepared him for this journey. His father had been tried as a spy by the French, and the ruin this brought on young Burckhardt in his teens conditioned him early to a life of exile. It also instilled a dislike of Bonapartists. He fled Lausanne at fifteen, attending schools in Germany, then Britain. At twenty-one he spoke and wrote fluently in German, French, and English. He could read Greek and Latin.

At Cambridge he discovered Arabic and must have done well. On leaving school, he was recommended to a group of London merchants seeking to open Middle Eastern markets. They paid very little, divining perhaps, that for Burckhardt the job was a pretext. Travel and language had come together in him from an early age. Out of school he seems to have given up almost at once to what he called his "traveling madness." He also began to express a flare for disguises. In 1809 he sailed from London, dressed as an Indian merchant.

He first wrote of his plan to visit Makkah in an 1812 letter to his employers. Meanwhile he had been studying Arabic and Islamic law in Damascus and Cairo. He had translated *Robinson Crusoe* into Arabic, mounted several trading expeditions, crossed the Sudanese Sahara, and rediscovered the lost ruins of Petra. By now he was using the name Sheikh Ibrahim and engaging in fine disputes with Muslim scholars. At twenty-eight, Burckhardt was what Alan Moorehead called him, a classicist in the wilderness, and one of the most observant travelers who ever lived.

When he arrived in Cairo to join the pilgrim caravan, his motivations were practical and religious. He had been a Muslim now "for many years," and the pilgrimage was thus an obligation. On the other hand, he also knew that the title hadji would open new doors for his employers. At Cairo he missed the caravan by weeks and set off up the Nile, hoping to catch it. By riverboat, then camel, he passed through Nubia and the Sudan, watching and talking and keeping careful records.

Burckhardt's chief discovery during this period was the temple of Ramses II, at Abu Simbel. His books, compiled posthumously from letters, show a curious and energetic mind. He was not by nature an archaeologist. He was an ethnographer, a humanist, and a writer with a scientific passion for small details. Broke though he was, his account was at its most autobiographical in the Hejaz:

> I had little time to make melancholy reflections upon my situation. For on the fourth day after my arrival I was attacked by a violent fever, occasioned, probably, by indulging too freely in the fine fruits which were then in the Djidda market. . . . I was for several days delirious; and nature would probably have been exhausted, had it not been for the aid of a Greek captain, my fellow passenger from Souakin. He attended me in one of my lucid intervals and, at my request, procured a barber. . . . In a fortnight after, I had sufficiently recovered to be able to walk about.

As it happened, the pasha of Cairo, Muhammad 'Ali, was nearby in Ta'if. The two men had met previously in Egypt. Burckhardt sent a letter now, describing his plight, but it took some days through the mountains to reach the pasha. Before it arrived, he had found assistance elsewhere, through a physician to the governor of Jidda. Nonetheless, about a week later an envoy arrived at Burckhardt's door with camels and a letter of safe passage from 'Ali. Burckhardt did not need help now, but a pasha's invitation was a summons. He arranged his affairs in town and went along rather than excite 'Ali's resentment.

*A*larm clocks were superfluous in Makkah. The five calls to prayer were piped through speakers all over the city—at markets, gas stations, on the roofs of banks. I read until midnight, slept a few hours, and woke to the *adhan* about three-thirty.

I found Fayez dressed and waiting in his room, reading the Qur'an on a rug by the window. A few hours' sleep had cleared his bloodshot eyes. He looked restored, ready for action.

On our way upstairs to see John, Fayez reported his latest discovery: he had found the perfect spot to sit in the mosque. The best seat in the house, he called it, tucked a few carpets back in the western cloister—where, out of the sun, beneath a Guinea fan, one had between two pillars a perfectly framed view of the Ka'ba. "A man can control the whole mosque from there," he told me mysteriously.

We found Abd al-Qadir standing near John's bed, preparing a thermos. He had seen the TV show on heat prostration and was tearing off the tops of sugar packets and pouring them into his water. John lay propped on pillows, reading *The Autobiography of Malcolm X*. Months before I had photocopied the chapters concerning Malcolm's hadj and slipped them into the binder John was holding. It was Malcolm's visit to Makkah, in 1964, that had boiled the racism out of his message forever. In a well-known letter at the time he wrote:

> You may be shocked by these words coming from me. But on this
> pilgrimage, what I have seen, and experienced, has forced me to *re-*

arrange much of my thought-patterns previously held, and to *toss aside* some of my previous conclusions. . . .

During the past eleven days here in the Muslim world, I have eaten from the same plate, drunk from the same glass, and slept in the same bed (or on the same rug)—while praying to the *same God*—with fellow Muslims, whose eyes were the bluest of blue, whose hair was the blondest of blond, and whose skin was the whitest of white. And in the *words* and in the *actions* and in the *deeds* of the "white" Muslims, I felt the same sincerity that I felt among the black African Muslims of Nigeria, Sudan, and Ghana.

Malcolm's radical transformation (which later cost him his life) was succinctly conveyed by his meeting with Prince Faisal:

Prince Faisal had read Egyptian writers' articles about the American "Black Muslims." "If what these writers say is true, the Black Muslims have the wrong Islam," he said.

Malcolm replied that for twelve years he had been working to build the Nation of Islam and that the hadj had helped him get it right.

Abd al-Qadir was squeezing a lemon into his thermos. "A lot of water's gone over the dam since Malcolm," he said.

I asked John what he thought of the chapters.

He said, "What Christianity did for Martin Luther King, Islam did for Malcolm. It let him repudiate racism. It hipped him to the brotherhood of man."

Fayez leaned against the desk, consulting his wristwatch. Prayers at the mosque were about to start, he said. Of course, we were free to perform *salat* here, in John's room; but being so near the Ka'ba made that silly. The sky was pitch-black. As we moved to the door, John produced a thermos and asked me to bring back some Zamzam water.

"He should come along," Abd al-Qadir said. "We can rent him a litter."

*   *   *

Coming down Malik Street, we passed a ruined Turkish castle tucked into the cliffs above the mosque. Burckhardt had mentioned this fortress, its towers and ramparts crumbling in the sun. It reminded Abd al-Qadir of a jail.

I asked him what he had meant the day before, about jail being a good place to think.

"Most prisoners I know," he said, "when they were on the outside, tried to belong to something and got arrested. Right now in Los Angeles one hundred thousand kids belong to gangs. If it isn't a gang, it's the fast lane they want to be part of. They want to sell crack and drive Jaguars. We had twenty-three thousand murders last year in America. A rape every eight minutes. We have two million guns in New York City. We have a million people behind bars. That's a lot of folks who threw in with the wrong forces. When you join Islam, it's a chance to wash your hands. It's like A.A. only better. You quit drinking and drugs. You think about your family. You make new friends."

The pedestrian traffic looked drowsy this morning coming down the hill. The sky turned lighter by degrees. In the encampments under the bridges African families were stretching, waking up. Coal fires licked the coffeepots on braziers. Vendors were setting up tables on the walk.

Where the road leveled out, Fayez went ahead. Wanting to show us his favorite spot in the cloisters, he walked us in by the 'Umrah gate, then worked through the naves to a hall of pillars deep inside the building. We stopped in the last colonnade and joined a carpetful of Algerians. The chandeliers in this part of the mosque had a greenish cast.

Fayez was right. The view of the shrine from here was unimpeded. Our colonnade ran right up to the courtyard, the floor dropping off a few steps where they met, like the curb of an ice rink. The stone looked cool. Our angle here was perfect.

Wherever you glanced around the mosque, a datable layer of history showed through. Every corner bristled with old stories. A seventh minaret, at the al-Wida' gate, for instance, dated back to the early 1600s. It had been added by Sultan Ahmed I of Istanbul, under duress, lest the six towers of his fabulous Blue Mosque appear presumptuous. And just beneath the history were legends. The Ka'ba itself is said to rest on a serpentine paved pad laid down by Ishmail.

The horizon turned purple. Outlines of hills emerged like streaks on glass. The imam began. We performed *salat,* and when the prayer was over, I thanked Fayez for showing us his spot.

The Ka'ba looked beautifully balanced from Fayez's corner. I saw it every day during this period, yet no matter how many I times I circled around it, its face remained impenetrable to me. The shrine seemed to stand for some necessary other set by choice at the center of my world. Perhaps it symbolized the human heart, as the Sufis put it. It was certainly potent. It stirred a stream of conjectures whenever I saw it. Its form affirmed God's oneness, but its veil was ineffably suggestive.

The *tawaf* around the shrine only stopped turning during prayers. It could otherwise be performed at any time, not only upon arrival or during hadj. The ring of pilgrims had already doubled its thickness since last night, and the outer rim of pallets was almost continuous. So many people moving in one direction could kick up a little breeze across the floor. In turn, the breeze stirred the *kiswa* and sometimes even made it sway. Because the *tawaf* is considered a form of prayer, this breeze is often attributed to angels. Angels, in turn, are considered products of prayer.

Early in the morning, with the sun just coming up, the *tawaf* was like dancing on a mirror. I finished my seven turns and came back to the carpet. Fayez was there, reading his Qur'an.

"This," he said, "is the perfect place to read it. You can open it anywhere, *al-hamdulillah,* and before you've finished a page, it's speaking to you. Look, I've been sitting here thinking about my grandmother. And what does it say?" He recited the line under his finger. " 'He coins for you a likeness for yourselves.' Well, that's all about your family, the generations. And here, look at this." He turned to another chapter and read: " 'I ask nothing for doing this. It is only as a reminder for the people.' "

Fayez returned to his reading.

I leaned down the aisle and tapped Abd al-Qadir. He passed me John Muhammad's thermos.

I carried it to a water tank on the *mas'a* wall. The tank was ten feet long and raised on legs, with basins on the side. Two janitors had just prized up its top and were tonging blocks of ice into the water. The chunks clanged on the steel sides going over. The water tasted spring-melt cold.

I carried the thermos back to the hotel and rode the elevator up to John's room. The cooks had delivered his breakfast tray already. He was sleeping. I set the thermos beside him and went to my room.

The message light was blinking on the telephone when I came in. I rang the clerk. Mardini had called, he said, and would meet me at eleven in the lobby.

I dialed up the air conditioner and stretched out on the bed to read more Burckhardt. His story appealed to me for two reasons. To begin with, he was infinitely observant, and his works provided an escape when the hours dragged. Reading him also brought home the hadj's transcendent nature. The city Burckhardt described was utterly different from modern Makkah; yet the rites of the hadj appeared unchanged. His crowds wore the same *ihram*. They circled the Ka'ba as I had done. They ran the *mas'a* course. They drank Zamzam water. I had the impression while reading him that human beings were vessels into which the hadj was being poured. The Saudis had ousted the Turks since Burckhardt's visit; cars had put the camel out of work. The rites went on unaltered. The hadj had not declined in the face of technology and science. It had flourished. A quick look out the window made that clear.

CHAPTER FOURTEEN

Allah's City, Man's Abode

Mardini rang me from the lobby at eleven. His friend Saleem was outside with a car. They were going to drive across town, he said, to visit Saleem's shop and meet his father. Saleem had invited me to come along.

The heat rose up in a wall on the sidewalk. We hurried across Umm al-Qura Road to a late-model Buick parked outside a bank. I climbed in back and was still pulling shut the door when the car roared off. The doors were heavy, the engine huge. The seats were in thick, fake leather. Saleem drove what at home we called a hog.

Besides being air-conditioned, it had a special sticker on the window that permitted us past the roadblocks around the mosque. We were climbing a ramp that circled the *haram* when I noticed below us the entry to an ancient-looking souk. Incredibly, it resembled a slice of the Marrakesh markets, nestled between new offices and hotels. Men in robes stood trading goods down there, as always. Then the car swung into a cloverleaf on trestles and we sped through a tunnel.

On the other side of Mount Qubays the view gave way to more familiar urban buildings. We rolled along in the sunlight down a modern four-lane road lined with the usual low white-walled apartments. Makkah, like Amman and Baghdad, is a contemporary city designed for commerce and the car. Lit signs began appearing in shop windows. Laundry fluttered overhead on poles. By the look of the skyline quite a few Makkans let out their flats at hadj time, camping on the roof for extra rent. Everyone seemed to be selling something to someone. The grocery shops and vendors' stalls buzzed. The walks were crowded. Three miles away we still were passing knots of white-toweled pilgrims walking in the direction of the mosque.

Saleem's family owned an engine repair shop in this district. His father had come from Sidon in the fifties and opened an engine repair business on this road. He had settled the neighborhood, set up two more shops, and raised a family. Saleem waved at a passing gate and said, "I was born here." It was hard to imagine him ever being small. His head grazed the roof as he drove, and he had to slouch turning corners, to keep the wheel from binding on his lap. There was no fat on Saleem. He was simply extra-large in all directions, with a tree-trunk neck and hands made to wrestle pistons. He towered beside Mardini, taking up two thirds of the seat.

Mardini, I now recalled, was from Sidon, too. He had worked for Saleem part-time when he first came to Makkah. I heard two stories about his tenure as we rode: one from a time when Saleem had won a contract to build an office building near the mosque and how Mardini had got him the permits and purchased his lumber, and one from later on, when Saleem had been owed a large debt and Mardini had seen it through court and got him his money. They were an unlikely-looking duo. Mardini stood five foot nine with soft, circular features. Saleem, more reminiscent of a bear, wore heavy glasses. They slid down the bridge of his nose every few minutes, and he was always pushing them back with the jab of a thumb.

Personally, I felt glad to meet a Makkan who spoke English. For Mardini and Saleem this was a reunion. They hadn't seen each other in six years.

I asked Saleem what kinds of engines he repaired. "Automobile engines," he said. "Mostly for big American cars, like this one."

From what I could see, big cars were in demand here. During the last few years cheaper Japanese compacts had nosed them out of the U.S.

markets, but guzzlers were still favored in the Gulf. Their weight and huge engines supplied the traction drivers needed in the desert, and their egregious fuel consumption bothered no one. They were used cars when they arrived, Saleem explained, and usually came equipped to "Texas specs," with oversize radiators and thick hoses. In this way the streets of Makkah resembled Houston. Broughams, Town Cars, and Signature sedans were everywhere. Fortunately for Saleem, enough of these specialized crates still boiled over to keep him in business. Besides repairing the ones already here, he and his father imported them to sell.

I asked the local price of the car he was driving. He thumped the wheel and said, "Twenty-four thousand dollars." The car was already five years old. Despite shipping costs, the profit margin looked impressive. I had worked on car lots once or twice myself. I reached for my wallet and showed Saleem my license.

When Mardini had seen it, he smiled and said, "Now Saleem's father *really* wants to meet you."

Saleem pulled up outside a row of shops and we got out. The call to *zuhr* prayer had already sounded, and traffic on the street was thinning out. As in most Gulf states, businesses closed down five times a day here. The sidewalks were empty. In the shop windows blinds were being drawn.

We passed through a door and stepped into a bright, fluorescent workshop lined with aisles of drill presses and lathes. The floors were oil stained, and twists of steel filings twinkled. Spare-parts racks ran deep into the building.

Saleem led us back to a partitioned space that served as an office. A dais stood in one corner. Old carpets covered a portion of the floor. We removed our sandals and joined a group of eight men for *salat*.

When *zuhr* was over, we all took seats around a desk. A workman brought in coffee on a tray. A six-foot waterpipe was lighted. Each man smoked and passed the tube and sipped his coffee.

Saleem's father, Samir, was overjoyed to see Mardini. They questioned each other at length in Arabic. I had already lost the thread of the conversation when Mardini turned and said, "Show him the license."

Samir had an ax-blade face, somewhat reminiscent of King Faisal's. He admitted a mild grin at the sight of my card. Shier than Saleem, he dipped his head and passed the card around, saying, *"al-Hamdulillah."* A discussion began, of ten or twelve minutes, between the six men around the table, and then Saleem explained that they wanted to make an order. I was passed a pen and paper. Samir began to speak.

They wanted to have shipped to them, from any U.S. port, ten white V-8 Chevrolet Caprices, five white and five black Buick Park Ave's, and three Lincoln Town Cars in black or charcoal. The cars were all to be four-doors, five or six years old, and loaded with extras. Saleem filled in the years and model numbers.

Where cars were concerned, Samir and I spoke the same language. Though the size of his order was mildly astonishing, my head cleared quickly as I wrote, for I felt I knew where to locate these vehicles, at prices attractive to both parties. Samir knew exactly what he wanted. He apparently hoped to strike while the iron was hot. In a town as remote as Makkah, with few manufactured goods, where even fresh fruit must be shipped in, the hadj provided a peak point for many merchants. Indeed, throughout the centuries—in addition to its spiritual importance—it has always been regarded as a trade fair. Makkah might be the Middle East's most isolated city, but once every year for a few weeks several million new prospects filled its markets, depositing a flood of cash and goods.

(Profitability flowed in both directions. Hadjis poorer and far richer than myself defrayed the cost of their pilgrimage by trading. Bukharans sold fine carpets on the sidewalks. Nigerians hawked kola nuts and beads. Oil deals and building contracts were structured between prayers, at the big hotels.)

A different kind of coffee went around now, brewed with green Arabian beans. Perfumed with cardamom, strained through a twist of palm coir in the spout, the ginger-shaded drink came in thimble cups. We sat and sipped for another fifteen minutes. Then Saleem stood up and everyone shook hands. We left the shop and drove across the city.

At the hotel reception desk, I wired a price request on Samir's cars to a wholesale buyer I knew in California. I had worked with this man before and believed he could help me. After sending the fax, however, I wondered if he knew where Makkah was. I hoped he wouldn't consider the order harebrained. I went upstairs to catch a nap before *'asr*.

The telephone by my bed rang before the *adhan*. It was a discouraged-sounding John Muhammad. He could not believe he had come this far to be bedridden. Now, after two days' rest, he had reached a decision to make an effort and not just lie around. If he pushed himself, he felt, things might improve. He had started slowly. Now, in spite of pain, he was managing to rise for every prayer. The muscle relaxants were helpful, he said. The other pills had run out. He needed refills.

I collected my medicines and went upstairs. John sat on the edge of the bed, his hair beaded with water from the ablutions. He had made it back from the shower stall and now was resting up before the prayer. I wasn't sure I approved of his exertions. When I'd been too sick to fast in Marrakesh, Qadisha had taught me something about religious obligations—that people were not made to carry more weight than they could bear. "The exacting faith" (Conrad's term) was full of merciful subclauses. A man in John's straits, for example, was perfectly free to say his prayers from bed.

John shrugged when I mentioned it. He said touching his forehead to the ground felt therapeutic. I counted out more pills, arranging them into fans on the bedside table. Before I left, he had me roll out a reed mat on the carpet and point it in the direction of the mosque. The first *adhan* was already beginning. I was saying good-bye when a tap came at the door. Sheikh Ibrahim and Fayez trooped into the bedroom.

Both men walked with a stoop and their nostrils were florid. Fayez's eyes looked worse than yesterday. His waking hours were loaded with supererogatory commitments. His catnaps in the *haram* were not enough. Today on the way to his grandmother's hotel he'd succumbed to sunstroke, fainting in the road. Ibrahim looked overworked and shaky. Both men complained of crashing headaches.

In the next few days prostration from exposure passed at a rapid clip through the hotel. Striking down groups of four or five, it moved from room to room and floor to floor. Soon the hotel began to resemble an infirmary, with dozens of guests in various stages of illness strewn around the lobby every night. Guides were not spared.

Every day the temperature climbed by one or two degrees. At midnight the mercury remained above one hundred Fahrenheit. Humidity at this altitude is low. The Tihama Plain walled Makkah off from the drenching coastal heat, and there were days of 10-percent relative humidity, when only a run in the sunlight produced a sweat. The night before I had washed a few *thobe*s and hung them to dry on the balcony. The gowns weren't wet long. The desert air had done its work in minutes.

Other factors contributed to the delegation's weakness. New foods, crushing crowds, a lack of sleep combined to exhaust a lot of pilgrims. Excessive enthusiasm ran others ragged. When the right state was reached, a flu took over. The first signs of this bug were bone weariness and mild fever. If one rested at the beginning, it was possible to keep the worst at bay. A couple of hours' nap served to restore me. The trick was restraint, and rest at the first indications. Rather than miss the buildup to the hadj, and perhaps the hadj itself, I became a little fanatical on the subject. I began taking aspirin to lower my body temperature. I carried bottled water on the street.

Sunstroke in June was so common during hadj that the Saudis, in their role as pilgrim hosts, had set up 150 centers equipped to treat it. In addition, Green Crescent nurses manned several hundred clinics in the town. The TV preached prevention every evening, and leaflets were passed out in the streets. The essential piece of advice—to avoid direct sunlight— went mostly unheeded. Visiting hadjis continued to choke the roads. Their guides had to work to keep up with them.

Our biggest adversary was the heat. Eventually it determined all my movements. To beat the sun, I began breaking up my trips to the mosque with long siestas—a three-hour nap between dawn and noon, another rest after lunch between *zuhr* and *'asr*. Canonical hours shaped everybody's day. Rather than fall out of step, I kept to the schedule. I slept between prayers while the sun was up and visited the *haram* every evening. Most of my time between dusk and dawn I spent at the mosque.

I became what Mardini called a midnight hadji. In June it was a usual regime. Every summer on the weather maps Makkah, Yanbu', and Jidda competed for the hottest spot on earth. Having spent two years in West Africa in my twenties, I arrived convinced that heat could not affect me. A few days in Makkah proved me wrong. The thermometer on the sill edged nearer 120 Fahrenheit every day. The sun, bouncing off the streets, added ten degrees. At night the buildings were radiators. Hejazi heat gave a new twist to Shabestari's famous couplet:

> *If the smallest atom were broken apart*
> *You would find the sun at its very heart.*

Stepping out of the air-conditioned lobby, one opened up the door on a roaring stove.

The mosque was surprisingly cool in the evening hours. A network of cold-water pipes ran under the floors, and some cloisters were air-conditioned. I often went there equipped to stay on until dawn, with a portable one-man prayer rug and my Qur'an. I found the mosque completely accommodating. There were water tanks in every hall, carpets to nap on, and food stalls on the street for midnight snacks. To simplify matters, I brought along a plastic bag to carry my foot gear. The *haram* had sixty-four entries, and once inside, I liked to stroll around so that exiting later by my original gate might mean a long hike across the building. Worse, the piles of shoes to be searched through became confusing. With my flip-flops bagged, I could come and go as I liked and be sure to leave wearing the pair I had come in on.

Every night the crowd and mood were different. Despite Fayez's claim, there was no best seat. The mosque, built on the round, provided countless perfect sight lines. Your view depended on time and elevation. The final prayers of a Muslim day, *'isha'* (just after sunset) and *maghrib* (dusk), occurred within ninety minutes of each other. I tried to be on the roof during these hours. The crowds were smaller than on the lower levels, and oftentimes a breeze came down the hills. One could watch the *tawaf* wind down and hear the *adhan* echo through the mountains. When the mike clicked on, the congregation rustled to its feet like wind in a wheat field.

❖ ❖ ❖ ❖

One day I was late for *'asr* prayer. From John's room I had rushed outdoors and was coming down the hill into the hollow when the second call began and traffic stopped. All at once I saw I couldn't make it.

A mosque is the choicest place, of course, but Muslims are advised to pray wherever the hour overtakes them. The imam inside the building cleared his throat. The crowds on the road began forming up their lines. I found myself on a strip of walk, near a money changer's office. The pavement was filthy, and I spread my scarf on the ground to protect my *thobe*. For two or three seconds the fabric framed an open yard of ground; then a pair of Egyptians squeezed in on my left, and I was left with a foot of cloth to bow on. Hemmed in by a wall, I could not raise my other arm. Fifty thousand people surrounded the building, merging in rows that ran back up the hill. The pair beside me occupied nine tenths of my *kaffiyeh*. As we straightened our line, they looked apologetic.

The entire street performed *salat* en bloc. We bent as one body, touched our knees, rose again, then knelt down on the pavement. We only found room to move by moving together. When it came time to press my forehead on the ground, a breeze raised the edge of the scarf, flipping back the corner. I could smell the grime on the street and count the pebbles. Then a hand shot out and adjusted the cloth for me.

When the prayer was done, the man and I shook hands, and he handed me a card with a Cairo address. His partner, meanwhile, folded up my scarf. They took my arms and insisted we go into the building together. They wanted to make the *tawaf* with me.

The crowds began to move, and we moved with them, wading downstream toward the mosque, but before we reached the gates, we were separated. I watched the two men be carried away, holding their hands in the air like people drowning.

Coming back uphill at dawn, when the streets were less choked, I had a chance to poke around the town. The roads still lay in shadow then, and things were at their coolest. Under the porticos on Bab al-'Umrah Street, coffee vendors set up tables on the sidewalks, and small bazaars were opening for business. Offices above them sprouted signs. Their English intrigued me:

EXPERIMENTAL ESTABLISHMENT
FOR PILGRIMS FROM NON-MUSLIM COUNTRIES
NO. 7

ONLY RIYALS

SACRIFICIAL COUPONS HEAR

"Only Riyals" was a gift shop. The government-coupon dispenser sold pilgrims sacrificial sheep.

The perfumeries sparkled like bright museums with tall cases of pastel-colored scents in cut glass vials. There were delicatessens, *thobe* and *ihram* vendors, pharmacies, trinket shops, and many bookstores. My favorite bookshop had dark wood shelves and seventeen-foot ceilings. It specialized in classic Muslim texts, printed in Beirut and Riyadh. It sold posters, too, writing materials, and postcards displayed on sidewalk racks.

I was browsing here one morning when a dozen Tadjik pilgrims came into the store. (Mostopha had predicted I would see Russians.) These men were among the first post-Soviet hadjis in seventy years. They wore brown wool hats and cream-white robes belted at the waist with tasseled cords. They entered warily, elected a spokesman, and walked him to the counter. They watched his lips, to be sure he got the speech right. They did not want perfume, they wanted books. If the ruble was worthless outside Russia, they were ready to pay in deutsche marks. The man produced a wallet filled with both currencies.

The Qur'an had been forbidden by the Soviets so long that a copy in Tashkent currently cost a hundred dollars. Here they cost five. The Tadjiks left the shop with a dozen copies.

I tried to beat the sun on these dawn excursions. By 8:00 A.M. the streets were white with it. I always reached the hotel in time for breakfast. After, I would go upstairs to read. When the skies were right, I could tune my radio. I tried, through the BBC, to keep abreast of troubles brewing to our north. Saddam Hussein, for example, had accused the Kuwaiti emir of stealing oil from Iraq and "waging economic war." Kuwait had walked out of a meeting on the subject. Now a second conference had been called. It would take place in Jidda, after the hadj.

Elsewhere, in the mountains of Zanjan, the earthquake toll was nearing fifty thousand. Moscow and Washington each had offered aid.

✧ ✧ ✧ ✧

*T*he day my fax arrived from California, Mardini phoned Samir from the hotel. Saleem drove over at noon to pick us up.

By now the mayor had imposed a citywide siesta, and bazaars on the street were rolling down their doors. Hadjis did not know how to cope with heat, Saleem said. Last year a few dozen shoppers had died, among them several pregnant women.

As he spoke, he puffed a meerschaum, and cherry-scented smoke blew through the car. Coming up the Marwa Bridge, he waved at a block of homes in Qushashiyah. The home of Muhammad's first wife lay down there. The Prophet had lived in that house for years, he said. I stared down the ramp and could not isolate it. (Historic sites and their locations were often in question. Having looked for Muhammad's birthplace for several days, I was told it lay "somewhere under" the city library.) Saleem dismissed the city with a wave. "There's nothing to see here except the mosque! I live here! Believe me! If it weren't for the Ka'ba, no one would come."

We did not use the tunnel today but continued north on Masjid al-Haram Street, taking the long way. We passed through Suleimaniyah. Construction crews were widening the road here, and Saleem had to shout over the jackhammers. A century ago this had been a quiet district full of Afghans. Burckhardt had found a hashish shop out here.

Today the intersections all wore stoplights. We were moving through fast traffic when a Range Rover nearly hit us at a crossroads. Both cars swerved. Saleem had run a red light. He waved dismissively.

"They were put up a couple of years ago," Mardini said. "Red doesn't mean stop. It means you slow down to twenty or so and look to see what's coming."

"You're kidding."

"Watch."

Mardini was scathing about Makkan roadsmanship. He called it the *insha' Allah* school of driving. He had lived here long enough to say this dryly. I tried to imitate his cool. Saleem, I told myself, was an expert mechanic. Automobiles were in his blood, his genes. A majority of drivers along this road apparently lacked such experience to draw on. I began to suspect they had trained on camel saddles. Most of the pavement in Makkah looked recent, modern, its surfaces uniformly marked with yellow lines, but drivers ignored them as much as the stoplights.

"It isn't like Michigan," Mardini said.

"It isn't like anywhere," Saleem said. "Have you seen any speed limits?"

I could not recall one sign.

The optimum rate of travel here seemed to be a mile per minute. If progress slowed, the correct response was to gain back lost ground fast, by any means, including high-speed weaving. Dropouts from the *insha' Allah* school sat demolished at the curb every few blocks, but nobody noticed. Horns blared. Rubber burned. I heard no traffic sirens. Policemen drove as badly as the rest.

A quarter mile down the road Saleem's pipe fell into his lap. We were sailing into a tight left turn when he dropped it. We had been discussing the proposed oil conference in Jidda. Now he brushed live ashes from his trousers and pushed back his glasses.

"Perhaps the emir will walk out again," he said. "He's in trouble at home. He's looking for a diversion."

"From what?"

"From democracy."

Saleem was full of cynical views about the region. His hometown, Beirut, had been reduced in his lifetime from the Athens of the East to a smoking ruin. He knew all about the local penchant for proxy wars.

In 1986, he said, Sheikh Jabir as-Sabah had suspended the Kuwaiti constitution. Now many of his subjects wanted it back. A petition, signed by thousands, had been presented to the palace. Last winter there were rallies every week. The police had reacted badly. To restore calm, the emir had gone on TV and promised a dialogue. These discussions broke down in the spring.

I asked what all this had to do with an oil conference.

Saleem said it did not matter how autocrats behaved toward each other so long as they remained in control at home. He also explained why the next conference would be in Saudi Arabia. The Saudis were gifted peacemakers, and they shared a neutral zone with Kuwait that was rich in oil.

"They can talk all day," Saleem said. "It won't matter. Each of these places wants very different things."

Samir's shop had closed for the siesta. Our car was the only thing moving on the block. Inside the office the air felt cool, and the shades were drawn. The same six men sat talking in the office.

Coffee was served and the waterpipe went around. Pipes the size of Samir's had electric coils in the bowls, to keep them lighted. Drawn at full blast, they gurgled like bullfrogs. The ceramic mouthpiece turned on a metal swivel. The pipe itself was too big to pass around.

A lathe whined in the front of the building. Samir began to speak about my cars. When talk turned to prices, I passed Saleem my fax. He set it on the blotter before his father.

I'd had a few days to think about this moment. I was not unaware that the hadj could be turned to a profit. The surprise was to find myself participating. Samir put on a pair of reading glasses. We discussed shipping points and import duties. He knocked a few dollars off two of the cars, then questioned me briefly, through Saleem, concerning air-conditioning.

Coffee arrived. The list went around the desk for consultation. We were still discussing fine points when the shop's front door squeaked open, and two men came into the office.

The first was an Egyptian named Hameed. Saleem's right-hand man, Hameed had a radiant face and a fast sense of humor. Today he could barely contain himself. He had stopped at the Transport Office, he said, to drop off some parts to be shipped to Jidda. He had found an American weeping on a bench there. The man had been trying to use the office telephone, but no one would let him. Hameed had driven the pilgrim back to Samir's.

At this point a German-looking man stepped up behind him. He had blond, disheveled hair and wide blue eyes. His *ihram* towels were sweaty and caked with filth. Apparently he had slept in them last night, lying on a sidewalk at the airport. The flight from Miami had taken eighteen hours, he said. Then he had been hassled going through customs. He had managed to locate a telephone booth, but no one could change his money. His name was Shafeeq. His story came out in pieces.

At home Shafeeq worked as a waiter in a Miami Beach hotel. A week before, he'd been serving dinner in the restaurant when a Saudi man had come in to eat and discovered Shafeeq was a Muslim. One thing had led to another, he said. Over dessert the man presented him with a ticket to Makkah. The idea had been that when his plane arrived, the man would be there to meet him at the airport. Shafeeq would not need a hotel room. He would not even need money. The man was a prince. The prince would be his sponsor.

The tale raised familiar nods around the table. Royal largesse during the hadj was well-known. Even I had heard reports, from Casablanca. When Shafeeq explained the outcome, however, the men leaned back in their chairs and whispered, *"Shu'ma."* Generosity was good, they said, but half a gift is nothing. The worst had happened. Shafeeq's prince had not shown up at the airport.

Shafeeq had a bag on his arm the size of a lunch box. This and a change of clothes were all his luggage. Inside the bag were two telephone numbers: one for a palace in Jidda, one for the prince's Florida hotel suite. Saleem became determined to get some answers. He walked a telephone across the room and gave Shafeeq a desk and chair. Shafeeq made the calls himself. He spoke Arabic fluently.

The first call confirmed that the prince was not in Jidda. Next he rang the Florida hotel and learned from a clerk that the prince was not taking phone calls. Shafeeq looked down at his sandals. "I'll try tomorrow."

"No, no," Saleem said. "Come with us. You can stay at my place."

* * *

Saleem's place was the family home, built by Samir in stages, on land that was barren ground in 1950. Rather than move on as his family grew, Samir had added structures, creating a compound. By now it consisted of three independent dwellings, the latest a three-story marble villa flanked by two small cottages for guests. Shafeeq was installed in a cottage. While he cleaned up, we waited in the main house.

Mardini seemed amused by what had happened. Saleem fulminated against the prince. Personally, I remained curious to hear what Shafeeq had told them on the way out here. The main discussion had been in Arabic. I could guess that Shafeeq did not have much to fall back on. I now learned that he had landed with a one-hundred-dollar bill. That was why he'd had trouble using the pay phones.

Saleem seemed impressed with Shafeeq. Mardini thought him naive to trust in princes. I sided with Saleem. When all was said, Shafeeq reminded me of the man who had ridden his horse into the sea in the pilgrim story. He had taken the plunge and ended up in Makkah. The guts of the performance justified him.

"But what if Hameed hadn't found him?" Mardini asked.

"He was found," Saleem said, his tone suggesting larger forces at work in the matter. "He was found and brought to us. He is a pilgrim. We are Makkans. The hadjis are our guests." Saleem was more or less quoting a *hadith*.

Mardini said, "Yes. He must go to the mosque now."

Despite Shafeeq's exhaustion, an arrival *tuwaf* was expected of him, too. Mardini would go along to act as guide.

Saleem took a ring road back to town. On the way we passed Jabal Nur, "the Mountain of Light," where Muhammad had often gone to fast and where the angel first addressed him:

> *Recite, in the name of your Lord*
> *Who created man from an embryo.*
> *Recite, for your Lord is generous*
> *Who taught man by the pen*
> *What he did not know.*

The voice had produced a spiritual crisis in Muhammad's life. In the words of Emel Esin, he

> rushed home in terror. He clung to Khadijah, trembling and saying: "Hide me! Hide me!" She covered him in cloth until his fears subsided, but still he could see the vision everywhere, even when his eyes were closed. He said to his wife: "I have heard a sound and seen a light, and truly I fear that I will become insane." But she comforted him: ". . . These are good tidings, Cousin. I hope you will be the messenger of this people."

Since then great numbers of hadjis have trudged up Jabal Nur to see the cave. When heat makes the climb impossible, you hear regrets. It is one of the very few sites pilgrims visit in Makkah. Even the iconoclastic Saudis seemed to give way before it. From here their religion passed into the world.

CHAPTER FIFTEEN

Midnight Hadjis

There was nothing I could do to conclude my car deal with Samir until after the hadj. I had handed him an initial set of prices; we would do more talking in the next ten days, but attempting to place an order was out of the question. Even had we agreed on a price and Samir signed a letter of credit, we would not have been able to transfer funds abroad. As more pilgrims poured into Makkah, the banking system's channels became clogged. I suppose there were complex reasons for this logjam. The main one I could see was the cashier's draft for $232, required of every hadji upon arrival, for tents, transportation, and so forth. Had the checks been for Saudi riyals, the business might have gone swiftly. Instead, they were mostly drawn against foreign funds in a thousand different banks around the world. In addition, the telephone system was overburdened. The international wires were jammed by hadjis, and the lines at the public booths stood double file. Mail backed up, too. I wrote a couple of postcards home, then walked almost a mile to have them posted. I could not be sure they ever left the city.

As the numbers in town increased, the crowds turned inward. Because of the heat the sheikhs had advised our delegation to stay indoors during the day. *Zuhr* was now being held in a twelve-by-twelve-foot room with industrial carpeting, in the basement. I adhered to my regime of two siestas, performing *salat* downstairs or in my room. As the hadj drew near, the TV was dedicated to long live broadcasts from the mosque. I could lie reading Conrad in bed at 2:00 P.M. and still keep tabs on events around the shrine. By now there was no discernible ebb to the crowds out my window. The streets ran at constant high tide. So did the mosque. Except at night, it was filled to overflowing.

Heat brought other hazards than prostration. Early in my stay Mardini had warned me not to wear contact lenses. One morning I disregarded this advice, annoyed by the sweat that collected on my glasses and ran into my eyes. I wore the contact lenses to the mosque but neglected to bring a vial of wetting solution. (Without proper moisture, a lens dries onto the eye.) Already mine were sticking to my pupils, affixing themselves like cloudy cataracts. It was a panicky, half-sighted walk back to the hotel for the wetting solution. Fortunately, when moistened, the lenses peeled off.

Another day, as I opened the window and leaned out to read the thermometer, I thoughtlessly left a cigarette lighter on the sill. Like all these plastic throw-away items, the lighter bore a warning label: FLAMMABLE GAS UNDER PRESSURE/KEEP BELOW 120F. Ten minutes later the lighter exploded. Bits of it lay melting on the veranda.

The desert air leached moisture from everything it touched, including life forms. Not only plants and people were affected. Climbing to the hotel roof one evening, I passed a two-inch lizard on the stairs. It was a sand skink. Its head was thrust into an empty water bottle. A few remaining drops clung to the sides of the container, and the skink's tail lashed the air as it tried to reach them. I crouched down to watch. The lizard's skin was translucent. I could see clear liquid pumping through its limbs.

The *tawaf* revolved day and night in the heart of the city. At any hour the oval floor was packed. I continued to walk to the mosque around five every evening, stayed until nine or ten, then returned after midnight. Transport was almost effortless. The constant stream of pedestrians moving past the hotel worked like a current, conveying us into the hollow and back home.

I'd been in a lot of crowds by now but never one so at ease or densely threaded. Most crowds acquire thrust by a destination. The hadjis moved as if they had arrived. In that sense, the *haram* resembled a roundhouse. Our pace became more stately day by day. This seemed preternatural in a city swollen to three million people, with lights and roads and horns and calls to prayer. Modern Makkah whirled around us, but the tempo was like a retreat. The city felt vital yet monasterial. When Burckhardt wrote that "in all my journies in the East, I never enjoyed such perfect ease as at Makkah," he was affirming the tranquillity of the hadj.

The delegation adjusted to new rhythms. We slept, we ate, we performed *salat*, we floated in robes along the street, moving with minimal effort, putting on lives of customary action. Like the airplanes over Jidda, we circled in holding patterns. We had managed to reach Makkah. Now we were waiting.

Every day thousands of new arrivals drove in from the airport. Performing the *'umrah* rites took longer now. The day Shafeeq and Mardini went down to the hollow, they were stuck at the 'Umrah gate for forty minutes. They did not complete the *sa'y* until after midnight.

I avoided the 'Umrah entrance after that. The *haram* complex had sixty-four gates, some in much more frequent use than others. I investigated one evening and turned up Bab al-Nabi. It lies on the east wall of the *mas'a*. It meant a long walk to the back of the building, but once inside it was easy to skirt Mount Safa and slip into the courtyard. Being nearest his house, Muhammad had used this gate often. There were always a few cats lounging by the door.

Coming in at whatever gate, you reached the Ka'ba by crossing arcades that radiate deep into the building. Despite its enormous population, I could always find room at the back of the mosque to sit. There might even be a pillar there to lean on. Far from the oval center, the cloisters lost their curvature and the architecture became conventional. It was quieter, but I could not see the shrine.

Occasionally it was possible to sit nearer. Where the porticos met the Ka'ba floor, three steps formed a ledge around the courtyard. These steps were broad and deep, like bleachers, and ringed around with steel water tanks. They formed a narrow perimeter where one could settle. I was relaxing here one night after making *tawaf* when Usama, one of the delegates, approached me.

Usama came from a prosperous family of Chilean merchants. He was very soft spoken; I had to watch his lips to catch his words. Tonight he'd come looking for me. He had been up on the second floor an hour ago and sat down by chance beside an old Moroccan. The man had been wearing the coarse robe of a peasant. A pair of tire-heeled sandals lay beside him. When Usama happened to ask how he had come here, the man replied that he had walked from Fez.

Usama was right to try and find me. He knew I had been in Morocco and that I took an historical interest in the hadj. Until about 1960, walking to Makkah was not unusual, particularly for poor Africans. They came from as far as the Senagalese Sahara and were joined by many more as they moved east, by Muslims from Chad, Algeria, and Libya. Having traversed parts of this route in 1970, I remembered passing compounds by the road adorned with poster-painted black Ka'bas. Even then it was a sparsely traveled route. The days of the camel trains were already over. Walking hadjis were a dying breed.

The man Usama met had taken longer than Ibn Battutah to reach Makkah. Because of his age and impoverished state, he had often stopped to rest and earn his money. He had cobbled shoes for seven months in Tripoli, for instance. He had worked as a watchman in Cairo.

To me, the old man seemed to step straight out of an illuminated parchment. I wanted the honor of shaking his hand. "Come on," Usama said. "He wants to meet you." But it took us half an hour to reach the right stairway. By the time we found the arcade, the man was gone.

I enjoyed sitting near the water tanks late at night, when the air was cooler. The ledge formed a natural curb above the fray, and it soon became my favorite place to rest. I had the Ka'ba in plain view, a hundred yards across the floor, and I had its precise reflection on the marble. Entirely serene, at times like these the mosque took on the mood of a summer palace—one of those ancient, well-appointed spreads designed to approximate Paradise, where poets and thinkers whiled away their evenings.

Groups of hadjis often paused to drink here. One night I saw a family of Pakistanis, three or four men with wives walking behind, followed by sons and daughters, cousins and nephews, fragile grandparents. The men wore the *shalwar kamiz,* a pajamalike top and blousy trousers, but when they spoke it was in British English—the children less rapidly, with Bradford accents. I had wrongly assumed they were from Lahore.

Another night in about the same place I met two young newlyweds from Atlanta. She was of Turkish background. He was blond, a novice insurance adjuster in his twenties. Both had grown up in the South, attended school there, just been married. I watched him fill a Zamzam cup and offer her a drink.

Haram honeymooners were not unusual. I sometimes passed them escorting each other through the galleries. Inside the mosque they practiced shy decorum. On the street, when the crowds were large, they might hold hands. Mardini said that in families who could afford it, the hadj was considered the best way to cement a marriage, before having children.

These two from Georgia were distinguished by their speech. When I asked whether they spoke Arabic, the man looked sheepish. His wife replied, "Ah do speak Turkish. But ah make ma prayahs in English."

*W*hen the Friday *jum'a* prayer rolled around again, I went down to the mosque with Fazeel Ferouz.

Fazeel came from Georgetown, Guyana. He had the ease of the Caribbean in his movements, a big man about fifty, and well read. His people came originally from India. When I mentioned an essay on Guyana by V. S. Naipaul, Fazeel said, "Yes, but the man is Trinidadian." He knew Naipaul's books. The hauteur of the travel essays galled him, but he praised the novels. His favorite "local" writer was Jean Rhys.

We left the hotel lobby two hours early. In thirty minutes, we had walked ten blocks. Fazeel appeared to enjoy the crowds immensely. His natural, languorous pace was a benefit to him. He had a method of lying back on the tide and letting it bear him along in the right direction. Going through a gate, we raised our arms like mountain climbers squeezing through a fissure. The ground-floor colonnades looked packed. I was ready to retreat to a different door when Fazeel's arm shot up to direct me. We made for a ramp. It led into a basement.

The crowds fell away as we went down. The hallways were cool, quieter here. Halfway along we reached a mezzanine, stepped through a door, and entered a curving gallery. We were ten or twelve feet beneath the *haram* now, almost level with the Zamzam well. Air vents as large as picture windows were cut into the wall here. To my surprise, they looked out on the Ka'ba floor.

We seated ourselves midway down the gallery. The rows were quickly filling in behind, and the swelter was dumbfounding. My *thobe* was soon soaked through at the back and neck, but Fazeel didn't seem to mind. Perhaps it reminded him of Guyana. He took a prayer book from his robe and began to read.

Water barrels with cup dispensers were stationed around the room. One sat beside a pillar on my right. I removed my head scarf, soaked it in a cup, and draped it over me. This felt delicious. A man nearby me saw what I was doing, and soon I was soaking his scarf, too. The barrel held thirty gallons. Whenever a hadji signed to me, I filled another drinking cup and passed it. People were very thirsty. When the barrel began running low, I waved to a uniformed janitor bearing two large buckets. He stepped down the rows, leaned on the barrel, raising up the lid, and poured in the liquid, splashing my face and shoulders in the process.

I protested.

The man said, "Zamzam! Zamzam!" and moved on.

"It's a blessing," Fazeel whispered. "Sacred water."

By now we were seated as tightly as teeth on a comb. The heat and the press were beginning to make me dizzy when a man of considerable size came inching down the aisle and squeezed in beside me. After a dozen adjustments to his knees, he turned and introduced himself: Gamel, of Tunis.

"It's the women's fault," he hissed. "If they'd pray at home where they belonged, we would have more room here."

Gamel was the kind of pious man who venerated Allah, then made up for the effort on his neighbors. Fazeel leaned over and whispered, "Ignore him. It's better."

"How," I hissed, "is it better?"

"In a mosque it is better to leave a fool alone. You can look at yourself in the mirror then, and God accepts your prayer. Who knows what will happen to this one's prayer?"

"May it go up in smoke," I whispered.

Gradually, as water to a boulder, the row began conforming to Gamel. I had forgotten him already when another man behind me tapped my shoulder. His owlish face was wrapped in a checked *kaffiyeh*. He had heard me speak French and English. He asked where I came from, then leaned down his row to tell the others. A half dozen heads turned in my direction. The man's name was Fuad. He and his friends were Jerusalem Palestinians.

"Have you been to Jerusalem?" Fuad asked.

"No," I said. "Is it anything like this?"

He laughed. "We like this better. No curfews, no tanks, no armed patrols, no jails."

I asked him about Islam and the PLO. What part did religion play in the Palestinian uprising?

"None," he said. "The PLO is not a mosque. The PLO is the identity of the Palestinian people. Religion has nothing to do with it. The problem is land and oppression."

Twenty minutes before the prayer a man stood up at the front of the room, faced the crowd, and began shouting. From thirty rows away his face looked tiny. Finally, even Fazeel glanced up from reading. The man held up an empty money belt.

Our sheikhs had warned against the thieves from Cairo who came here every year to work the hadj. This man was the first victim I had seen. The robbery had taken place outside. The man stood weeping, recounting the crime, and waving his money belt. Now and then he pointed out a long slash in the pocket. The thieves had cut it open with a razor.

It took nerve to pursue this line of work here. The stigma attached to robbing pilgrims is extreme. The deterrents are biblical. Saudi law retires a first-time pickpocket by cutting off one hand. Very few locals were fool enough to risk this. Almost all the hadj thieves that summer were out-of-towners. Every year new teams arrived from Cairo, and every year they robbed, and some were caught. They were usually young, since rashness is required and since it is not a profession at which one ripens. The man with the money belt favored extreme measures. As he spoke, he sawed the air with his arm as an illustration.

Gradually people around the gallery reached into their wallets. A trickle of cash began moving up the aisles. I collected alms from Fazeel and the Palestinians, added some notes of my own, and passed them on. In five or six minutes the man had collected several hundred multicolored bills.

✧　✧　✧　✧

I had read a few books about the Saudi legal system. In the more contemporary studies Sheikh Abd al-'Aziz bin Baz was often mentioned.

Sheikh bin Baz was the kingdom's most public theologian, the religious senate's senior figure, and the final arbiter of canon law. A scholar and a legate, he also served on the governing board of the World Muslim League. This last post made him, distantly, our host.

Bin Baz had been an adviser to three kings. He had various reputations—in Saudi Arabia as a judge and scholar, in Iran as a social reactionary, in the West as an ultraconservative and a mouthpiece. Because his views were at variance with non-Muslim behavior and because he had once declared the planet flat, American reporters liked to emphasize his blindness—as if the condition explained Islamic law. More accurately, Sheikh bin Baz represented a counterweight to the modernizing forces released into the kingdom by its fabulously rich oil reserves. I was intrigued when the sheikhs announced we would pay him a visit.

After breakfast we crossed the road and piled into a row of Toyota vans. This was our first group venture since the *'umrah,* and the mood was like a day-camp outing. Ibrahim called the roll from a clipboard. One driver was missing. While we waited, sunlight beat down on the roof. Patches of sweat began breaking through our *thobes.*

The driver arrived and the caravan sped off. Sheikh bin Baz was receiving guests that year at a palace in Al-'Aziziyah. A soldier at a guard-house waved us over. We got out and walked up a gravel drive. The palace appeared modest for the Gulf, a long, one-floor building like a campus dormitory. The walls were white, the roof tiles green, the shutters orange and weathered. There was a flagpole.

On the porch we crossed paths with a dozen pilgrims from China, emerging from a prior audience. They all were Uighurs. Forty million Muslims lived in China, and almost none were allowed to perform the hadj, because the practice of a religion made them suspect in that country. I wanted to speak with these people, but it was impossible.

We were ushered into a tennis-court-size hall with high, plain ceilings. Upholstered armchairs lined three walls, and sunlight slanted through a bank of windows. The hall was spacious, reminiscent of a mosque.

A dozen clerics stood at one end of the hall. We were seated on carpets. Tea arrived. Then a man passed out pens and pads and made a speech. As we were delegates from the modernizing West, it had been decided to open our meeting to questions. The Americas, he said, were far from the Prophet's birthplace. Perhaps we had questions concerning the conduct of the hadj. If so, we should write them down and pass them forward. They would be read out and answered by the sheikh.

A first set of questions was gathered this way; then Sheikh bin Baz was shown into the room. I could not see his face. The hood of a *burnoose* covered his features. He sat down quickly. A microphone stand and a telephone were near him. These and several office fans were the only Western objects in the room.

A cleric read each question, first in English, then in Arabic. The sheikh began speaking the moment the cleric stopped. The microphone caught every whisper. The translations were unstintingly precise.

When Abd al-Qadir posed a question concerning a man in prison, I looked up. The man had committed a murder when he was young. After many years in a New York jail, he had become a Muslim. He performed *salat;* he kept the fast; he learned to read the Qur'an in the original. Naturally he hoped to fulfill the hadj before he died. Seeing he would never be able to travel, he had asked Abd al-Qadir to do it for him. The question concerned "the proxy hadj."

This exchange had everyone's attention. Sheikh bin Baz knew the hadj laws inside out. He had even written a miniature guide to be handed out to hadjis at the airport. To my surprise the proxy pilgrimage not only existed, but it had its root in a *hadith* that Imam Muslim had recorded in the ninth century:

> Abdullah b. 'Abbas reported that while al-Fadl b. 'Abbas had been riding behind Allah's Messenger (peace be upon him) a woman of the tribe of Khatham came to him (to the Holy Prophet) asking for a religious verdict. . . . She said: "Messenger of Allah, there is an obligation from Allah upon His servants in regard to Hadj. (But) my father is an aged man; he is incapable of riding safely. May I perform Hadj on his behalf?" He said: "Yes."

Bin Baz began by quoting this *hadith*. He related the story word for word, waited on the translation, then cited three opinions on the text. There was an admirable elegance to the logic. With each citation he found new ways to tie the Prophet's words to the prisoner's problem, extending their application from family to acquaintance, from sickbed to cell. Then he directed a question to Abd al-Qadir.

Was there any chance of the man's release? he asked. Could the man ever hope to perform the hadj himself?

Abd al-Qadir answered that the man was serving five consecutive life sentences. He did not expect to see Makkah before dying. The sheikh nodded.

"Are you already a hadji?"

"No," Abd al-Qadir said. "This is my first time."

There were no further questions.

"For the proxy hadj to be valid," bin Baz said, "the man performing it must be a pilgrim. He must have made the hadj himself, you see, before taking on another man's obligation. Otherwise the proxy has no value. You are not yet a hadji. Since no one can make two pilgrimages at once, your course is clear. Fulfill your own hadj. Then, God willing, come back another year and perform your friend's."

A sigh settled on the crowd, as if we'd just witnessed an especially fine return at Wimbledon.

The final question concerned Naguib Mahfouz, the legendary Egyptian author. Mahfouz's realistic novels, set in modern Cairo, are best-sellers. His characters are bywords in Egypt, even among men who cannot read. The occasional ban on his books and films has not affected his popularity. Recently he had received a Nobel Prize. Shortly after the award a militant politician had threatened Mahfouz's life, for a share of the spotlight. Sheikh bin Baz was being asked about Mahfouz's writing. There was no reply.

Mahfouz had nothing to fear from the Saudi clerics. The sheikh had never heard of him.

✧   ✧   ✧   ✧

Outside the others climbed into the vans and left the palace. Mardini and I caught a taxi to Saleem's.

Mardini complained of a headache on the way over. Guiding Shafeeq on the *'umrah,* he said, had worn him out. I looked out the window while he rested. Every vacant lot we passed was filled with sheep. The end of the hadj is marked by a three-day feast, when every family makes a sacrifice. In the space of a few dozen blocks, I saw thousands of animals.

When we reached Saleem's, I walked Mardini slowly up the drive. Saleem met us at the door, and we went into the kitchen. He sat us down at a wooden table and produced an ice-cold jug of limes and water.

"Do you have any cucumbers?" Mardini asked.

Saleem drew a half dozen cucumbers from a cold box. He set a knife and plate on the table, beside a yogurt tin. Mardini began to slice the vegetables.

His head was pounding.

Saleem offered aspirin. Mardini declined.

"It's dehydration. I'll need some salt."

The cucumbers were short and squat. He sliced them thinly, filling half the bowl, then added the yogurt and salt and stirred the mixture.

"I wouldn't have made it back to the hotel," he said.

Saleem and I talked business over yogurt. I had passed a shipping office yesterday and stopped in to check on freight costs from Charleston, South Carolina, to Jidda. The charges were less than I had imagined. By now the scent of money had affected my thinking. I saw, I thought, a way to blend work and travel, to write my own ticket after the hadj, from Jidda, say, to Bombay, then on to Malaysia, learning Arabic as I met new people, selling willing buyers dinosaurs. The idea was wacky enough to appeal to me. I had the shipping figures in my *thobe*.

When Samir came into the room, I gave them to him. He smiled and thanked me. I could see dark, blue circles under his eyes, and his voice sounded weaker than before. Mardini had said that Samir suffered from emphysema. When he noticed a package of cigarettes on the table, his face turned impish.

"No!" Saleem cried, but Samir had the box and was going out the door. Saleem went after him.

"Just one! For tonight!" Samir giggled.

Saleem grabbed his father's hand and removed the box. Samir left, laughing.

Mardini called yogurt and cucumbers the Makkan cure. Saleem had a bowl, too, and we went on talking. When I asked after Shafeeq, Saleem had him sent for.

Shafeeq came into the kitchen a new man. On his first day here his towels had been grimed with dirt and his cheeks were tear streaked. Now his hair lay slicked back from a shower; he wore a clean *thobe* and seemed at home in his surroundings. On the strength of an idea he had cast himself into the wind, with a plane ticket in his hand and a hundred dollars. The fact that his prince was missing didn't matter. He had crossed paths with Saleem and now had a house and car at his disposal. He had just spent sixteen hours in the mosque.

Getting to Makkah was all that really mattered. Shafeeq could have made his hadj without Saleem. The price of a room might have kept him on the street, dining under trestles in an encampment, but thousands of people performed the hadj that way. Thanks to Saleem, he had landed on his feet. His gratitude was casual, accepting, Islamic.

Saleem seemed pleased to have Shafeeq around. With Mardini tied to the delegation, with Samir looking ill, a surprise guest became the extra hand he'd need to help him make the pilgrimage next week. *Al-Wukuf,* "the day of standing," took place outside town on the Plain of Arafat. This all-day vigil was the centerpiece of hadj. Saleem went every year with his wife and children. Arafat, he knew, had its grueling moments, complete with crowds and traffic jams and searing heat—a sacred place, but a place as well where the threat of flat tires or running out of water made one glad to have an extra hand. Saleem did not mention saving Shafeeq's hide, then or later. He didn't see it that way. Shafeeq was *sent.*

CHAPTER SIXTEEN

Following the Hadj

*A*s the hollow of Makkah filled to the brim, the authorities sealed off the city. The Jidda airport locked its gates on Thursday. The western, coastal roads were closed off, too. Cars and buses still rolled in from the north and east—over the Madinah road, down the Taif switchbacks—but by Saturday morning, arrivals had dwindled. Reporters went out to the passes with video cameras; for once an *absence* of traffic became big news. It was down to a trickle, mostly composed of Saudis, Kuwaitis, Iraqis from Basra, and other neighbors near enough to dash down via Riyadh at the last moment. Pilgrims coming from any appreciable distance were here already. The buildup was ending.

In addition to pilgrims, there were a hundred thousand soldiers in the city. They wore the latest in camouflage fatigues—the universal brown-green splatter pattern—and they tooled about the streets in trucks and jeeps, CBs squawking. They were mostly unarmed—only here and there you saw a pistol—and even Saleem conceded their usefulness. They directed traffic, ferried trucks of water through the crowds, and were helping to put up the tent village at Mina. Their numbers seemed high until I saw the village. The extent of it could not be imagined.

Mina figured prominently in the next stages of the hadj. It lay five or six miles to our east, over two bare ranges and a patch of desert. Freeway tunnels had been blown straight through the hills, and a car could cover the distance in thirty minutes. In the days of the camel the journey took six hours. Ibn Battutah, Burckhardt, Rutter, a thousand years of witnesses record how at dawn on the appointed day the caravans would form above the hollow, parade in a pageant toward Arafat, and manage to make Mina before *'asr*. Burckhardt called this "following the Hadj." Perched on cliffs at the head of a long valley, the town formed a natural midpoint for their camp. Here the caravans would rest until morning, then continue on to Arafat. Today Mina still plays this ancient role of halfway station. With one main street and a scattering of buildings, it seemed an unlikely hub for the giant hadj.

For fifty weeks of the year Mina looks like nothing—a "deserted and derelict village," Harry St. John Philby called it, overlooking a mile-wide valley stretching out of sight between low hills. Things had not changed here much since 1930. The road was wider, the king had built a palace on the cliffs, but the houses of Mina, while more in number, still formed "the strangest collection of little fantastic khans in the world." Open at back and front, they were not really houses at all, but just what Rutter called them, stone-built tents. At the western end of the street sat a few new buildings and a largish mosque. It all looked provisional. The valley, not the village, made the view.

It ran as far as the eye could see, a level corridor of bone-white desert curbed by granite ranges on both sides. The impact as it stretched away was spectacular, its extent made more apparent by the few public buildings it dwarfed along the way. Five paved roads divided the length of the valley. Like the airport, they were only used for the hadj. For eleven months the only things that moved here were bales of tumbleweed and herds of goats. Then, one day at the end of month eleven, pilgrim agents pulled up in trucks loaded with tents and mallets, stakes, and rope and proceeded, with help from the soldiers, to pitch a few hundred thousand twelve-man tents.

They tied and stretched and tapped day and night for a week, and in the end a canvas city rose up on the sand, from the Makkah tunnels east past Muzdalifah. Encampments blossomed in quarter-mile quads, complete with food bars, market stalls, electric light, outhouses, and clinics. For a few nights during the hadj the valley blazed, after which the teams appeared again and trucked the dismantled city back to Makkah. You had to see it to believe it, young Ahmad said.

We were supposed to leave the hotel Saturday morning. From the beginning there were adjustments and delays. Coming down to the lobby after breakfast, I found the window couches lined with pilgrims. The rites were due to start again, and the room was buzzing. All the men were wearing their white towels.

Out on the street the interminable human river had changed directions. It was now flowing *out* of the hollow, leaving town. The roadblocks above the mosque had been removed, and the curbs were jammed with yellow buses, vans, and trucks, their rooftops piled with luggage. Crates and chests were being handed up and lashed with ropes. Passengers rode the rooftops, too, as if the trucks were open omnibuses. The pace was halting, self-entangling, the whole recessional progressing sideways, looping forward, slithering through the hills.

Moving a few million people into the desert produced inevitable delays. Nothing went as anybody planned it. Our vans were trapped across town. The sheikhs revised their schedule hourly. After the first few delays I decided to walk down to the mosque. I wanted a final glimpse of the Ka'ba.

For months the shrine had been everyone's destination, part magnet, part beacon. People called it the Qibla of the World. It looked a bit different every time I saw it. Its uses shifted, too, as time went on. The arrival *tawaf* turned it into a pole. The *kiswa* made us read it as a book. As the hadj changed gears, the Ka'ba served new functions. Today it worked like a great revolving door, spinning pilgrims through their final circuits, out of the mosque, uphill, away from town.

I wanted to see this. I stepped outside and waded into the traffic, but the street was a surging slough of heads and shoulders. The current of the hadj flowed away from the mosque now. Turning downhill proved impossible. I tried to cross to the median strip, thinking to turn downhill from there, but it was hopeless. Looking back, the hotel lay *behind* me. I was being carried up, not down, the street. I gave up on the Ka'ba. I settled for a curb two blocks away, then worked my way back up the sidewalks to the lobby. Ibrahim gave me a sharp look when I finally reached the foyer. I did not try to go downtown again.

The second stage of the hadj was a movable pageant conducted between the eighth and twelfth of the final lunar month. It described an eastward loop of twenty miles, from Makkah to Arafat and back again. This was not in fact a second stage at all, but the pilgrimage proper. The hadj revised itself as time went on. Our arrival *tawaf* and *sa'y* were preliminaries, making us eligible "to go on hadj." Until now there had been no need to leave the city. Today the entire town was on the march. The series of rites that comprised our hadj were to be performed *in passing*, at various sites in the hills outside Makkah.

I got back to the hotel about ten-thirty. Two sheikhs in the lobby were fixing name tags to a stack of luggage. The lobby itself was almost empty now. Delays had made the delegation restless. By this time they were dispersed through the hotel. I climbed the stairs to the vacant dining room. In an unused conference parlor down the hall I found Usama, the Chilean, slumped in a chair before a bowl of cornflakes.

Usama's health had been perfect two nights ago. All through the week, while others fell by the wayside, he had not. Now his turn had come: his face looked flushed, his bones ached from the inside out, he said, and he disparaged the bad timing of his body. He seemed much sicker than Fayez had been—and Fayez was a youngster. Usama was nearly sixty. When I put a hand on his shoulder, the towel felt sweat drenched.

I tried to encourage him. Everyone here fell ill for a day or two. It was like an inoculation against the weather. He was only a little later than the rest. As for his age, I reminded him of the walking pilgrim from Fez. I offered him pills, too. Since the day Mardini had weakened at Saleem's, I'd been carrying a vile of Cipro with me. This was the miraculous medication supplied by Yusef in Tangier. I had used the pills myself the other day. A couple of doses dragged me back from the brink of a fever. Yusef had called it the H-bomb of antibiotics. Today a wrapper containing twelve pills was tied into the tip of my *ihram*. I loosened the knot and put four tablets on the table.

Usama eyed them doubtfully. The heat, the crowds, his exhaustion combined to remind him of his age. The prospect of four days on the desert terrified him. He thought he might die out there.

I said he would be fine. It wouldn't be a desert like the old days. The better tents on the plain were air-conditioned. There were field hospitals at Mina, too, with clinical labs and even surgeries. If the ride out proved too much for him, I said, there were lying-in vans with eight beds each, to ferry him in comfort, with nurses on board and every medicine.

In the end he downed one pill with a glass of water and agreed to take another in four hours. I turned in the doorway. *"Insha' Allah,* you'll be all right," I told him.

He tossed me a look that frightened me a little. "You haven't been on the hadj," he said. "You don't know how it is."

Our week in Makkah had been a period of acclimation. Whatever else had happened, our bodies were adapting to the heat. Some adjusted more quickly than others. Cucumbers and sleep restored Mardini. By now Fayez had recovered, too. Even the delegation dark horse, John Muhammad, was on his feet and full of resolution. When I came into his room, he and Abd al-Qadir were laughing near the window. "Tell him," John said.

Abd al-Qadir repeated the joke. "Have you heard about the agnostic, dyslexic insomniac? He stayed up all night, wondering if there really is a dog."

John looked hearty. The hospital had sent over more pills. His limp seemed improved, and he no longer walked with his palm pressed to his backside.

We went downstairs to the dining room for lunch. When the meal ended and everyone had gone, I sat down to read at a table by the window.

For twenty minutes the only sounds were an occasional thunk and ping of an elevator. Then Fayez and Sheikh Nasser swept into the room. The others were downstairs, they said. The vans were leaving.

"When?"

"In about an hour."

Nasser handed me a passbook with blue covers. It contained two pages. One described the stops we would make, with suggested times of arrival. The other, headed ROYAL PROTOCOL, had been sealed at the bottom with a signet ring. The cover was gold-foil stamped with two crossed swords.

"The others already have theirs," Fayez said.

I slipped the pass into my Conrad book.

"You must keep this with you always," Nasser said. "If you lose your way or have problems, show it to a policeman or a soldier. We don't want to lose you." And he plucked the pass from my book and gave it to me. "Keep this in your money belt," he said.

Nasser's delivery was always gruff. Toughly built, with a pock-marked face and ready smile, it was his voice that distinguished him, a sandy, crackling baritone that at close range gave new meaning to the word *stentorian*. In a different life he might have made a good racetrack announcer. Nasser was a professor of religion, from a village near Riyadh. He knew the *hadith* as well as Ibrahim, but was more assertive. As the hadj picked up, Nasser emerged more often from the background. He alone among the sheikhs spoke decent English.

"What's this?" he growled.

"An English book. A sea story."

He read the title. "And who is this Lord Jim?"

I said I had only begun the book. In the early chapters Jim appeared as an officer on a hadj boat bound for Makkah. I did not go on to describe Jim's desertion of the vessel in mid-journey. Although the mainspring of the book, it seemed more full of meanings here than even Conrad had intended.

Nasser looked pleased. "When did this happen?"

I said the tale was based on events that took place in the 1880s.

"Yusef Conrad. Is he Muslim?"

"No," I said.

Nasser looked disappointed.

"He died many years ago," I said.

Fayez finally put an end to the awkward silence. "This man was a great writer," he explained. "I read another book of his, in school. *Heart of* . . ."

"*Darkness.*"

Fayez thought Nasser ought to read *Lord Jim*. This appealed to me, for many reasons. I offered to give him my copy when I finished.

"*Insha' Allah,*" Nasser said. "But, please, don't keep your passbook in it. Are your bags downstairs?"

"One bag," I said.

"Good. Just bring what you need for a few days at Mina. We'll be back soon."

*A*ccording to contemporary records, in the first days of the last new moon in 631, Muhammad led a caravan of thirty thousand Muslims into Makkah, on what was later called the Farewell Hadj.*

They performed *tawaf* and *sa'y*, drank from the Zamzam well, and prayed with their Prophet, following his footsteps. During this visit the ancient hadj was liturgically transformed. Saluting the black stone, the two-part pace of *tawaf*, dropping one's towel off the shoulder all date from this period. Muhammad assigned a new order to the rites. His words and gestures were witnessed and recorded, creating precedents in force today.

On the eighth of the month he led the hadj out of town to Arafat. This journey was accomplished in two stages. When his camel stopped at Mina the first evening, the people set up tents and spent the night there.

Sheikh Nasser said that we would do the same.

The sky was growing red as we climbed on the bus. We had been coming to this moment for a week now. We were leaving for the desert. As the bus

---

*Muhammad died three months later, in Madinah.

swayed forward through thick traffic, the mosque fell behind. At times the pedestrian crowds moved faster than we did. With stops we averaged fifteen miles an hour.

It was hard to imagine a time when the hadj had not been up on wheels. Four-lane bands of glinting chrome snaked up the hillsides. Crowds dashed between bumpers. Vehicles spilled off the modern roads, taking shortcuts over sand and scabblings. In a little more than fifty years a medieval city had been utterly transformed by modern transportation. I wondered what would come when the car was gone. It would take a lot more than a face-lift to rearrange things. The town had been remade for the rubber tire, the wider axle. A massive infrastructure of tunnels, freeways, and overpasses swooping impressively through granite hills physically walled us off from the 1930s, when the hadj was still an occasion of the camel. Harry St. John Philby wrote then of the Mina caravan,

> As I moved forward with the royal cavalcade it was chiefly the camel that impressed me. All over the immense plain, suddenly in motion towards the valley leading back to Mecca, it was the lines and phalanxes of camels that caught my eye. There must have been 50,000 of them at least, and all moving forward together at the silent, hurried pace characteristic of the chief carrier of Arabia. . . . For all the light of the moon it soon became impossible to see anything clearly in that moving mist, but the white shrouded bodies of men raised high aloft on their giant steeds.

Today's chief carrier ran on gasoline. Bumper to bumper the trade-off appeared pathetic, and yet we were not figures in a frieze. The hadj had been motorized for fifty years, and we were products of that history, a part of the blaring horns and squealing rubber, not the sweep of padded feet.

A camel can carry four hundred pounds of cargo, cover sixty miles a day for twenty days without a drink in temperatures of 120 degrees Fahrenheit—and still go five more days before it dies. Only a fool is not respectful of the camel. On the other hand, almost no one on the bus knew how to ride one. Rafeeq, the Libyan, who did, only joked about it: "Imagine yourselves on that wooden saddle, wearing cotton towels!"

As we entered a mile-long tunnel, the chants of "I am here, Lord" were replaced by the roar of huge electric fans mounted in the ceiling. They hung side by side every quarter mile, looking and sounding like jet engines. Their purpose was to clear away exhaust fumes, for besides the cars, a steady mob of towel-clad pilgrims moved down narrow walkways in the dark. At night they slept with their feet to the traffic, laid out like lumber in the headlights. The giant fans permitted them to breathe.

Halfway through the tunnel Nasser began to tell me the story of his first visit to Makkah. He had arrived with a couple school friends well after midnight, he said, in the middle of winter. The streets had been empty—no cars, the town pitch-dark. They had walked to the hollow, shivering with cold, and found a dozen people at the Ka'ba. The greatness of the hadj, he said, was not proved by high attendance. The night had been cold and perfect, as today was perfect. He and his friends had performed *tawaf,* then found rooms for the night at a local school.

I asked when this had been.

He said, "In 1958, before all the airplanes."

On the other side of the tunnel the road joined an overpass. It crossed the top of Mina Valley for two miles, then dropped into the main street of the village. We turned and rode along the cliffs and met a roadblock. While the driver jumped down to negotiate our passage, we sat in silence, staring out the windows. The valley under the cliff road glittered with a million tiny lights. I strained my eyes to the east, and there was no end to it. Ahead, up on the cliffs, there sat a palace.

*T*he building we were assigned to formed part of the palace guesthouse several hundred feet above the town. The lobby, much larger than a hotel's, blazed under chandeliers as we came in, but the rooms upstairs were spare, furnished with cots. Mine, on the eighth floor, faced a valley as broad across as San Francisco Bay. I moved a chair to the sill and could see just a few degrees of the encampment. The valley was expansive, the windows small and sealed against the heat, like square portholes.

At ten o'clock I went down to the lobby. Plush couches were arranged along the walls, on Persian carpets. Here delegation members sat immersed in conversation with other hadjis I did not know. Of the several hundred residents installed here, some were figures of real distinction—muftis from Lur and Samarkand, Nigerian oil magnates, a chancellor from Maiduguri University. There were judges, scholars, exiled leaders, too. Later I would meet some of these people. Right now they were the last thing on my mind.

We had been plunked down on a microdot in the biggest peaceful assembly on the planet. I wanted to get out and see it, as quickly as possible. I stopped Mardini at the elevators and tried to enlist him in a stroll. He advised against it.

"It's a battlefield out there," he said. "Why rush? The important thing now is to get some sleep before *fajr*. At dawn we leave for Arafat. We'll spend all day there, standing in the sun, then move back up the valley to Muzdalifah. We'll have time to see Mina later. We're going to spend three days up here."

I boarded an elevator car and rode it up six flights to Usama's room. Awake in bed, he looked almost restored, having doubled up on Cipro. I gave him more tablets.

"It's the hadj," he said. "You'd have to be dead not to rise to it."

From Usama's room I went to the top floor, found an unlocked door, and climbed a stairway. I felt I deserved at least an overview. At the top of the stairs I slipped through a laundry room with many basins, past a row of men asleep on mats. A steel door stood open to the rooftop. It was covered in gravel right up to the ledge. A metal water tower rose behind me, with a ladder bolted to its side. I went up the ladder and sat down on the turret.

An unbroken panorama blazed below. In the dark the expanse of the valley resembled a harbor. The tents like capsized hulls ran without end, up the sides of the cliffs and down the narrows, all the way to Muzdalifah. Electric lights rippled in the heat haze. Campfires glittered on the hills. Beneath the occasional bleatings of penned-up sheep ran the dull throb, like a dynamo, of several million men and women milling, talking, breathing in the night. Across the ravine, under half a moon, an oblong slaughterhouse poured its neon lighting on the land.

For a camp that had not existed a week before, the vista was impressive. I gazed a long while at it, feeling vaguely unsettled, not sure why. Then it hit me: if all the hadjis really were at Mina, that meant Makkah must be empty. The idea seemed impossible to me. I looked back in the direction of the city. At the top of the valley contiguous lines of bumper-to-bumper headlights still spilled from the tunnels through the dark.

While I sat watching, a sand-bearing breeze came down the cliffs and passed over the tower. I felt a rasp at the back of my throat, the first sign of a cold perhaps, and remembered Usama's warning. "You haven't been on the hadj," he had moaned. "You don't know how it is." The hadj was a battlefield. You had to keep your head down. On the pillow.

CHAPTER SEVENTEEN

When Men and Mountains Meet

*T*he road winding back to town from the cliffside guesthouse was lined with families camped out for the night. I woke before the others and went out into the hallway to a window. Darkness continued to simplify the valley. From the upper floors it was hard to pick out shapes. High on the ridge a few small campfires glimmered. A scattering of mountain-born Yemenis had pitched their tents along this jagged cliff, trading the soft sand for a perspective.

As the predawn call to prayer ran up the hill, lantern lights came on inside the tents. Gradually gray figures stepped out onto the rocks and formed neat rows. This narrow wedge of a view from one hall window was representative of the whole valley. The whole population of Mina would be on its feet now, three million people lining up for *fajr* in the dark.

Throughout the guesthouse doors were clicking open. John Muhammad limped out of a bedroom, followed by Abd al-Qadir and Mardini. Usama appeared. Fayez looked wide awake.

The delegation filed into the hall, lined up on a rug, and faced Makkah. Nasser cleared his throat and began the call. I have already said that Nasser's speaking voice was rough. It bounced along the corridor this morning like pea gravel strained through a bullhorn. But when he began to sing, it was angelic. I had heard my share of muezzins by now, but never one with such a clean vibrato. The Muslim *adhan* is a highly developed art form; Nasser's vocal talents were first-rate. What is more, for anyone who knew him, there was the added pleasure of so much tenderness pouring from a man with the voice of a Klaxon. I never got used to it.

After breakfast we went downstairs with our passbooks. I carried it in a shoulder bag today, along with four or five books, a packet of medicines, and a camera wrapped in a scarf to keep out sand. On top lay the player on which were recorded the prayers of all my friends in Marrakesh. As we moved outside, an officer noted the numbers in our passbooks. He examined the contents of my bag and waved me on.

The sheikhs had devised a careful plan to minimize exposure to the sun. The plan fell through the moment we left the building. Our vans, which ought to have met us at the door, were trapped in the valley. The road ahead lay choked with pilgrims. The guides formed a huddle. The huddle broke up. Nasser waved an arm. We began to walk.

At 7:00 A.M. all of Mina was in motion. Winding downhill to the parking lots, I had my first clear view of the whole valley: a mile-wide dun-colored corridor forming one continuous plane between two ranges, from its western edge against the spine of Makkah due east to Arafat, five miles away. The sky was still faintly pink in that direction, and traces of morning ground fog smudged the view. Past Muzdalifah the visible end of the valley tapered off. Most of the way the land ran with tents and glints of chrome.

I had been through Super Bowl gridlock in San Francisco. I knew the rush-hour tunnels of New York. I had witnessed Woodstock and marched on Washington. I had never experienced a throng approaching this one. It was as if the twentieth century's thickest tie-up had embarked on an epic traveling back into Roman times. A tricky desert sky hung over everything, compressing volumes, curving distance, befuddling the eye.

As we boarded vans, a block-long hulk of yellow helicopter appeared above the cliffs over the road. It hovered long enough to drop a basket on a cable, then pluck a prostrate pilgrim from the crowds. It reeled him up and vanished over the hillside. Mardini referred to the craft as a flying hospital. The Saudi army had seven of these contraptions, with landing pads all over the valley.

We inched our way down the drive to Abdul Aziz Street. The encampments in this quarter were mostly filled with Pakistani peasants. The numbers of mothers with infants startled me. The hadj in July with a baby on each hip seemed inconceivable. Nasser guessed that the children were here because of economics. Their parents could not afford to leave them with nursemaids.*

The pressing heat and constant need for water weighed down older people, too. The camps were peppered with them, men and women seventy and eighty, bent over walking sticks, toothless, squinting. They were here by choice, of course, to do their duty and to soak up the hadj's grace before they died. The women looked bird boned. The men in white towels, creaking down embankments, appeared to have one foot in the other world.

At the bottom of the hill the crowds thinned out, and the cars and trucks and buses and vans took over. For several minutes I saw nothing but steel hoods and blazing trunk lids. Then the road ran up into a viaduct and gave us a bird's-eye view of Mina Valley.

Night had all but erased the surrounding mountains. Now they dominated everything. Their bouldered bases tumbled to the sand's edge, forming up the narrows of the valley. The contrast of gray-blue rock on sable was exact, as if cut with a scalpel. Terraces in the rock face higher up formed tier upon tier of shelflike lofty bleachers holding single ranks of canvas tents. The shelves zagged like roads in a pit mine. The tents were distant flecks. The treeless ranges appeared to have poked up yesterday, but they held legends. The Prophet's cave on Mount Hira lay to our west. To the north stood Mount Thebir, where Abraham went to sacrifice his son, and where Gabriel stopped him.

---

*Taking a child on the hadj does not fulfill its obligation. Grace always attaches to the journey, but the rites are void without mature intent, or *niya*.

"Do people still go up there?"

"A lot of people go up there," Mardini said. "To visit the site."

"What is there?"

"A big, flat rock. Split in two, very cleanly."

"Does that mean something?"

"They say it's where Abraham dropped the knife, when the angel stopped him."

It was no surprise to find the father of ethical monotheism at Mina. Muslims, like everyone in the Middle East, see his life as a metaphor for universal guidance. In their view, Abraham's story had two phases: an initial stage in Palestine and a second one in the Hejaz. In many ways the hadj commemorates this final chapter: pilgrims leave their home (as he left Ur), resign themselves to a pure life *(ihram)*, circle the shrine he built with his son, and run between the *mas'a* hills, like Hagar. Today we were trooping past Mount Thebir, another stage in the Abrahamic drama.

The van rolled down off the escarpment, taking a crossroad to the middle of the plain. Here we joined one of the many numbered ribbons of new pavement linking Mina to Muzdalifah and Arafat. These long, sand-leveed roads ran high and dry across the desert, like taffy stretched out in the sun. They paralleled each other through the sand, splitting the valley in quarter-mile channels, so that crawling along at a snail's pace, we could gauge our progress by vans across the way on our left and right. Sometimes we saw whole vehicles. More often we made out only roofs, viewed over sand humps topped with hanks of thorn brush. There was something submarine about the valley. Low dunes lapped the canyon floor, as if a sea had boiled off it in the night.

A pedestrian walkway shaded with green roofing ran down the center of the plain. Thousands of hadjis flowed along it, keeping pace with the traffic, stirring up dust clouds. It ran unbroken for about three miles, dumping out crowds at the eastern end of the spillway. Seen from the air, the walkway would be a prominent feature. From the van it was hard to distinguish across the sand. Had Mardini not pointed it out, I might have missed it. It was difficult to hold any view in focus, especially where dust became involved. Heat waves curled off the sand. The sky was scored with corrugated ripples.

Where the valley narrowed, we crossed a riverbed, the Wadi Muhassir. Over its dry banks we joined a track reserved for special cars. The traffic gained speed here, in keeping with a tradition that the Prophet spurred his camel through this pass.

The road climbed slightly, hills fell off to either side, and we entered the mile-wide basin of Muzdalifah. Again the valley ground was packed with tents, the hills dotted white like Mina's. In the acid light objects melted to shades of solar brown. Lost between slopes, a worn gray runner of masonry and stone wound through the clinkers. This was an eighth-century aqueduct built by Princess Zubaidah, wife of the caliph of Baghdad. Easing the hadj for centuries to come, Zubaidah had paid to sink a hundred wells from Al-Kufa in southern Iraq all the way to Mina. She and her husband, Harun ar-Rashid, had performed the hadj nine times along this route, once across a field of carpets rolled out every morning on the sand.

We had traveled about four miles in two hours; it was nine o'clock when a chevron of army motorcycles appeared out of nowhere. Whether they were meant as an escort, no one knew. The sirens made one feel singled out. The touch of protocol just slowed us down. We crept through a crossroads. Soon we were mired in a major tie-up. The van sank down in the sunlight. The soldiers revved their bikes and roared away.

As often happened during stalls, John Muhammad and Abd al-Qadir began chanting. The rest of us sat looking through the windshield while three Turks jumped from the truck ahead and climbed onto its roof to survey the traffic. They squinted and shrugged and shook their heads and climbed down again. While we sat and sweated, a yellow school bus inched up beside us in the right-hand lane. Whenever its driver hit the brakes, they screeched like donkeys. The bus, a large old clunker, teetered with fifty pilgrims from the Punjab. Water bags hung from its bumpers. The rooftop luggage rack was full of men clutching umbrellas. They, too, were chanting "I am here."

Files of pedestrians swept by on roadside paths. Some waved staves with make-shift banners. With the men in *ihram,* it was hard to tell families apart or confirm nationalities. The banners helped to keep the groups together. I saw Moors from Spanish North Africa, Libyan Berbers, blacks from the Sudan, Syrians, Palestinians, Kurds and Iraqis, Mongols, Circassians, Persians, Baluchis, Afghans, Malays, and Sinhalese. I became so immersed in this pageant I did not mind our lack of forward progress. Even hadj congestion had a planetary character. The chunk of road we looked out on was as racially dense as a UN parking lot on Flag Day.

In a while the driver stepped down from the bus beside us, climbed onto the bumper, and raised the hood. Then he got down and untied a water bag on the fender. I saw him unscrew the cap and squint into the liquid, but instead of topping off the radiator, he made a circle around the bus, pouring water over all the tires. The passengers up on the roof strained forward, as if to will their old crate back to life. The rubber steamed. The driver slammed the hood and climbed back in.

The bus inched away by stages, and a TV truck began to take its place. The cabin of this vehicle bristled with aerials. On the bed in back two men worked their gear beneath a shade tarp. The camera lens peered out from the canvas, turning on a dolly. While it panned, an enormous Nigerian woman strode from the crowd, waving a handbag hoisted on a stick. It was strange to see pilgrims vie for the camera's attention. However, the main events of the hadj were broadcast live, all day, around the world, and everyone knew it. These people were waving, by prearranged signals, to watchful families thousands of miles away. Qadisha, I now remembered, had urged me to carry a bright purple umbrella, hoping that it would help me to stand out. I waved to her three or four times as the truck crawled forward.

We were heading toward a boundary line that divided Muzdalifah from the plains. Arafat proper, the site of the hadj, lay a mile away. As the van gained ground, the enclosing ranges tapered, then opened like an hourglass below the waist. We passed a pair of whitewashed pillars at the mouth of the valley, marking the edge of sacred territory. Another dry river, the Wadi 'l-Arak, extended for some distance to our left. It was filled with a shrub that the Makkans prize for toothpicks. Behind sparse green tops we picked out the spires of Namira mosque farther down the valley. Its minarets stood out like ships' masts in a harbor. There were four.

The enormity of my assumption, that words could take the measure of the hadj, caught up to me on the Plain of Arafat. I saw now why men as observant as Rutter and Burckhardt had given it two pages. At Arafat the hadj became too big to be a subject, too sprawling, too amoebic. There were no hooks by which to hoist the vista. Its edges outran the verbal frames we place around things. Its center was everywhere, confounding reason, opening the heart.

The four-mile bowl of sand we entered now was lined with tents enclosed by granite mountains, identical white canvas rows, forming quads that lapped out of sight, fusing into dots on the horizon. Sweeps of momentarily homeless millions were divided here and there by two-lane roads winding through the camp like canals through Venice, coming and going in the mist. As we rolled to a stop in one of these canvas rivers, I gave up and slipped my notebook into my bag. I relinquished my post at the fort of objective inquiry. Chants of "labbayk" welled up from the plain.

The van rocked and pitched as we watched at the windows.

> *You wanted a look*
> *At Death*
>   *before you faced it?*
> *Now you have seen it*
> *with your eyes.* *

If Arafat *was* a dress rehearsal for Judgment Day, one thing seemed certain: no one would be alone there. The crowds on the road gleamed like figures from two worlds. The hadj was at its most ethereal right now, vibrating between the real and the symbolic. Out on the sand a man in towels marched past the van with a green flag. Suddenly it was as if we had driven into a Wallace Stevens poem. The figures in the street became figures of heaven. Men grew small in the distances of space. The blown banners seemed to change to wings. Then the van jerked suddenly forward, the crowd swam into focus, and we floated along together down the plain.

The plain is not entirely a desert. At the eastern end of Orina Valley, I caught a glimpse of some leafy, planted rows bounding the long west wall of Namira mosque. This stretch of verdant farmland shocked the eye after

---

*Qur'an 3:143

what we'd come through. In the sixteenth century all of Arafat was cul-
tivated. Today we had this tidy patch of green, dwarfed by lunar sweeps of
barren gravel. The garden only added to the land's surreal aspect, bean rows
jutting up from nowhere, flanked by boulders shaped like body parts. The
only missing touch was the Daliesque pocket watch.

A few blocks from the mosque our driver nosed the van into the
wrong end of a blacktopped one-way alley lined with buses. This aisle was
fitted out to form a market. Tents on either side were jammed by pilgrims
buying juice and fruit and small provisions—bread, umbrellas, head cloths,
beads, canteens. People beyond the berms of the road looked blissful,
complacent. On the pavement, however, a heated throng of shoppers
bulged onto the road and blocked the way. Ahead a man on a crooked staff
had fallen to his knees, and a crush of sheep and hadjis stood around him.
Muhammad once called pilgrimage an "honorable equivalent of battle."
From here it had all the tumult of a campaign.

I wanted badly to get out and walk now. We hadn't moved a yard in
fifteen minutes. The Namira mosque was the same distance away. When
Nasser barked an order and the long side door rolled back, I got to my feet.
A gust of fresh air blew through the cabin. Before I could move, however,
the van lurched forward and the door slammed shut. Our driver had found
a gap in the oncoming traffic and was gunning the engine, bouncing down
a sidetrack, honking, shouting. The delegation cheered. Rounding the
mosque, he swung a hard right and rejoined the traffic. We continued
nudging forward through the crowd.

*T*he roads were little veins of pandemonium in the larger, calmer body of
the hadj. Once we had found our parking lot and left the van behind, I
marveled at the quiet in the campsites. Laid out in quads, they occupied the
largest part of the valley; the roads were no more than perimeter stripes
around them. Each quad was further broken into blocks, great sandy
courtyards edged by canvas tents and gravel walkways. The tents sat backed
against these paths. Stalls and vendors collected at each crossroads.

In contrast to the roads, the camps felt cool and crisp and organized. Here life's minor rhythms carried on. A young man crouched to wash at a plastic bucket. Three Iraqi women sat around a Primus stove, sipping coffee. A baby whimpered.

The first real breeze in a week blew down the valley. It whipped up scraps of paper as we walked. The air smelled strongly of ozone. Tissue-thin, high clouds dulled the sun. After ten days and nights in the hollow, the plain felt cool. It was ninety-three degrees Fahrenheit at ten-thirty, a low unheard of in summertime Makkah. Usama, in particular, looked relieved. Yesterday at the guesthouse he had been dying. Now he kept pace with the sheikhs as they marched along. A few rows back came Abd al-Qadir and Ahmad, forming their usual guard for John Mohammad. John walked with a shuffle. Ahmad held an umbrella above his head.

It was impossible to place ourselves in relation to the landscape. The corridors of tents blocked any view. Cut off, with no point of reference, I wondered if it were possible to attend the hadj and miss it. Passing a rank of buses by the road, I stopped to look. They were locked, painted white, with sky-blue trim. At the back of one a ladder ran up to the baggage racks. I let the others pass and climbed the ladder. From the roof, I had a good view of Jabal al-Rahmah.

It lay at the closed end of the valley, butted against the foot of Mount Namira. Broad stone steps zagged up the eastern side to a gentle summit two hundred feet above the plain. This modest pile of boulders was the focal point of the hadj. Every structure on the plain, tents included, faced or flowed toward it. A tall, whitewashed obelisk marked the summit. It looked the size of a matchstick from the bus.

I felt oriented the moment I saw Jabal al-Rahmah. The name means "Mount of Mercy." Hadj encampments ran right up to its sides.

I had a long look, then caught up to the others, following Ahmad's umbrella to a pavilion. Nasser was making a speech when I came in. Men milled about him idly, listening, blinking, adjusting to the light. The enclosure was simple: a sixty-by-ninety-foot roof on concrete pillars, open on three sides but casting shade. A low wall ran around it. Nine-by-twelve red carpets lay on gravel. The gravel was level, loosely packed, and gave with a little crunch when I sat down. To the rear, behind tall screens, there lay a kitchen. Stacks of dishware rattled. Fans churned above me. The shade made the air delicious.

Nasser concluded his speech by announcing that this would be our base camp until nightfall. He warned us twice to stay out of the sun.

❖   ❖   ❖   ❖

*T*he pavilion was out of earshot of the traffic. With an hour until *zuhr*, the delegation lounged. A few told beads. Others read or talked. I was lying on a carpet reading supplications from a handbook ("We have halted in your courtyard," one began), when Abd al-Qadir and Dr. 'Ali, a delegate from West Africa, started talking. They were seated on either side of me. Their conversation, taking place across my body, resembled a Platonic dialogue.

Abd al-Qadir was pondering human suffering. He had seen, on the TV news the night before, some film clips of forest fires in California. The hills around Santa Barbara had been burning for a week, and hundreds of homes had gone up in flames, leaving families homeless. Tragic news on a holiday like this one—it nagged Abd al-Qadir. He asked 'Ali whether God created evil.

'Ali replied that God created everything. "The good, the bad, the whole shebang," he smiled.

Dr. 'Ali was an elderly Ghanaian lately relocated in Detroit. He spoke butter-smooth Gold Coast English and possessed a sweetness of disposition that intrigued me. He had a way of beguiling people while holding them at bay with his confident firmness. Though he rarely spoke much to anyone, I had seen total strangers cross crowded rooms to shake his hand, perhaps in the hope of absorbing his charisma. I never learned what his degree was in. 'Ali was a doctor of something very attractive.

Hearing that good and evil derived from Allah, Abd al-Qadir fell silent for a time.

"Maybe there's no such thing," he finally said.

"No such thing as what?"

"As evil."

"You are wrong," 'Ali replied. "God created the evils of air and water, for example."

"Of the air?"

"Tornadoes, for instance."

"A tornado isn't evil."

"Oh, yes," 'Ali said in his gentle way, raising a finger. "Crops are destroyed. People suffer. Children die. It is bad. And men feel badly."

"But tornadoes are made by pressure, not by evil. Name one thing that's really evil."

'Ali shook his head at this. "Bad things *do* happen. And people feel awful because of them. When one of the Prophet's children died, he wept. The others said, 'Why are you crying? It is God's will.' The Prophet said, 'God put mercy in our hearts. We are human beings.' If a city burns down, and no one mourns, it would be as if nothing had happened."

'Ali smiled sweetly while Abd al-Qadir chewed this over.

"But why would Allah make evil?" Abd al-Qadir asked.

"Perhaps as a way of telling people apart."

The sun angling over the roof put the grounds in shadow. The pavilion rippled beneath the fans. A little while before the call to prayer, I walked across the road in search of a bathroom. I needed to wash up before *salat*, and I wanted cold liquid. Even in the shade a liter of iced water turned tepid quickly. The bottles provided on our arrival were now hot to the touch.

Nasser asked where I was going, and I told him. He gave me an umbrella.*

It is a whimsical pastime, strolling around in bone-dry heat beneath a cloudless sky with your parasol open. The breeze had picked up. The ruler-straight gravel lanes were mostly deserted. They intersected every twenty yards, forming mazy corridors of canvas. A cinder block latrine rose

---

*Hadj law forbids male pilgrims to cover their heads, but umbrellas have always been permitted. Being much larger in the old days, perhaps they were classified as tents. Burckhardt mentions a group of several thousand men under green umbrellas. At a distance, mounted on camels, they "bore some resemblance to a verdant plain."

on my right. Inside, the walls were dotted with brass spigots. Men crouched in the shadows, washing. Others waited. A cement trough carried off excess water. The room was dark.

Outside again I paused on the stoop to let my eyes adjust. The plain appeared as a sheet of white-hot metal. It put me in mind of Valéry's motto for a sundial: *"Lux dux."* I was still getting used to it when a tiny man stepped up and squeezed under my umbrella. Withered and toothless, he took up so little room I hardly noticed. He carried a basket of oranges on his arm and while we stood there began nonchalantly handing fruit to the men emerging from the building. It was the sort of small, inspired gesture that so often endeared me to Islam. No one could have mistaken him for a vendor. He smacked his lips. He glanced away when someone thanked him.

Walking back, I passed a drink cooler on a picnic table. It was filled to the top with bottles, cans, and ice. This gleaming, snow-capped mound looked out of place here on the desert. The table was untended, the ice audibly melting around the drinks. I worked a liter of orangeade free. I laid my hand on the ice until it ached.

By the time I reached the shelter, the call to prayer had started. The delegation stood facing Makkah. As prayers began, a low, steady hum engulfed the plain. A few million people were whispering in concert. A soft roar beat about the edges of the shelter.

The brevity of the session was exceptional. At Arafat *zuhr* and *'asr* prayers are joined and shortened. Instead of eight *rak'ah*s, today we made four—two groups of two cycles, with a third call from the minaret between. Prayer required *wudu'*, and *wudu'* required water, which in the old days camels lugged over the plain. Condensing the sessions cut these needs by half. It also gave people an unbroken afternoon to use as they pleased on this day of days, and extra time before dusk to prepare an exit.

"You saw the roads this morning?" Mardini asked.

"Yes."

"Well, that was nothing."

"You mean everyone leaves at once?"

He said, "They try."

I remembered the recording of the prayers from Marrakesh. Preparing to play it, I fished the recorder from my bag and switched it on when the air around the pavilion roared with static. A moment later the voice of the imam of Makkah shook the plain. I knew this must be the Arafat sermon, but I had not expected it so early. I fumbled a blank cassette into the recorder and passed Mardini the tiny microphone.

Later, replaying his translation, the imam's voice overrode everything.* It ran out at the top of his lungs for forty minutes, full of advice and theatrical emotion, sometimes breaking into tears. The delegation listened solemnly. The hectoring tone disturbed me. Loudspeakers boomed above the quads.

The imam's address was an annual occasion. It marked a brief, more memorable sermon made by Muhammad on the Farewell Hadj. This was the Prophet's last public speech. Deservedly famous, its contents are memorized by schoolboys. I had seen the words on plaques in Moroccan homes. The first lines made it clear that he knew he was dying:

> Listen closely, people. I do not know if I will meet you here next year.
> From this day forward, until you meet your Lord . . .

In taking his leave, he abolished blood feuds and usury between Muslims. He exhorted people to stay together after his death. He reminded couples to honor their spouses and to use reason:

> Listen to what I am telling you. Any Muslim is a brother to every other.
> Only take from one another things that are freely given. And do not do
> injustice to yourselves.

Muhammad had stood near the peak of Jabal al-Rahmah. The crier Rabi'ah stood below him, repeating his words to criers on the plain. The amplifiers replacing this ancient system were no great improvement. As

---

*For some audible parts of Mardini's translation, see Appendix A.

often happened in the Middle East, the volume was turned too high. The speech sounded shattered.

After the sermon our rows broke into smaller groups. Dishware clattered behind the kitchen screens, then a group of Saudi boys in *thobes* appeared. They carried yard-long cylinders of white cloth in their arms, dumping them down like firewood at one end of the shelter, rolling them out on the carpet with soft kicks. Platters of food were placed on these improvised tables. We scooted into lines and began to eat. The meal consisted of curried rice and lamb shanks, bowls full of oranges and bananas, water, green coffee, cups of tea. The desert receded. For an hour the hadj became a communal picnic. "Once you eat in a place, you belong there," 'Ali said. Sheikh Nasser nodded.

The combined effect of the food and heat was stunning. A handful of pilgrims nodded off. Fayez and Fazeel, at opposite ends of the shelter, recited to themselves from bin Baz's book. There was little movement on the rugs between. As the day settled over us, I took out my camera and snapped several photos. A few men in our party objected to portraits, on the grounds that Islam's taboo against icons extended even to likenesses by Kodak. Most people had cameras of their own.

In a little while Mardini came over to borrow my radio. He was going for a stroll, to visit a tentful of notables, and he wanted to monitor the hadj as he walked along. I was feeling the heat by then and declined to go with him.

The blue sky past the roof looked painted, static. The black fan blades barely turned. I felt no desire now to move at all. If the pilgrimage had a pinnacle, we were on it. The sun appeared pinned into place, the mica glinted. In the prairie quiet the protean hadj became a vigil.

People may do as they like at Arafat. There is no required liturgy, no clutter. The point of the day is to be here. To inhabit the plain is sufficient. You may talk if you wish, or walk, or pray, or chant, or doze. There is nothing compulsory, no set pattern of behavior. No special spot to flock to. No metaphors, no verbs.

The *wukuf* is a chance to let the spirit breathe. For men like Fayez, it was also a day of answered prayers and God's rewards. They bent to their job, not wasting a moment, seeking blessings for friends and families. Hassan Mubarak, who worked in Detroit at the Clare Muhammed School, borrowed my Qur'an and lay down to read. Fazeel sat chanting. Dr. 'Ali fingered beads. I did an amount of all these things, then played back the Marrakeshis' prayer tape. Their familiar voices blended with the murmurs on the plain.

When the pebbled carpets became too hard to sit, I moved around the shelter, working out creaks, performing knee bends. At one point I crouched beside Fazeel. He glanced up from his chanting, cotton mouthed, and squinted at me in a distant way. I passed what remained of the orangeade. He drank it off.

"Is there more?"

I pointed across the road.

Soon we were weaving through the solar flares. Fazeel, I noticed, was as high as a kite from the chanting. He walked with a rolling motion, looking glassy. All at once a brisk wind came down the plain and tore the umbrella from his fingers. I chased it briefly, then we watched it go, tumbling inside out across the sand.

We returned with a half dozen soft drinks and distributed them to the men. By now I had run through my store of supplications. While the others prayed or chatted, I puttered for fifteen minutes, straightening rug ends, depositing empty bottles in a trash bin. I checked on John Muhammad. I gave him a tablet. I noticed a pilgrim getting up to leave.

Abd al-Mu'id was an interesting case—an Algerian computer engineer who lived in Colorado. That summer, after four confusing years, his marriage to an American was ending. The rift had begun when his wife joined a Bible group. It ended one night in his living room with the group trying to convert him to being Baptist. Abd al-Mu'id had confided to me that his hadj was a declaration. He had come here to get back in touch with who he was. He alone among our group had revealed a deeper motive to his journey. I watched him leaving the pavilion. I was tired of sitting on gravel, cut off from the crowds. Telling myself that he might get lost, I followed Abd al-Mu'id.

He turned down a corridor, walking toward Jabal al-Rahmah. The backs of the tents faced us here, the stays hammered into the sand formed vacant alleys. Again I was struck by an absence of commotion. The air hummed with a muffled drone. The tents faced inward on their courtyards. Directly ahead I saw only Abd al-Mu'id. His gait was easy. His white umbrella bobbed.

Following behind at fifty yards, I passed a group of air-conditioned tents with half-ton units pumping from their backsides. These intrigued me, God knows why, and I stopped long enough to peek into a tent through a chink in the canvas. The enclosure was empty, the hot air musty. The air conditioner was running at full blast.

When I turned back up the path, Abd al-Mu'id was gone. Now I remembered Nasser's warning about the sun. Seeing a clump of movement in the distance, I walked toward it. I was weaving from side to side to get my bearings, like an ant on a blueprint. The corridors cut by the tents curved in the heat.

At a road intersecting two camps, a government truck had backed into the road, and three soldiers stood on the tailgate, handing bags of water down the sides. Around them fifty or sixty hadjis reached up for the water. It came in shapeless packets, small and clear and blue when the sunlight hit them, and stamped in three languages: DRINKING WATER. GIFT OF KING FAHD. A soldier on the truck tossed me down a liter. I nipped the plastic end and drank it off.

I stopped at every crossroads to look for Abd al-Mu'id. The lanes between the tents were becoming more populous. Soon I entered a Pakistani quad. *Chipati* (flat-bread) stalls marked out the border. I peeked into one of the courtyards, where men and women lounged on carpets, shaded by orange saris propped on poles. They looked self-absorbed or relaxed to the point of dozing. A few sipped tea from bowls.

The Pakistani enclave continued for three blocks, then gave way to a district of Moroccans. The bakery odors turned to savory drafts of stewed *tajine*. Cheekbones changed. Tea was served in glasses jammed with mint. This was like stumbling onto a wedge of the old Maghreb, and I crouched beside a flap to take it in. At Mina, where tents served as private dwellings, I might have been run off for trespassing. Here no one noticed. I made a rapid once-over of the crowd, then looked closer. I was searching for

someone, I dimly realized. In an attack of misplaced nostalgia I was comb-
ing the yard for Abd al-Hadi, the electrician from Marrakesh. At this
realization I backed away from the tents, shaking my head.

The camps continued on for fifteen minutes. Every few blocks another
ethnic margin marked a clear-cut border as I walked, like bands in a
rainbow. Little India led on to Little Egypt. I looked up again and found
myself in Thailand. In each case the plain *ihram,* designed to wipe out class
distinction, heightened the contrast, setting races naturally apart. This was
the mosaic that Malcolm X remembered:

> There was a color pattern in the huge crowds. Once I happened
> to notice this, I closely observed it thereafter. Being from America made
> me intensely sensitive to matters of color. I saw that people who looked
> alike drew together and most of the time stayed together. This was
> entirely voluntary; there being no other reason for it. But Africans were
> with Africans. Pakistanis were with Pakistanis. And so on. I tucked it
> into my mind that when I returned home I would tell Americans this
> observation; that where true brotherhood existed among all colors,
> where no one felt segregated, where there was no "superiority" com-
> plex, no "inferiority" complex—then voluntarily, naturally, people of
> the same kind felt drawn together by that which they had in common.

I was now on one of a dozen lanes that ran like spokes toward Mount
Mercy. Wider than the aisles through the camps, these lanes were filled with
hadjis like myself from the back of the enclave. Although the whole plain
was Arafat, the *jabal* represented the heart of the action. Muhammad had
stood on its peak. People wanted to see it.

A ring road circled the hill's perimeter. It looked less like a road from
where I stood than like a moat full of shepherds. Ahead the feeder lane was
a lake of hands. Another government water truck had backed into the road,
and hadjis stood around it with their arms raised. I worked my way past
them, wading through cast-off plastic. On the other side I stood facing the
mountain.

Broad stone steps ran up the southern flank, making a left, then a
right-hand turn, leading to the summit with its column. Halfway up lay a

pad with a wall around it. This, it was said, marked a spot where the prophet Adam first performed *salat*.* Hadjis leaned at the wall, enjoying the view there.

Earlier that week I had visited this hill when no one was on it. Now small figures perched on every rock. Some stood still like sentries, faces growing smaller near the summit. Others chatted under parasols or read from prayer books. Every few minutes a patch of two hundred people would stand together, wave their shoulder towels, and chant, "Labbayk! Allahummah, Labbayk!" An answering chorus rose up off the plain.

Behind the hill a higher shelf of cliffs overlooked the quads. It formed a gallery fringed with tents and cars, where hundreds of thousands of locals were assembled. Makkans considered these perches the best seats in the house, and they drove out from town in packs to claim them early. Shafeeq and Saleem were probably up there now, camped under a lean-to near his Brougham. Their view across the plains would be superb.

Very few tents stood on the *jabal* proper. Bodies packed the rocks on every side, but the slopes were too oddly pitched for real camping, and the boulders looked jagged. A few stunted mimosas poked through cracks.

On the outer rim of the road the crowds grew thinner. There were unexpected pockets of open ground and no trucks or cars. People strolled easily. Some walked arm in arm. Here and there I heard a vendor calling. Just then the crowd was moving in a counterclockwise direction, but this was coincidental. Circling Jabal al-Rahmah was not a required rite of the hadj. A minute later the crowd's flow changed direction. Something offhand, even idle, about the procession distinguished it from the purposeful *tawaf*.

On the inner edge of the road, near the base of the hill, emotions ran higher. Walking there, I passed a dozen Filipino women. They were weeping. Farther on a distracted Kazakh pilgrim in a brilliant hennaed beard stood lost in meditation by the road. On the hill itself blocks of *ihram*s went up, and the chanting swelled in sections. Mount Mercy induced a notable

---

*The name Arafat derives from a root meaning "to find, recognize, or know." It denotes the spot where, after their expulsion from the garden, Adam and Eve crossed paths and became reacquainted—a primal lost-and-found for souls.

self-effacing ardor. The nearer I came, the more my mind went blank and the place took over.

I continued around the drive and soon crossed paths with an old Yemeni woman selling apples. Remembering events at the latrine, I impulsively bought all the woman's fruit and walked along the road passing them out. The apples were small and red, perhaps from San'a. They gave my hands something to do while I strolled around. I saw nothing out of the ordinary, really—shoulders, elbows, bare heads, tear-streaked faces. The mood was self-possessed, not at all trancelike. Now and then I felt a swell move through us—the unifying agency of the hadj.

Time passed quickly at the mountain. When my supply of fruit ran out, I started winding back to the pavilion. The sky grew hazy as I went. The sun declined toward the Makkan hills.

CHAPTER EIGHTEEN

The Rush

*A*bd al-Mu'id was back at the pavilion, sitting on a wall, when I returned. I kicked off my sandals. Nothing much had changed. After the effort of arrival most of the group was glad to take it easy. And the sheikhs had warned us: the dust, the heat, the risk of a separation were not worth it. Nasser checked off my name as I sat down.

The heat had drained me, and a blister was starting up on my left foot. Still the walk had been worth it. I knew where we were now, and seeing the many divisions of the quads brought home the uniqueness of our delegation. Our little block was a mixture of all the others. I appreciated more our ragtag makeup. In about equal numbers we were New World Muslims and Old World émigrés with Western passports. We had no common speech or skin among us. Exotic in the extreme, we were a sampler of the hadj under one rooftop, a patchwork quilt that drew on every quad. We were also the New Americans. Racially, nationally, despite the cotton towels, our party resembled a random slice of urban Rio or Los Angeles.

I lay down by the wall to take a nap. I was nodding off when a couple of local boys in ragged *thobes* began shrieking behind me. They were ten-year-olds with a stick to fight for, playing on the sand. Pilgrims along the wall looked irritated; I waited for someone to speak. When no one did, I silenced them myself, then fell asleep.

At about five o'clock the plain and everything on it began moving. I woke to bus horns in the distance. The tents on every side had emptied out, and the alleys around the pavilion ran with hadjis. The sky flushed pink. The sun rolled down. The Namira minarets glowed pale emerald. Standing barefoot on the wall, I saw a dust cloud blanketing the plain, thick as a fogbank, obscuring the bases of the hills. Only their peaks stood free, like clouds at sunset.

The dust was a part of the rush Mardini had mentioned. It was not fog but wisps of sand and diesel fumes raised by the first thousand buses setting out. The hadj was under way again. The daylight vigil at Arafat was over. A second, nighttime vigil lay ahead, at Muzdalifah. The short march between these points was called *al-nafrah*, "the pouring forth, the rush." To approximate its confusion, one might imagine two dozen Super Bowl games letting out at once and every fan heading for one exit. From here on until we doffed our towels, our progress to Makkah was slowed by tie-ups. None would be as massive as the rush.

Grains of sand and dust swirled through the shelter. The delegation was on its feet, and Sheikh Ibrahim had begun to lead the first group to the buses. Hassan passed by and gave back my Qur'an. Mardini returned the radio. I packed my things, took a pull of tepid water, and looked for my sandals. They were not on the wall. They were not in the pile of thongs behind it. I studied every pair of feet around me. I scanned the grounds for the ten-year-olds, then gave it up. Nietzsche said that everyone brings to the desert what he finds there. Thinking of Nietzsche at Arafat amused me. My feet were burning.

Mardini devised a simple means to get me to the bus. He went along with the second group, and five minutes later a runner brought back his sandals. They were several sizes too small, but I put them on.

The route to the parking lots lay deep in litter. Scrap paper lay mounting in the lanes, ankle high in places, or raked into piles the wind was blowing. Religious screeds and handbills skittered by. Crushed water bottles, trodden plastic packets lapped the margins. Mixed up in the sand and mica lay lots of soft drink caps with glinting points. Here and there I caught a whiff of chlorine.

The four-mile ride to Muzdalifah took two hours. Traffic ran bumper to bumper all the way, with longer halts as we neared the neck of the valley. Buses stalled, boiled over, ran out of gas with regularity. Here and there a maddened trucker turned his heavy rig onto the sand to try a shortcut. Buses wound up buried to the hubcaps. The lighter vans, with four-wheel drive, fishtailed down the dunes with piercing lights. All too often cars were mired, too.

Burckhardt faced similar chaos in 1814. He and many others lost their camels in these crowds. It should be said that the indescribable confusion of departing Arafat is the result of traditional ardor, not automation. Everyone *does* want to leave at once. Burckhardt wrote, "I was therefore obliged to walk to Mezdelfe."

We turned left at a roadblock, past a dozen unroofed vanloads of Iraqis. These vehicles bounced along like lidless carts. Someone had blowtorched the ceilings off their door posts. When I asked the purpose of this adaptation, Nasser replied that head coverings were not part of the *ihram* garb. It took me a minute to understand what a steel roof and a knit cap had in common. Certain of the sects, he said, customized their vans to uphold custom.

Down the road he pointed out a bridge where, in 1968, sixteen police cars had been destroyed in a slow-motion pileup. I wondered why that year had been so catastrophic. He looked amused and said, "It rained. Flash floods." Any addition by nature to this disorder was hard to grasp. I tried to imagine a rainstorm here. I couldn't.

The sun was down now and the air felt cooler. Courtesy lights had come on inside the bus. I took out my contact lenses, opened the case, and squinted at its little oval mirror. I was weary of wiping white sweat from my glasses. I washed my hands from a water bottle, then dried them on my scarf. While Mardini watched, I balanced a lens on my finger.

"They're blue?" He laughed.

The lenses were tinted.

I showed him.

"Why?"

The lenses were a sort of joke in earnest. The previous winter a friend in California had advised me to wear brown lenses on my journey, to keep me out of trouble with the Arabs. When I mentioned feeling safer in Morocco than in Manhattan, my friend replied that perhaps I should move to Morocco. A week before leaving, I bought the brightest blue lenses I could find and wore them to his house to say good-bye. In Marrakesh I wore the lenses often, without comment. Most Americans were wrong about the Arabs, just as they were wrong about Islam. The only Arabs they seemed to know were the mug shots of men employed by shabby tyrants. As for Islam, they knew nothing about it and did not want to. They drove around with their windows rolled up. They watched TV. They believed in what they saw.

The delegation began to chant as the bus pulled into the campgrounds. Across the valley a lit city of tents spread up the hills. Because it had not been here this morning, I mistook this for the camps at Mina. The hills were pocked with the same cells, like electrified honeycombs. Over and over along the way sprawling quads of flaps and stays were being raised, then struck, as we moved on.

We stepped out into a parking lot at Muzdalifah. Mardini went ahead again. I stayed with the driver by the bus. We smoked a cigarette and waited for the sandals. A makeshift pen had been set up across the lot, and a herd of perhaps a hundred sheep stood loosely roped against a chain link fence. We watched the sheep. They faced every which way, bleating. Their rear left hooves were dyed blue for some reason.

When the sandals arrived, I started climbing. I was glad for the moonlight. The long path up to the camp lay deep in gravel. Halfway up I had a full view of the valley; the plain of lighted tents lay like a mirror of the sky. I had never seen so many shooting stars—every thirty seconds another tracer arced over the hillside. Some appeared to fall among the tents.

I liked Muzdalifah the moment I saw it. The night was as soft as the day had been metallic. I felt more on my own here than at Arafat, and darkness gave the place a subjective basis. The quiet was palpable.

At the top of the hill a concrete wall enclosed a lighted courtyard. The grounds inside sloped down a slanting grade. To one side stood wooden serving tables. We performed the dusk and evening prayers together, then went to the tables. They were set with bowls of lamb stew, rice, vegetables, and salads. We filled our plates, then crouched by the wall to eat supper. There were no carpets, no banquettes.

John Muhammad came to eat beside me. His back, he said, had stopped hurting at Arafat. I supposed the desert air was better for him, that the hotel air-conditioning had not helped. John shook his head. He had a different theory.

"Arafat is a power spot," he said. "Usama's better, too. The minute we crossed the boundary, things got better."

The food made me drowsy. When John got up to leave, I did not mind. My right foot was throbbing. Mardini's sandals were too small, and the blister between my toes, where the thong slipped in, was becoming dome shaped. I washed it, heated a pin, and drained the blister. Then I laid out my rug and tried to nap, but the surface of the camp was graveled. I tried to get comfortable in two or three positions. In the end I opened the Qur'an and read a chapter called "The Cave." I was coming to the parable of Moses and the disappearing fish when a young boy approached and crouched beside me. He scanned the translation, clicked his tongue, and scurried off to a group of men across the compound. When they glanced my way, I did not recognize them; nor could I make out where they were from. I waved politely and went back to reading.

A minute later Mardini appeared and pointed to the group.

"They can't place you," he said. "The boy thinks maybe you're Russian. They want to meet you."

We went over to the group. They had their own carpets and lay in a cozy sprawl around a brazier. They were Saudis from the southwestern region of Abha, a mountainous land of brooks and trees near the Yemeni border. As a district, Abha was as far as one could get from the modernizing habits of the Saudis. A quick turn off the paved road there plunged you into an ancient land of steep, terraced cliffs and tribal fiefdoms. Cars, TV, electric light had reached it, but the people remained remote. Hearing these men were Ghahtani piqued my interest. The tribe is mentioned in the book of Genesis. Each one stood and introduced himself. We all touched hands, and several of the nearer ones embraced me. They were part of a family and seemed entirely at home.

Coffee was poured. I set the Qur'an on my knee to take the cup, and an old man picked up the book and began to page it. The book went from hand to hand, until the translation was identified as English. Mardini explained my nationality, and the group leaned forward.

"We know all about you," one said with animation. "From television."

I posed a couple of questions and was told that a satellite dish had just gone up on the cliff above their village. Now they could watch CNN world news. They were full of questions, alas. My interest in Abha fell by the wayside. Did the sultan of Washington really use cocaine? Did Republicans take drugs? Did Nancy Reagan? And what about AIDS? Were all Americans infected?

The questions came thick and fast, in one direction. My suggestion that they did not have the whole picture met with disbelief from the Ghahtani. After all they had seen it, with their eyes. We slogged the fens of trivia—was Michael Jackson a Muslim? What about this wife of his, Madonna? We traipsed the bogland of stocks and bonds—the Ghahtani dismissed accrued interest as a Satanic instrument. We even trudged the thicket of Western marriage. Loaded topics, all, were lobbed across the fire with goodwill. Having to translate my answers bogged down the discussion. To my relief, Mardini took over. He joked, he defused, he promoted understanding, he did what he could to maintain peace during the hadj. When it came to Salman Rushdie, he outdid himself.

Rushdie (whose latest book was then being burned in the Middle East) had been sentenced to death by the ruler of Iran. The story was followed closely in the press, and everyone I met took sides that summer. Some people felt the judgment fit the crime. Some saw the thing as political and blamed Khomeini. It was easy to find both points of view in Makkah and clear that the furor was fed by wild writing and worse reading. Yet the burning of a book is never a literary matter. Rushdie's work and institutional Islam formed a perfect fit, like a spear through a breastplate.

The Ghahtani felt no allegiance to Iran. They only wondered how such a book had ever come to be published. It was insulting. Why would people want to read it? Mardini attempted to explain. He said that in his experience most Americans did not read books, that almost no one he knew there had heard of Rushdie until the Iranians put a bounty on his head. When they heard, they bought and read the book and, becoming more confused, asked their critics and professors why it was so awful. They were told that it dealt irreverently with the Prophet and the Qur'an. As a result, a lot of Americans bought translations of the Qur'an. Here Mardini paused with great effect while the Ghahtanis broke into smiles, for the only book they really cared about appeared to be benefiting, thanks to Rushdie's.

Throughout this exchange a quiet boy about eighteen sat at the back of the group, paging my Qur'an. His incipient mustache bobbed as he read. In a while he came over and sat down. His name was Ghafel Mansour. We spoke in whispers.

"This Qur'an, where did you get it?"

"In America," I said.

"Can you send me one like it, later? I'll reimburse you."

Ghafel spoke English well and he read it with relish. He was a sophomore at King Saud University and a literature major. He tried out some titles on me: Henry James's *Washington Square*, Steinbeck's *The Pearl*, Mark Twain's *Huckleberry Finn*. The Twain, in particular, threw me. What did he make of the dialects? I wondered. Or of the scene where Tom led Huck on the raid of the "A-rabs"?

"The whole book's controversial," he said.

"What about Washington Irving?"

Ghafel had read "Rip Van Winkle" and the "Legend of Sleepy Hollow." "Your first short story writer," he said.

Irving had also written a fine book on the life of the Prophet Muhammad. When I told Ghafel this, his eyes bugged.

"Can you send me that, too?"

Ghafel had just won a scholarship to study English in Washington, D.C. He was anxious to see the Library of Congress. He was frightened, too. It would not be like Abha. I asked what scared him.

"Well, I don't want to die there."

"Who said you will die?"

He looked at me with pity. "Many people die there."

"They do?"

It was the specter of AIDS and drugs again, beaming down the cliffs. Ghafel's view of America was as distorted as most Americans' views of Arabia. So much, I thought, for the global village. TV was a wall, not a window.

"Besides," he said, "my father forbids me."

"To?"

"Go to Washington."

"Well, you know what they say: 'All Arabs are terrorists. All Americans have AIDS.' "

His mustache wobbled.

"A joke," I said. "Go to America. My God, you speak the language! See for yourself." I rustled *Lord Jim* from my bag and gave it to him.

✧   ✧   ✧   ✧

When the interview broke up, Ghafel and a few of his friends led me out of the campground. I followed them into the hills on a twisting path. My feet slipped in two or three places. There were no lights. In time the land leveled out, and the moon took over. The walk became easier. The last half-moon I'd seen was above the villa in Tangier. I remembered the Sharf topped with its mosque and the taxis of old men riding up to pray. The hill we walked tonight was shaped more like a cupcake. Gradually I began to notice other hadjis. Singly or in small groups, the slope was dotted with them, popping up between rocks, then stooping over. They were picking up pebbles.

"This is a good place," Ghafel said.

He bent down and began to gather stones, dropping them one by one into his palm. I did the same.

We were arming ourselves for the next hadj rite. I had read about it, of course, but it seemed elusive. According to bin Baz's handbook, three pillars stood up the road at Mina. They marked spots on the way back to Makkah where the angel of darkness had tempted Abraham's family and where they had thrown stones to drive him off. Pilgrims still memorialized these rejections in a series of flings at the pillars, called *jamarat*. The rite was reportedly rowdy. Yet there was precision to it, too, as is often the case with ancient rituals. The throws were assigned set hours and days, the number of stones and their size were fixed, and they had to be gathered at Muzdalifah. Ghafel, I noticed, was counting to himself.

"How many do we need?"

"Forty-nine," he called. "Unless you stay an extra day."

"And if I stay?"

"Seventy."

I kept glancing up at the hadjis in the distance. Bent down in twos and threes, rippled by heat, their garments stood out against the moonlit boulders. Despite its rugged surface, Muzdalifah was ineffably serene. This was my kind of vigil: meditative but on one's feet and with a hunt in progress. I felt I could stay here indefinitely, collecting pebbles, counting falling stars.

Ghafel had already started down the hill. When I caught up at a spigot near the campsite, his pebbles had been placed inside a Coke can and he was shaking them up and down, pouring off the water. The moisture brought out their greenness under the streetlamps. When I showed him my collection, he critiqued it, tossing out a few stones as too large, substituting others from the driveway. I washed and tied them into a corner of my towel.

By ten o'clock the moon had rolled and mellowed. I lay down in the yard and caught a nap. My exhaustion was not only physical. It owed something to the fact that the hadj had surpassed its outer limits. Our line of march after Arafat now looped back to the west. The procession was becoming a recessional. We were heading for Makkah. The old books called Arafat "the completion of yearning," but even completion is a stage. In this sense the hadj remained true to life's inexorable motion. It was not a destination, as people thought, but a direction: a circular loop of temporary stations, from the Ka'ba to Mount Mercy and slowly back. Chaucer's palmers would have felt at home here—"And we been pilgrymes, passing to and fro."

You went "on" hadj, not "to" it. You approached, you reached out, you rushed forward, but none of its stations was a place to stay, least of all rocky Muzdalifah. You arrived to go. The Qur'an was frequently quoted at these junctures: "Unto Allah is the journeying."

A shuffle of feet over gravel woke me up. The Ghahtani were at the gate, about to leave.

They had lost half their group in the frenzy of the *nafrah*. Now word had arrived from the stragglers, and the Ghahtani were going down to meet them. I shook hands with Ghafel and offered to speak to his father for him. I felt strongly that he should come to Washington and not be timid, especially as he had a scholarship. Unhappily, his father was with the missing party. I wondered what would happen to these people. I left the yard and watched them file downhill.

I was leaning on the courtyard wall, applying a patch of moleskin to my blister, when Mardini came over.

The flap of skin was toughening already. With the patch on top, the thong barely rubbed at all. I took a few steps and nodded.

"The dry air heals things fast," he said. Smiling broadly, he dropped a fresh set of flip-flops on the gravel. "The Ghahtani left them," he said. "Someone brought along an extra pair."

I was very glad. The loss of my gear had set up a chain reaction in the group. Mardini had lent me his sandals, which were too small. Then he had borrowed the driver's, which were too narrow. Neither he nor I was comfortable. The driver, unable to move at all, was holding a barefoot vigil down in the parking lot.

The new sandals fit almost perfectly. I clomped around. I stamped my feet.

"Good," he said. "Let's get going."

As far as I knew, we were meant to spend the night here. Nasser had said so, and I liked the place. Mardini, I soon discovered, had reasons for leaving. John Muhammad was limping again, he said. The *nafrah* had not been easy; worse lay ahead. By morning the *jamarat* area would be a mob scene.

This was the bridge from which one stoned the three pillars.

"Is it really that bad?"

"They say a hundred pilgrims died last year."

I had heard this, too. *Jamarat* victims were mostly infirm or lame. They stumbled in the crowds and were slowly trampled.

"How long would it take us to get John there?"

"Tonight? An hour. Tomorrow, three or four, if he can walk."

I glanced at John. He was sitting alone across the yard with his back against the wall and a cane beside him.

"Do you think he can make it?"

"Let's ask him."

CHAPTER NINETEEN

The Jam

Solvitur ambulando.
It is solved by walking.

*T*he last of the moon dropped behind the hill as we traipsed down to the parking lot. Mardini went first, raking the path with a flashlight. I brought up the rear, staying a couple of paces in back of John. Once or twice he slipped but did not fall. The forward thrust of the hadj seemed to raise his spirits. Lying on the pebbles had been torture. Walking was better; it chased the numbness from his toes.

The parking lot was clogged with vehicles. The streetlamps were out, and it took some extra minutes to locate our driver. We found him perched on the gate of the red Suburban, paring his fingernails. Mardini explained our decision. The driver nodded. We climbed into the wagon and roared off.

Mina lay two miles up the valley. A couple of slipways above the sand were the only ways to reach it. I sat alone in the backseat, watching the view pour forward as we rode. Orion glanced off the windshield. Glowing quads of tents flowed by the road.

Climbing a broad bridge thrown across a wadi, we saw a dozen vans streak down the channel in a dusty midnight drag race back to Makkah. Their lights cut crazy arcs over the sandbanks. Inspired, our driver pressed the pedal to the floor.

A conversation started up in the front seat. Now that we were under way, John doubted the rightness of leaving Muzdalifah. The Prophet had kept his vigil until dawn. What were *we* doing? Was it proper?

I, too, wondered about the pilgrim laws. The forms of the hadj seemed so open; yet now and then you came upon a rule that could wreck your efforts if you broke it. You performed *sa'y* after *tawaf,* never before; if you reached Arafat too late, your hadj was void. Mardini now repeated a *hadith* that allowed the weak to beat the crowds to Mina. His studied quotation impressed me. I had so often thought of Mardini as my room-mate, just one more pilgrim in the party, that sometimes I forgot his erudition. All the sheikhs addressed him as imam.

The minarets of the Khaif mosque shone mint green in the distance. Across the valley lay a slaughterhouse. A triangle of sheds on five or six acres, it was the largest complex in the valley. The abattoir was already in full swing. It had to be, to accommodate tomorrow's feast, the 'Id al-Fitr, when half a million sheep were sacrificed. This rite that ends the hadj is observed throughout the Muslim world, but nowhere on a grander scale than in Makkah. Herds had been building up in town all week. At Mina every hillside had its pens. They lined the sides of the potholed road we traveled. The bleating grew louder as we climbed.

All at once the driver began shouting, thrusting his head out the window, gunning the engine. I sat up, squinting. A flock of sheep stood in our headlights up the road.

Perhaps they were blinded. Perhaps sheep are even dumber than they seem. As the van bore down, they rushed forth to meet us. It looked a lot like suicide to me, until just before impact, when the flock divided smoothly down the middle and flowed around us like a school of fish. In the end it was our driver who overreacted. He cranked the wheel hard as the sheep skipped by, and the wagon fishtailed. We felt the back end slide; we heard two thunks, as if rolling over a tree trunk.

Looking back, I saw a figure on the road, chasing the van with a wooden staff and shouting. Undoubtedly it was the owner of the sheep. Our driver saw him, too, in the rearview mirror. We picked up speed and flew around a bend.

"The sacrifice is not until tomorrow," Mardini whispered.

The driver berated Satan, then himself, after which he sank into a funk. A minute later, near the summit, he came to an intersection of three roads. Traffic gelled. He threaded and bullied, leaning on the horn, sideswiped a concrete wall and tapped some fenders. Mardini showed his disgust for this by ignoring it. "When the Makkans get out to Mina," he said, "they lose their minds. And they don't have insurance."

"They don't?"

"Of course not." He chuckled. "What fool would sell insurance here?"

Our towels were caked with sand. My skin felt chalky. When John suggested a shower at the guesthouse, Mardini reluctantly agreed. I did not share his urgency that evening. I did not understand yet how grueling the *jamarat* rite could be. Mardini would not have had illusions. Already John was limping, and we hadn't tossed a stone. He was anxious to get through the rite while John could walk.

Upstairs we showered and changed into fresh towels. The moleskin between my toes was filthy. I peeled it off and applied a new one. I was packing my bag when Mardini stopped me. "Leave everything here!" he said. "Just take your stones."

We were back outside in twenty minutes. I was bathed in sweat before we left the drive.

Mina's main street filled a narrow valley. The hadj encampments lay below and to our right. Burckhardt had paced this road at fifteen hundred yards. It was many times longer tonight and bathed in lamplight. One or two ancient features had not changed. Before the days of traffic tunnels, this street's only connection to Makkah had been by a stone step path over the mountain. I passed these steps, which pre-date Muhammad, near the Aqaba Jamara. They were lined with pilgrims going up and down.

Because the pilgrims paused here for three days, the road was lined with tent kitchens and soup shacks. We had hoped to beat the crowds, but the street was deluged. The farther we went, the more the numbers grew.

The right of the weak and the halt to go ahead strongly affected the look of this population. Inordinate numbers of people moved on crutches, and there were many misshapen limbs and bandaged heads. The street resembled an engraving of the old Lourdes road. Mixed in with the special cases went many younger, healthy-looking men. Perhaps, like us, they were here as protectors. Perhaps they were on fire with devoutness and could not wait to get on with the rites. One, rushing by in tattered robes, looked like a ringer for the man John Bunyan described in *Pilgrim's Progress,* running with his fingers in his ears and crying, "Life, life, eternal life." There were others too, Sudanese, Egyptians, Moroccans, and one tall, intensely vibrant Yemeni with tangled hair and a rope around his waist like John the Baptist. He did not look behind him but fled toward the middle of the town.

A two-tiered curving, futuristic bridge on concrete pilings paralleled the road as we moved west. It lay on our right, converging with the pavement. Where the street forked, we followed a rail and went down. A sign on the arch read JAMARAT in four languages. The ramp led steeply to a lower level, and the bridge's upper tier became a roof. There were lights below and a broad, covered walkway over which the crowds strode, hip to hip. The design of this two-story boulevard recalled the *mas'a,* but here we saw no marble, no expensive touch of any kind. Rough and plain, it looked less like a shrine than an underground car lot. The *jamarat* arena was a no-frills operation.

This rite began the closure of the hadj. Relief was apparent in the early crowds. In addition, the prospect of pelting a slab with stones, even to ward off evil, contained a certain element of sport. The wheelchairs rolled along in double time. Smiling, laughing faces outnumbered the others. Our procession developed a packed and slipping rhythm, like many conga lines bouncing together.

As we came within sight of the pillars, the noise level rose. The roof collected our echoes, raining them down on us. Mouths mimed "Allahu akbar!" but no apparent sound came out. It was all absorbed in an oceanic roaring. More and more people raised and waved their arms. More faces looked ecstatic. In the crush John's eyes grew wider. I kept myself at his back, to break the shock waves. Mardini went before him with folded arms.

Our goal was the big third column at the far end of the hall. Except in size, these pillars are identical. Set up at intervals of a hundred yards, each one rises from a ground-floor base, tapers up through a hole in the overpass, and soars a further eight feet into the air. The new bridge seemed to me a stroke of genius. Its two-tiered construction split up the crowds, letting twice as many hadjis at the pillars.

The jostling grew intense as we passed the first two columns. I dug in, to shield John. Progress became a tricky combination of taking half steps forward while resisting pressure from behind. There was no overt violence in the crowd, only an unpredictable swell of forces. I have said that the throws are athletic, that people feel relief at the end of the hadj. There was another cause of the turmoil in our procession. In the popular mind the *jamarat* pillars are associated with Satan.

In Morocco I had heard this rite called *rajm as-Shaytan*, "stoning the devils." During the hadj men referred to the pillars as Shaytan. Although assigning a name to a stone is traditionally frowned on in Islam, and while the Saudis, very correct in all these matters, had placed signs near the columns, calling them pillars, the pilgrims performing the rite showed fewer scruples. They expressed themselves very clearly. They were stoning the devil.

A dense ring of pilgrims surrounded the third and largest pillar. As I worked my way forward, I loosened seven stones tied into my scarf. The bodies were packed here, and I had to dig for room to raise one arm. Naturally left-handed, my right-hand throws were not as strong as some. To compensate, I edged nearer the column. Aiming on tiptoe, I somehow hit the pillar seven times.

Mardini and John remained a few rows back, lofting the last of their pebbles at the column. As I moved toward them, a hand shot up behind John and knocked off his glasses. As Mardini stooped to pick them up, John took a second blow around the temple. While I struggled to reach them, Mardini pointed away from the pillars, hauling on John's arm. He had the glasses.

*   *   *

Away from all that now, back up on the high road, we continued away from Mina and the crowds. The streetlights faded quickly at this end of town, and there were no buildings. The hills butted sheer against the mountain. Black boulders loomed above the road.

We moved unsteadily, it seemed to me, like staggering sailors washed up on a beach. John's eyes had the same glazed look I'd seen in Fazeel's at Arafat. One never knew when the hadj high might come on. In John's case, the timing seemed perfect. Just when things were at their roughest, it enclosed him in bubble wrap. The blows to his head and neck rolled off, absorbed.

I felt exhausted. Lack of sleep, the crowds, the miles to go joined themselves into a single question. If that was the jamarat rite *before* the crowds, I kept thinking. I couldn't finish the sentence. We stopped at a fountain to wash John's glasses.

The road widened, then dead-ended into a car park near the tunnel. A second, pedestrian tunnel branched off to the right. Mardini led the way to a line of cabs.

We followed the standard protocol for renting Middle Eastern taxis: you never stepped into a cab without settling the fare. The first driver quoted a price nobody liked. Mardini cut it by half, and the man began shouting. Mardini ignored him, walked away, and began to price the second cab in line. The line, of course, existed to prevent this. The first man rushed up to interfere. I closed my eyes and leaned back on the taxi. When I looked again, Mardini had left the parking lot and was walking into the foot tunnel leading to Makkah. John went after him. I went after John.

"What happened?"

"They wanted fifty dollars."

"We'll walk," Mardini called. "It's safer."

His words were beginning to echo; he was twenty yards ahead of us, entering the dark mouth of the tunnel.

It was cool in the tunnel, but dusky. The ceiling fans whipped up scraps of paper on the road. There were also occasional acrid whiffs of chlorine.

Maintenance crews spread a white powdered disinfectant on any road spill, and the tunnel concentrated the smell. I watched my step here. Fluorescents hung from the ceiling in some sections; other stretches of the road were dark. We clung to the side of the right-hand wall and walked quickly.

The road debouched under a hill on the other side. Another taxi rank was set up here, but we kept walking. Apartment buildings rose around us. Where a roof line slipped, I saw a minaret lit up like a rocket. The familiar bowl of Makkah glowed below us. I tried not to look at it or think of the *tawaf* and *sa'y* ahead. I had been through these rites and knew what they exacted. I could not imagine John performing them. By now we'd been going nonstop for twenty hours. Mardini seemed unaffected, but that was normal. Mardini lived on another plane. My own legs were aching. In the small of my back I felt a familiar throb.

Fortunately the way was all downhill. When we stopped for a traffic light on Second Street, I asked Mardini the direction of our hotel.

He pointed. "And there's the *haram.*"

Mardini wanted to finish the hadj tonight, to pay our required visit to the mosque, while John was able.

"Then we'll be hadjis."

I nodded, waiting for John to throw in the towel.

Whenever headlights passed us by, I scanned the road for taxis. Coming into town, we met a crowd of local Makkans in scarves and *thobe*s. Some were leading goats on lengths of clothesline. Others carried trays of un-baked bread. We passed a café set up in the ancient style. Backless chaises longues lined a front veranda, where men reclined and puffed on water pipes. It looked like a slice of paradise to me. I suggested going in, but the place was a rough house.

The road descended, then leveled out again. We passed a telephone-company building on a mall. The office windows throbbed with fluorescent lighting. Inside a night clerk stood behind a desk.

For several days Mardini had been trying to telephone his sister in Sidon, but Lebanon was deep in civil war. It was hard to imagine the phone lines withstanding all those rocket launchers. The waits were interminable and every call had failed.

Tonight the clerk was optimistic. He jotted down the number and fiddled his switchboard. Mardini went into a booth and shut the door. I sat down next to John. The room was tiled in white, and the lights were painful. I closed my eyes. I heard more doors close. Muffled voices bounced around the walls.

When Mardini woke me, I was lying on the bench, toppled over sideways.

"Hotel?" he said.

I squinted.

The pilgrimage went on and on and on. It was not a place at all. It was a hemstitch in a landscape, a thread on a human needle, plunging and rising. It had stages and points of emergence. It did not stop. Only hadjis, who made up the march, fell by the wayside. You woke where you stumbled. You picked up the trail. I did not want to be the one to break our progress. On the other hand, with the hadj there was always more. What did it matter? I argued the two points back and forth in my head while Mardini waited. Finally, I nodded.

He didn't even blink. "Easy. No problem. We will visit the mosque tomorrow."

Now that I had seen the hadj firsthand, I began to think there was nothing familiar about it. My studies and meetings in Marrakesh had led me to view Islam as a Western cousin. Events in Makkah changed my mind. The nature and shape of the pilgrimage made plain the Arabian root of Muhammad's teaching. Like the isolated chain of the Hejaz, it drew a line between Jerusalem's urban vision and the more nomadic outlook of Arabia. The Qur'an linked Islam to Jewish and Christian sources, but the hadj bound it firmly to Makkah.

The hadj is unique among Islam's five pillars. Declaration, prayer, fasting, and alms share an ethical basis. The hadj went beyond them, past society. Its significance is as a turning point, a rite of passage accomplished on two feet. I especially admired the way the sweat and the symbols flowed together. By an act of imagination and exertion, a spiritual rite of some duration fulfilled a private quest. For all its public aspects the experience was intensely personal. By giving the pilgrim a chance to choose his moment, it provided a service missing in the West since the days of the medieval palmers: it offered a climax to religious life.

I woke about one the next day with stiff joints and a backache. Dressed already, Mardini sat by the window, slicing cucumbers. Instead of the *ihram,* he wore slacks, brown shoes, and a sport shirt open at the collar. I showered and dressed casually. Wearing loafers especially pleased me. I'd had it with rubber sandals for a while.

Down in the lobby John sat stiffly on a couch, greeting a couple of delegation members. These men had just returned from the stoning grounds, and they looked bedraggled. Most of the others were still in Mina. John seemed pleased to be ahead of the crowds. The men went to shower, and he stood up. I noticed, going out, that he wore a back brace.

During the night the hadj had shifted keys. Truck horns blew as we left the building. The jammed streets pumped like a passage from Stravinsky: tumult and digression, passionate yearning, obstructed quests. Strident blows. Abruptness. Reconciliation. The hadj was now symphonic. The hollow, when we reached it, overflowed.

There was no point in trying to round the mosque or reach my favorite gate at the back of the building. We were here to perform the *tawaf,* and we went right in. We waded the aisles, reaching the key in twenty minutes, and gazed across the floor at the Ka'ba. After our days in the desert the authority of this simple structure astonished me. The angular lines created a towering effect. It sprang up through the pillars like a freight train in a forest.

Inside the horseshoe wall on its southern side lines of hadjis stood at Hagar's grave. The worshipers at this popular spot were always changing. Right now they were mostly Africans. I thought how at ease I had come to feel in this temple without pews, where the races mixed freely. Malcolm X had found relief here, too.

We stepped into the crowd and began our circuits. In the time it took us to go around six times, the numbers of pilgrims seemed to triple. Our elbow room compressed with each turn, driving us closer and closer to the Ka'ba. Robert Frost's couplet ran through my mind:

> *We dance round in a ring and suppose,*
> *But the secret sits in the middle and knows.*

Then I went back to shouting *"Allahu akbar."*

By the end of our third circuit, we were close enough to the velvety black *kiswa* to reach out and touch it. I had never been so near the shrine before. I was fascinated by everything—the pores in the rock, the texture of the embroidery. I was frightened for John, too. In our final lap the roar of the crowd became so confused that I had to shout for Mardini to hear me. I pointed to John, then to the rim of the circle.

Mardini nodded. Shielding John, we worked our way out of the center. At the edge of the ring lay a final barrier—a solid wheel of elderly hadjis on litters, bobbing around the rim, fencing us in. A person who stumbled here was sure to be trampled. We pumped in place like limbo dancers, ducking under the boards to the other side.

Leaving the crowd behind, we went up a rise, turned to face the Ka'ba, and performed two bows. The order of these events was familiar now. We stopped for a drink at the well, then proceeded across the mosque to the *mas'a*.

The racecourse was constructed on two levels. Today the lower course was packed. We went upstairs to the second floor and strolled between the hills seven more times. When the *sa'y* was complete, Mardini produced a tiny pair of scissors. We clipped a few hairs from the backs of our heads, then slipped through the Prophet's gate into the street. The formal duties of the hadj were over.

The old market quarter lay nearer the mosque than I had imagined. At the entrance stood a row of barber shops. Pilgrims sat inside, having their heads shaved. We stopped to watch, then passed under an arch into the souk. What remained of this quarter was very, very old. The alleys were cobbled, the bazaars mostly small and specialized. We passed a spot between two carpet shops where Abu Bakr, Muhammad's first male convert, once kept a store. We window-shopped. We were hadjis.

At an ice-cream shop we toasted our status with three vanilla cones. In a jewelery store, while Mardini bought a wristwatch, I admired a display of gold pendants, hanging in a glass case, pinned on felt. These were perfectly cast in the shape of the Ka'ba. I asked the clerk to weigh a small one, about the size of an airmail stamp, and finally purchased it for fifty dollars.

We emerged from the souk on the east side of town and caught a cab to Mina. By now John's back brace had begun to give him trouble. The exhilaration of the hadj was wearing off.

At the guesthouse, I expected a celebration. The hadj had formally ended, today would be a feast, but by now all the other delegates were in Makkah. I saw no familiar faces in the hall. Down in the lobby a handful of pilgrims sat whispering on couches. The room's abnormal quietness confused me. At the reception desk I found a message from Saleem. He wanted us to dine with him that evening.

We settled John, then showered, and left the guesthouse without speaking to anyone. Main Street was completely devoid of traffic. On King Khalid Road we waited without success for a passing cab. In the end we walked.

The pedestrian tunnels were not like those for cars. They had fewer lights and were not split into lanes. Being about a mile long, fresh air was still a problem. The same huge fans were mounted in the ceiling.

Going in, we clung to the right side of the tunnel. The sun, now low in the sky, backlit the road. We were almost the only pedestrians that evening. For some reason the fans had been switched off, and the scrape of our steps ran in front of us. Otherwise the place was very quiet. The absence of people puzzled me again. The farther we walked, the more withdrawn I felt. Midway down the tunnel the air grew tomblike, and my head began to ache. The road lay littered with refuse. Depressed, I found myself thinking, Why don't they clean this up? Mardini glanced at the fans. We walked faster.

The tunnel fed into Aziziyah Road. This was the busiest street in

Saleem's district. During the hadj of 1853, Sir Richard Burton had found rooms here. Today steel traffic galloped up and down, and the walks were filled with university students. I was glad to see them. My throat was burning. We caught a cab and hurried to Saleem's.

❖   ❖   ❖   ❖

*O*ur early departure from Muzdalifah had put us out of sync with the *'id*. The focal point of the three-day feast was Mina. In Makkah we missed its early phases.

No religious blame attached to this. Only the actual sacrifice was required. I had arranged for that some days before, buying a ticket for thirty-eight dollars from a street vendor. The stub (I was told to guard it) ensured that a sheep would be offered in my name. The rest of the ticket and half a million like it were sent off to the Mina slaughterhouse.

The slaughterhouse had been mechanized for two decades. Whereas carcasses used to be buried in common graves, currently even hides are put to use. Today's *'id* looks surprisingly efficient. A family receives enough meat for the three-day feast. Acres of packers and freezers take care of the rest of it. Even in scorching summer weather the resulting unused tons of meat are boxed and shipped as gifts to poorer African and Middle Eastern countries. I had seen the freezer trucks on the Jidda road.

In the 1920s, when Rutter was here, no separate facility existed to handle the sacrifice. The narrowest Mina side road ended in sacrificial fields, and the sand about the tents was littered with corpses. By 1970, the increase of pilgrims made clean-up measures mandatory. Not only the stench but the threat of insect- and buzzard-borne diseases became overwhelming. Today the sacrifice is sanitary.

In the 1960s these matters were not always so well arranged. Jalal al-e Ahmad, an Iranian author who made the hadj in 1964, described the slaughtering grounds as a devil's punch bowl. With the exception of red bulldozers, he saw things as Ibn Batuttah must have seen them, a few years before the scene was swept away. The killing fields on the far side of the valley lay covered with fresh carcasses of sheep and goats. The killing was done by hand, often with dull knives. Muscles quivered. The earth ran red and frothy. Ahmad raised the hem of his garments as he walked, like a man trudging through a painting of purgatory. Every step bred fresh hallucinations. At one point a young man brandishing a knife stood up abruptly from inside the ribs of a fallen camel, stopping Ahmad in his tracks. As for the carcasses, small servings of cookable meat were stripped away by professional butchers and carried back to the pilgrim camps on foot. The rest was laid out to dry in the sun or sprinkled with lye and bulldozed. For the urban intellectual Ahmad, this visit to the abattoir was the worst part of the hadj. He nearly passed out on two or three occasions, and his journal is full of frantic recommendations against waste and carnage. He berates the Saudi government—a favorite game in Iranian writing—and he considers vegetarianism. He remarks that had the directors of *Mondo Cane* included a scene from Mina in their movie, the film would have made a fortune.

✧   ✧   ✧   ✧

*A*t Saleem's we sat down to a table decked with mutton—barbecued joints on platters and succulent organs floating in fine broth. There were salads and rice and vegetables and baskets of warm bread. We were eight this evening, including Saleem's wife, Sari, and two children. Samir took the head of the table. As we were sitting, Shafeeq came through the door in a new white *thobe*.

As we ate, Saleem recounted their day at Arafat. His routine tone surprised me. Whereas I had traveled around the globe for this, Saleem had left his home on Sunday morning, taking his family and a house guest with him, like an Englishman picnicking on the moors. They had reached the cliffs above the plain at sunrise and pitched camp. It had been the best weather for the hadj in eleven years, with a touch of cloud cover and a breeze. Later on in the morning he and Shafeeq had propped drop cloths off the Cadillac Brougham. By then the ground lay thick with acres of cars.

Saleem's one regret was drinking too much water. As time went on and the sun climbed, he drank more. After lunch he set out for a bathroom. He waded through rows of bumpers, arrived at the edge of the cliff, then doubled back and finally came to a line of portable toilets. The queues were long. He waited, inching forward, bladder bursting. When his turn came, he threw open the door and clambered in, but the outhouse had not been designed for his bearish figure. He cracked his forehead on a crossbeam. Tonight his brow was gashed and his guts were aching. He sat on two pillows as we talked.

Shafeeq was pink from the sun, and his wet hair gleamed. He looked somehow beside himself, steeped in the afterglow of hadj. I felt fortunate to be here, but Shafeeq! He had ridden his horse into Biscayne Bay and come up in Makkah.

We talked and ate and, when the meal was done, adjourned to the *majlis.* Coffee arrived and Saleem lighted his pipe. Soon the room was wreathed in fruity smoke. Sari complained of the smell and lit a Marlboro. Samir turned on the TV, very low.

It appeared we were going to chat about cars over coffee. Samir had done some research on my price list. Knowing how commerce blended with the hadj, it did not seem irreverent to get down to business. But before we could start, Saleem glanced at the TV and turned up the volume. On the screen, through layers of smoke, I began to make out twisted steel beams and shrouded bodies. The camera jerked unsteadily, then fixed on an announcer in a *thobe.*

There had been a stampede in one of the Mina tunnels, at a place called al-Moaisim. No one knew yet what had caused it, but the passage was clogged at both ends, and some pilgrims were trapped there. Their number and condition were unknown, because no one could get to them. Meanwhile a localized power failure had somehow cut the current to the fans. People were rumored to be choking.

Every few minutes we learned a little more. Gradually a theory began emerging: that car traffic had started the stampede, that a handful of hadjis had fallen from a bridge at the mouth of the tunnel, that people had panicked, blocking the entries. A large crowd had been camped inside, it was said. *Asphyxiation* crept into the broadcast. After several minutes a wave of stretcher bearers started in.

I had never been anywhere near the Moaisim tunnel and couldn't visualize its situation. The television pictures, limited to a single hand-held close-up of the announcer, did not help. The fuzzy arch in the background resembled the tunnel we had walked through, but of course, it wasn't. Moaisim lay on the other side of the valley, near the slaughterhouse.

The faces around me were turned to the screen at very different angles. Shafeeq's looked concentrated, overtaken; Saleem's, suspicious of the official story. Samir muttered apologies, pained as a Makkan that such things could happen in his city. On the screen a doctor was giving a speech on asphyxiation. Saleem erupted. Where had this talk about car traffic come from? The facts were not in; already we had explanations. And what about the fans? These tunnels, he said, had back-up systems in case the power failed; he knew the engineer who had designed them. Mardini put in that the fans had been off in the King Khalid tunnel, too. At that Samir stood and left the *majlis*. He was going to telephone friends, to see what had happened.

I kept hoping the cameraman would move around more. Without a view I felt disoriented. Like Shafeeq, I found it hard to absorb this finish to our week. The hadj had started out with the Zanjan earthquake. It had continued with prayers for the dead five times a day. It was peopled by pilgrims in cotton shrouds rehearsing scenes for the afterlife. Now it had ended with a real-life demonstration, close up, impersonal. "Sufficient unto the day is the evil thereof." But it was night now. I could have done without it.

These were my first reactions to the tunnel. For the most part I sat numbly with the others, eyeing the television. Eventually Saleem switched off the set. The children were roughhousing in another room, and Sari went in to calm them. We did not talk business. It was time to leave.

CHAPTER TWENTY

Independence Day

*T*he mood at the guesthouse over the next two days depended on the subject under discussion.

I heard wide dissatisfaction with the crowds. Mina was normally a one-horse town—a few thousand people lived here out of season. Now several million bodies were plunging through its canyons, and the risks were great, especially for old people. Arafat had raised our spirits to a high point. The jam at Mina threatened to bring them low. The gap between a pilgrim's inner condition and the crush he faced every time he stepped outdoors was a real challenge, emotional as well as physical.

The *jamarat* area had been in full swing when Fayez arrived with his grandmother. The melee he described sounded familiar, but the throngs were twice as dense as those I'd seen. The worst offenders, in Fayez's view, were droves of rough-and-tumble Pakistani farmhands. Pathans and Indian shopkeepers ran a close second. Fayez grew livid on the subject. "Completely uncivilized," he sighed. "They need an education."

"Education?"

"A training course," he said, "before they get here. In Malaysia they have a scaled-down *haram*, with an entire pilgrim route laid out around it. You know: 'Here is Mina. Here is Muzdalifah.' You walk around it, in miniature. You get your bearings." The Malay hadjis were wonderful, he said. Yemenis, however, ran every which way. He had seen two old men trampled.

We traded stories about the *jamarat*—I behind John, he with his grandmother. The woman was not so frail as he'd feared. She had refused to go ahead of the daylight crowds. She had made it across the stoning ground unharmed.

If Fayez was angry, Rafeeq, the Libyan delegate, looked depressed. I found him withdrawn in a corner of the lobby, eyes cast down, avoiding human contact.

Rafeeq was a barrel-chested man with a keen intelligence. His father, a legend in Libya, had led a revolt against Italian occupation. Rafeeq had come to New York at age eighteen and put himself through school by driving taxis and sweeping out bus stations. He had studied economics, then gone on to teach at Tulane, Duke, and Georgetown. In the service of his country he had also become an adviser to the International Monetary Fund. Perhaps this post had cost Rafeeq his Libyan citizenship. I could only guess at the twisting road that had carried him from his shepherd's youth in Cyrenaica to a scholarly, early retirement on the Potomac. His feet were badly blistered now, and he had the raspy cough everyone caught here. Usually we got on well. This morning Rafeeq did not want to see me.

Information concerning the tunnel continued to trickle in, via two TVs in the guesthouse lobby. The quantities of dead had increased overnight, from a vague few hundred to 1,473, mostly elderly Asians. In my experience this was a lot of people—about the same number as in the village where I lived. On the other hand, the body count amounted to less than .0005 percent of the hadj. I could not make sense of the matter from either perspective. Philosophical and horrified by turns, my mood swung about like a compass needle. Luckily there were Muslims around me. Raised on Islam's unitarian views, they had a knack for facing facts without jumping to conclusions. Their naturalness at this made the trait seem genetic.

"It's in Allah's hands."

"What is finished is over."

Dr. 'Ali raised his eyes in silence.

Equanimity tempered our talk about the tunnel. At first I mistook this for coolness. It was poise.

The ending of the hadj was a different subject entirely. When that came up, the corners of men's mouths rose and they smiled. Especially for first timers the hadj was the crowning moment of a lifetime. To have got through it required celebration. Muslims, who drink no alcohol, tend to celebrate by meeting, chatting, embracing, and strolling arm in arm. An amount of all this was going on in the lobby, fueled by trays of coffee at each couch. No one spoke now of how hard it had been to get here or of what the trip had cost in health or money. The most common emotion was gratitude, a genuine gladness to be here. I heard pat phrases designed to calm complainers. One man in the elevator touched a downcast pilgrim on the shoulder. "If it was not hard," he said, "it would not be the hadj."

A few sections of the guesthouse were set aside for foreign dignitaries. As the building had only one lobby, I saw these people often. They swept in through the big glass doors, accompanied by guards. In an entourage they appeared serenely distant, but one to one they were forwardly warm, even starved for talk. You saw the relief in their eyes when they addressed you. The trappings of power cut men off, I thought, and the hadj was a chance to dispense with class divisions. Most of these men and women were multilingual, at ease in their roles, and informal. In short, they deserved the title royal guest.

I came downstairs before the *zuhr* prayer and found Mardini chatting on a couch with an assistant to the Lebanese prime minister. I decided not to interrupt their meeting. A long, near-vacant couch stood across the room. I sat down and opened a small diary.

The guesthouse had been a palace years before. Its upstairs rooms looked spartan, but the lobby was spacious, ornate as a UN lounge. An acre of handloomed carpets dampened the sounds of socializing. The marble walls resembled thunderclouds.

I was writing up last night's walk through the King Khalid tunnel when I noticed a woman seated on my right, watching me intently. She wore a cream-white robe and a gray silk shawl. Perhaps she had been there all along.

She introduced herself as Mrs. Mojadidi. She and her husband resided in Jidda, she said, but they were Afghans. They had lived abroad for twenty years, in Tripoli to begin with, until Qaddafi became impossible, after which the Saudis brought them here. Quite a few of her people lived in Jidda. I longed to hear more about Libya. The Western press had virtually written off the country, and I knew nothing of the way Libyans lived. Mrs. Mojadidi did not oblige me. She shook her head and changed the subject. She asked whether my hadj had been *mubarak*. I said that it had been and repeated the politeness. We sat smiling matching smiles on the sofa. Mrs. Mojadidi's English was dissolving.

Before very long her eyes began to dart. "We must find the princess," she whispered. "Please, wait here."

A minute later she returned, leading a younger woman by the hand.

"This is Princess Na'im," she said. "Her husband and his family served our country."

The good humor of these women was contagious. The princess carried the conversation. Soon I was being invited to London for Ramadan, to attend the retreat of her teacher, Sheikh Nazim. Nazim was a Sufi in the Naghsbandi lineage, a Turkish *pir*, or guru, based in Cyprus. I had met a few of his students in California. They were gentle, purposeful people.

"Unlike you, I was born to Islam," she said. "But only lately have I *got* it. Peace of mind is so difficult to locate! Being around Nazim has shown me something."

I told them about myself. I said I was married.

"You must bring your wife to London," the princess said. "I'll take her shopping." And she held up a gold and lapis ring on her right fourth finger. It was twelfth-century Persian. "I found it in Bond Street," she said, "for next to nothing. Tell your wife!"

I remarked on her fluent English.

"Of course! We have lived in London since the coup." She looked thoughtful. "You really must meet my husband. He's so bored here."

Aziz Na'im was a tall, slender man with silvering hair. He had a beardless face and unlined skin and spoke above a whisper, in ruminating sentences that purled toward their goal, like Edward Gibbon's. Even his posture was patrician—he seemed to curve slightly backward, like a reed.

We spoke about food and the weather. After the women had slipped away, Na'im took me into his confidence. The hadj had been wonderful, he said, but he was bored now and beginning to feel cornered. The Saudis felt such concern about the safety of their guests that he and his wife could not set foot outside without a guard. The *jamarat* rite had been judged too chaotic for them. Their outings had been limited to shopping. He did not like shopping, especially when the women overbargained. I suggested things might be changed, but he shook his head. He had been here last year; he knew how it went. After the hadj you were more or less trapped in the lobby.

Aziz had been stationed in London for many years, working with the Afghan foreign service. He had stayed on in England after the 1978 Saur revolution.

This was the palace coup his wife had mentioned. It had ended the royal republic of Prince Daoud and led to a decade of Soviet occupation. I knew from my reading that Daoud, his brothers and cousins had been controversial figures in their country. As its first Western-educated rulers, they had forced the king to step aside, installed a constitution, banned the veil. Near the end Daoud was harshly criticized for relying too much on secret police and succumbing to sycophancy. His death brought about the end of the Naderi dynasty.

Daoud and most of his family had been murdered in the coup. There was no tactful way to ask Na'im what had happened. Instead, we spoke abstractly about change. In Aziz's view the only real Islamic revolution had taken place nearly fourteen hundred years ago. Its basis, he said, was in Muhammad's emphasis on equity and the pursuit of truth. Its source was Qur'anic. Muhammad's first revelation had been a command to read, to seek to know. After his death subsequent caliphs had followed this commandment, constructing a loose-knit confederation founded upon universal law. For a period of six centuries the Qur'an and the constitution were synonymous. The Mongol invasions destroyed that unity in the 1200s. Decadent Mamluk and Turkic rulers fractured it further. Later, Western domination had stunted the very ability to govern. This long Islamic dark age was ending now.

Rebirth, Aziz observed, is always messy. In his own country's case, decades of colonial influence had so deranged the process that even populist candidates were "mostly reactionary—not revolutionary at all." They knew best what they did not want; they had forgotten what they wanted. They argued over which movement was more Islamic. But a movement could not be more or less Islamic! A movement was either Islamic, or it was not. Despite the confusion, Aziz was hopeful of a renaissance. Because Islam was not at heart regressive, matters, he felt sure, would be worked out. He confessed he had no idea how this would happen.

✧   ✧   ✧   ✧

I met Fayez at the elevators after lunch. He suggested we go to the *jamarat* together, for the second of our three required throws. The afternoon heat, he believed, would limit the size of the crowds there. I had planned to go later, alone. Fayez objected. "Safety in numbers," he told me. He referred to the *jamarat* area as "the jam."

I wanted a shower first. Fayez rode along in the crowded elevator. Upstairs we met Rafeeq limping down the hallway. He did not seem to know us when I stopped him. His bare left foot was swollen, red and yellow, and his head drooped. I gave him a tube of Neosporin from my bag. While he rubbed on the ointment, he launched into a speech against the crowds, but Fayez interrupted. "I saw you at Muzdalifah!" he chided. "You were smiling!" Rafeeq released a grin and hobbled off.

We visited John Muhammad, too. The long hike back to Makkah had landed him in bed on a field of pillows. A doctor had already come to chastise him. There was no question of his throwing stones today. He had appointed Abd al-Qadir to do it for him. Abd al-Qadir, who had missed his chance with the murderer, seemed destined to be a proxy in some way.

Before we left, I gave John two Halcion tablets.

"You're a regular walking pharmacy," Fayez said.

Fayez looked edgier than yesterday. His left eye blinked more than the right. His jaw was rigid.

"Do you know why the hadj is so hard?" he asked. "Because you're working off your sins. At the end of it, if you've done things right, you should come out as clean as a baby."

I said did he mean that innocence was gained?

He nodded. "And it makes me nervous. Because everything I do from here on really matters. It's a dangerous position."

Main Street was a cataract of shoulders and umbrellas bobbing toward the bridge in drenching sun. The high noon heat had not put off the pilgrims. I lost track of Fayez by quick degrees. The crowd had a trick of opening, then closing down around us. His arms disappeared in stages as he slipped ahead. Next his shoulders went, and then his neck. Soon all that remained was a pistoning pink umbrella, shrinking as we were swept along.

The pebbles tied into the tip of my scarf swayed with every step like a bandolier. The stones, people said, were little bits of *bismillah*. They protected you from the evils of Shaytan. Others compared them to bullets. With every throw, one shouted "God is great!" like a *mujahid* freedom fighter firing a rifle. The pace was athletic. We did not skip a beat. When a man to my right lost a sandal, he kept going. The thrust from behind made stopping dangerous.

The *jamarat* bridge had a high road and a low road. Being alone made me cautious. I chose the subway level, which I knew. Where the bridge cut off the sun, the heat grew thicker. It welled out of the ramp way. Going down, the raw look of the *jamarat* area impressed me. A lot of cement had been poured to widen these walkways, yet it was a cut-rate undertaking, befitting Satan. Safety and convenience mattered, not much else.

Yesterday we had thrown at just one pillar. Seven little pebbles and we were gone. Today and tomorrow all three columns would be pelted— twenty-one pebbles per session, forty-nine in all. This kind of symbolic precision seemed to me part of the genius of the hadj. It provided a focus in a crowd inclined to frenzy. The right-size pebbles had to be cast a specified number of times in the proper direction, or the act was void. Intention still counted, but so did magical exactness, an unerring adherence to getting it right, as others had done before you. It was a perfect piece of religious psychology. Hitting the mark with a pea-size stone was just enough of a task to keep tempers from flaring. The press of the crowds, the nagging heat became unimportant. We had our pebbles to consider.

I had counted out my day's ration at the guesthouse, including an extra seven in case some missed. I loosened the stones as we marched and shifted them into my right hand. The pilgrims stood twenty deep around the column, like contestants in a massive penny toss. I worked my way into the circle. Ten feet from the pillar I came up short in a clog of elbows. The press was too great to move nearer. I had to wriggle for room to raise my arm.

I started throwing, giving a lot of loft to every stone. The pebbles were very light and hard to follow. There were shouts of *"Allahu akbar!"* yet the air inside the circle was strangely still. I could hear the plink of arcing gravel raining on the pillar. Now and then a stone from behind fell short, striking my neck like grapeshot. Pilgrims were missing! I closed one eye. I aimed and hurled. People around me whooped as their throws connected. Faces cracked into smiles. I heard laughter. For a moment the scene resembled a booth at a county fair. Then it was over, and we flowed forward.

Lapidation is the most arcane of the old religious rites. Its roots are said to reach back to the Mesolithic period, to a people who fashioned the bow and tamed the dog. Whatever age had brought it in, the version we performed today expressed itself as an act of restraint and protection. It was less a matter of casting *at* than of casting out. We were not warding Satan off but compelling him to knuckle under. I had liked picking up the pebbles in the moonlight. I enjoyed aiming at targets with them, too. We were taking part in an exercise that for Westerners had vanished with the Druids. It was as sociable and precise as a good athletic event.

Ahead I saw no end to the pilgrim river. It slowed like protoplasm at the spires. It thickened and streamed around them, moving on. When my pebbles had all been thrown, I continued walking, letting myself be washed along, sticking to the center of the current. The ragged edge of the *jamarat* crowd was its least agreeable section. Most accidental tramplings occurred in these eddies, and I learned to avoid them. The safest place lay deep inside the throng.

The crowd broke down and spilled me out near the tunnels. Doubling back by a row of wooden shacks, I stopped to snack on kabobs near the Bayah mosque.

✧   ✧   ✧   ✧

*T*he clouds and breeze of Arafat were gone now. The canvas city sagged into relapse, and leaden heat pinned down the valley. Through the afternoon hours nothing rose much higher off the ground than lamb fat curling up from campfires. At the guesthouse a steady trio of elevators ferried weary pilgrims to their rooms. I lay on a cot until sunset, dozing and listening to the BBC.

Word of the tunnel disaster had reached the outside world. At the top of each broadcast the same gruesome story led the news. It shocked me to hear about Makkah on the British air waves. Our Hejazi isolation was not so complete as I'd believed. The report conveyed new details. Eighty percent of the victims had been elderly. Most of the dead were Turks and Indonesians. The word *stampede* cropped up. Fifty thousand pilgrims had been trapped inside a tunnel made for a thousand. These were new, disturbing wrinkles. I tossed on the mattress and did not sleep much.

Mardini and I returned to Saleem's that evening.

We went by taxi. Knowing what I knew now about Moaisim, I did not want to trudge through another tunnel. The cab ride proved unsettling enough. Our driver was an especially high-speed version of his type, and the hadjis who slept in the tunnels had learned nothing. They reclined too near the pavement, as before, legs extended inches from the traffic. As we emerged into the twilight, Mardini began to discuss the price of cars.

When prior to the hadj, Samir had revised my first quotation downward, I had sent a second wire to my California buyer, requesting a lower price on half the cars. Now he had sent back a compromise. He was also looking into cheaper shipping. To my surprise, the deal was going forward. We were dickering amiably for middle ground. I felt delighted and remotely optimistic. Any arrangement by which I might profit through selling cars in

Makkah seemed too good to dwell on. I did not want to think of it too much.

We found Saleem in the *majlis,* puffing a hookah in front of the TV. He looked unhappy with the local coverage. "We stare at the screen and we stare at the screen," he said. "They tell us the same story every hour. It adds up to nothing." This reminded me of some lines by Robert Frost:

> *The people along the land*
> *All turn and look one way.*
> *They turn their back on the land.*
> *They look at the sea all day.*
>
> . . . .
>
> *They cannot look out far,*
> *They cannot look in deep.*
> *But when was that ever a bar*
> *To any watch they keep?*

Saleem loved poetry in any language. Politically he was a skeptic, full of doubts. In this case, he thought it peculiar that the broadcasts said so little. Yes, there had been a stampede; but what had caused it? The official word, a traffic jam outside, seemed suspect. Samir had telephoned around the town. There was talk of a bombing.

I was shocked. "Who would do that?"

"Any group wanting to make the king look weak. It wouldn't be the first time," Saleem said.

This was true. A few years before three hundred Iranians had died in a street demonstration near the mosque. Their protest had been viewed as a provocation. There were other examples, too, including attempts to embarrass the Saudis by violence. The point of a bomb scare in Makkah would be to prove them incompetent to run the hadj.

Mardini scoffed at this theory. "Was anyone arrested near the tunnel?"

"Not yet."

"Were there traces of explosives? Did the roof cave in?"

"No."

Mardini sat back. "You see? Saleem has a big imagination."

All this served to remind me that we were in the Middle East. Remote, heady Makkah tucked into a bowl among treeless peaks could make you forget how near you were to trouble: to Beirut, with its wildfire wars; to Israel's barbed wire camps; to an Iraqi supercannon. Makkah drew devotees from all these hot spots. None was more than a few hundred miles away. On a map the connecting roads resembled fuses.

Saleem switched off the set after the news. In place of the bandage on his head he now wore a Band-Aid. We began to talk business. I had questions concerning import taxes, shipping costs, insurance on the cars. Saleem produced a binder with his figures.

At 11:00 P.M. he drove us back to Mina. Even under way the big car's doors retained the heat, scorching my arm when I draped it out the window. The hadj had not returned to its nighttime schedule. The tunnel lay empty of traffic going in, and the sleeping hadjis beside the road looked eerie. Then the tunnel curved, a rush of hot wind from nowhere rocked the car, and an entourage of six Mercedes 560 SEL sedans blew past, moving at a hundred miles per hour. Saleem swerved as they shot ahead of us. The cars remained in view for a few more seconds, then vanished down the gullet of the tunnel.

"A million dollars worth of steel," I said.

"Perhaps. But it's nothing to them."

Mardini had seen the same sedans that morning, parked outside the guesthouse. The cars belonged to a group of Kuwaiti princes. They were here for the hadj, and for the oil talks next week. I repeated what I had heard on the BBC: that Iraq had accused Kuwait for the seventh time of pumping oil from fields inside its border. The emir was looking forward to "constructive talks" at Jidda.

"Their meetings will get them nowhere," Saleem said.

Talks seemed only to lead to more talks. The differences were mainly economic. Since December, Kuwait, through overpumping, had helped drive down the barrel price of oil by seven dollars. So far, each of these drops had cost Iraq about a billion dollars, devaluing the dinar to one twelfth its former worth. The principal parties were now engaged in diplomatic chess. In a late defense Kuwait had raised the matter of a war debt, amounting to about ten billion dollars. A few weeks after, matters worsened. I was on my way back to the States when I heard the announcement. To strengthen his hand at the bargaining table, Saddam had ordered thirty thousand troops into the desert south of Basra. U.S. satellite cameras had picked them up, forty miles from the Kuwaiti border. The emir of Kuwait dismissed this as a bluff, and perhaps it was. On July 31, however, discussions broke down for good. Baghdad denounced the emir's "fiscal arrogance," and two days later Iraqi troops crossed the border. Kuwait was invaded. The stage was being set for a Gulf war.

After the march from Arafat to Mina most Makkans returned home for the *'id*. The Makkans had cool houses to recline in. They did not bother signing up for tents. This was lucky. Had another five hundred thousand pilgrims jammed the valley, the tiny village would have split its seams. Once a day the *jamarat* rites brought the locals streaming back through the tunnels, but not to stay. They slipped into Mina long enough to throw their stones, then rushed away again to escape the melee.

I woke late on Wednesday morning and went up to the roof. From here I could overlook the long, sunlit defile of Mina Valley. Uniform acres of canvas still wavered in the heat. More camps overflowed the valley walls, spilling uphill toward Ta'if, where they melted like dots in a pointillist composition—about a half million flecks in all.

The tents were emblems of the hadj's shifting essence—the *insha' Allah* factor, I called it. In less than a week the whole set would be struck, packed into trucks, and carried off to storage. Viewed from the roof in a melting sun, the scene resembled an insubstantial pageant, ready to fade at a moment's notice, the fabric of a dream.

I breakfasted downstairs on tea and rolls and went into the lobby at eleven. Fayez passed by and sat down on my couch. He had just returned from the streets, his robe was smudged with dirt, and he trailed depression. He wore a streak of chlorine on his jaw. Had we been in tents, like millions of other hadjis, his mood swings might not have seemed pronounced. As it was, the relative comforts of the guesthouse emphasized them, in contrast to the chaos of the roads. Today he was in a rage over the traffic. The exchange of the car for the camel, he said, was going to bring the downfall of the hadj.

Conducting a spiritual quest in a state of gridlock vexed everyone I met. Day and night Main Street lay choked with buses. The four-mile ride to Muzdalifah took four hours. I understood Fayez's reaction. I shared it. Combining the hadj and the car in a Saudi desert had produced the biggest traffic jam on earth. The auto's main attribute, its speed, was completely subverted. The invention seemed useless. The hadj would have been easier on foot.

Fayez's wanted to replace the cars with trains. He suggested a circular subway system, linking Makkah to Arafat and Mina, permitting pilgrims to travel below ground. The passage would be more orderly. They would not be in the sun.

This was not a completely new idea. Trains had been under discussion for fifteen years.

"It's either that or the hadj will die out," he said.

A lot of people before Fayez had predicted the end of the hadj. Burckhardt and Burton, forty years apart, each had reasons to think it would die in their century. Burckhardt based his assessment on a growing indifference to religion and on the rising costs of travel. Burton, an imperialist by nature, foresaw a day when necessity "will compel us to occupy in force the fountainhead of al-Islam." In a more passive vein, General Lyautey, the brilliant French resident general of Morocco, had suggested in 1916 that the hadj "be permitted to fall into disuse," as a political expedient. In fact, all these men were gazing into a mirror. It was not the Muslim pilgrimage that would crumble, but the French and British empires. The hadj has prevailed into modern times, for reasons that are clear. Society continues to validate it. Modern transport encourages it. Modern economics, in the form of petrodollars, sustains it. It has not been reduced to a metaphor. It remains a public means to a personal quest, a practicable rite of brief duration that, by an act of intelligence or imagination, enters hearts. It would survive the gasoline engine, I supposed.

Prince Na'im stopped me in the lobby after lunch. I had my pebbles tied into my scarf and was heading outside again to stone the columns. The prince wore khaki slacks and a short-sleeved shirt. He looked dressed for a golf match. His eyes were furtive.

"Take me with you," he whispered.

"Sir?"

He scanned the room. "Kidnap me."

In his hand he held a plastic water bottle full of stones. He had been out in the parking lot collecting pebbles. He was ready to throw, but his hosts would not allow it, he explained. On their first day out the Na'ims had almost been trampled. As a result, the Saudis had assigned them a couple of soldiers to act as proxies and carry out their rites. This was permissible under pilgrim law, but Aziz thought the gesture ridiculous. He wanted to throw his own stones. He wanted to come and go and take part in the hadj. The night before, he said, they had waited for their driver for three hours, then coaxed a local Makkan to take them to dinner. This protocol breach had so upset the Saudis that now a driver trailed him everywhere, even in the guesthouse. Because of this, Na'im and I were strolling in wide arcs around the lobby, speaking in whispers.

I could sympathize with the prince's confinement. The hadj, which dissolved class barriers, had hemmed him in. Despite an unwanted affront to my Saudi hosts, some part of me longed to take him with me, to slip past his guards into the crowd.

"Do you know what day this is?" he asked.

"The third day of the *'id.*"

"In your country," he said, "it's July the Fourth."

As I took this in, his eyes seemed to beg me to free him. It was Independence Day.

The *jamarat* road ran thick with pilgrims out for their final throw. I left the prince behind and went alone. Across the road tents were already coming down in sections. Food stalls were closing, too. At one intersection two cooks dumped a pot of soup into a gutter, then scattered a patch of chlorine on the stones. Whiffs of disinfectant burned my nostrils. The pavement was hotter than a match head.

Where the route split into a subway and a bridge, I took the high road, coming up a ramp into the sun. Except for a view of the granite hills, this level was not much different from the other. Perhaps the crowds were packed more densely. The walls of the bridge were lower. Paper scraps lay piled by the road. As we reached the first pillar, a helicopter swooped over the hills, kicking up dust. The noise of churning rotors beat our eardrums, thunka-thunka-thunka, like machine guns. I mistook it for an army gunship. In fact, it was another flying hospital. Each of these monsters carried a medical team and a fully stocked clinic. They mainly served the weak, the prostrate. If someone were trampled, aerial surgery could be performed. They were a boon, but I never liked seeing them. They boded ill and caused confusion. This one appeared to be out on a false alarm. After a minute's hesitation, it swung away abruptly, vanishing as quickly as it came.

I allowed myself to be carried to the first column. I threw my stones and rode the crowd again. I was no longer walking. Rather, I was being swept forward, using my feet as rudders. The *jamarat* rite was nothing if not energetic. There was a certain humor in it, too—once again people were whooping as they saw their stones connect. The ritual had the feel of a contest, no matter how sacred. Beneath the commotion it seemed to blend the challenge of the *mas'a* walk with Fayez's notion of innocence won through labor. The throws were elating, but this was hard work, too, performed in a melee. It required precision, aim, and quick departures to keep from being crushed.

A crowd pressed me from behind near the second column. I braced my hands on the basin to keep from ramming into it and took this chance to peer over the rim. It was filled with stones and many unmatched sandals. Some foot-long sticks lay down there, too, but it was the sandals that impressed me. In an excess of enthusiasm some hadjis had left themselves barefoot on the bridge. The rule called for pebbles no larger than a fava bean, but excitement got the better of some pilgrims. Over my shoulder a rubber flip-flop spiraled through the air. Cloudbursts of pebbles broke around me. We were throwing to beat the devil, hollering *"Allahu akbar"* in the sun.

I knew that we were dealing here in a world of unseen things, of ideas and traditions that required imagination. We were embedded in a very ancient story. The word Satan still felt strange to my tongue, and yet a lot had happened since my first walk here. With a suggestion of bombs in the tunnels, with hints of war to our north, things looked different. Today I saw the devil from a bridgehead. He was the shadow of man's most destructive instincts.

Every faith addressed this matter somehow. Whether the prince of darkness was Shakespeare's Gentleman or Conrad's "soft spot" or the mute neuroses pointed up by Freud, the fact remained that his presence required action. Islam, with its usual wisdom, understood this. Intellectual resistance was insufficient. One ought to put one's body into it. To steel one's nerve, to objectify the struggle, one threw stones collected in the moonlight.

CHAPTER TWENTY-ONE

Walking On

O n the third night of the *'id* we returned to Makkah. Most pilgrims were already back in town.

As the city filled, we resumed our nighttime schedule. For a day or two I stayed near the hotel. After our time in the desert the urban heat felt oppressive. My thermometer shot back up into the hundreds. Many more people were fainting on the street.

The hotel lobby was almost cool. From behind the tall, glass windows I had a good view of the road. A juice bar sat in one corner. A bank of couches faced a color television. From here I could watch my companions cross the foyer. They stepped outside looking showered and clean and returned wilted and drenched from head to toe. I could welcome them back from the heat of the city. I could offer them mangoes and listen to their stories. When I cared, I could turn on the TV.

*　*　*

People looked physically different after the hadj. The *ihram* was gone, for one thing. And half the male pilgrims had shaved their heads. The clipping of two or three hairs at the back of the neck is required by law, a part of the desacralizing process, but the more public statement of baldness was also popular. Like the "raisin" on the forehead, a completely razored skull was considered a sign of deepened faith. Rough barbershops sprang up around the mosque to perform the service. They were busy day and night.

I had never noticed how many types of human skulls there were: the oval, the flat backed, the double lobed, the pineapple nubbled, the nearly square, the spade shaped, all covered with skin of a hundred different shades. Without hair the faces of men in the lobby looked more neotenic— childlike, round featured, relieved. Perhaps this was also because the labor was over. The thing had occurred. We were hadjis.

Coming down from Arafat a pilgrim is said to resume, however briefly, a state like Adam and Eve before the Fall. In my case, the effects were less dramatic. I felt like a prospect for faintly big improvements. Sometimes I felt precariously perched. Fayez had already pointed out the risks of a "purified" position. One of these was hypersensitivity. The world, that part of it that touched me, seemed more raw. The casual, daily violence I'd been used to felt intrusive. Every day I listened less to the BBC, with its litanies of grief. That somewhere beyond these hills men and women merrily labored to cheat, debase, and kill each other seemed preposterous. And then there were the rumors of a bombing— here, inside the sanctuary walls.

The TV had gone back to broadcasting the hadj. The programs, including aerial shots, were intercut with prayer hours at the mosque and with beautiful recitations of the Qur'an. There were also soccer games each afternoon. The World Cup was being played in Europe, and the lobby filled up for it, with a lot of hadjis sprawled out on the rugs. People seemed to have made their peace with the tunnel disaster. The hadj, I suppose, had prepared us for death's fears—in that sense the rites were like setup exercises. Soccer helped, too. We cheered, we took sides, we forgot ourselves and the tunnel. As the crowds at the window blended with the players on the screen, I felt more human. Then, on Wednesday morning, Nasser proposed a different recreation.

✧   ✧   ✧   ✧

*O*pinions diverge among Muslim scholars as to whether pilgrims should leave Makkah quickly, as soon as they have fulfilled the rites of hadj, or whether it is better to linger for a while in the Holy City. Every book of religious practice contains some discussion of this subject. Usually the commentary starts with an observation made by the second Caliph 'Umar that a person should not remain too long in Makkah, lest familiarity breed indifference, and Allah's house become like every other. The gist was to leave the shrine before it left *you*. Whether Nasser subscribed to this view I do not know. At breakfast he announced a trip to Madinah.

The mosque in Madinah, containing Muhammad's tomb, is Islam's second most venerated shrine. An early tradition quotes Muhammad saying, "Anyone who comes on the hadj and does not visit me is being churlish." To visit the tomb is not a requirement, but a great majority of pilgrims do so, whether they are novices or not. No hadj tour would think of omitting Madinah from its package. The town, two hundred miles north of Makkah, has a huge airport. Many would-be pilgrims land there first and spend a week, or a month, before going on the hadj. Abd al-Qadir, the vendor in Marrakesh, had advised me to make it my base of operations. When I asked Dr. 'Ali his view on why people went there, he said, "You go to Madinah to get to know the Prophet."

There was plenty to know. In contrast to Jesus, whose personal life is a postmortem reconstruction, the life of Muhammad reads like an open book. His position in spiritual history is unique in this respect, an historical figure who founded a world religion and whose every move and a lot of the words were recorded by multiple witnesses during his lifetime. It is a story worth repeating for two reasons: Madinah makes no sense without it, and those who haven't heard it are surprised.

We know from the writings of pre-Islamic Arabs that a temple stood at Makkah centuries before Muhammad's birth. In biblical times it was customary for tribes from Yemen to Iraq to make a yearly pilgrimage to the spot, where a market flourished. Here men and women conducted a thriving trade in Arabian products, performed their rites, and circuited the

Ka'ba. At the time of Muhammad's birth, 360 idols surrounded the temple. By then Christianity had reached the Hejaz, too. A stone cut into the likeness of Mary and Jesus figured in the Makkan pantheon.

Muhammad was born in 570 c.e. His tribe, the Quraysh, were the keepers of the Ka'ba, responsible for supplying pilgrims with safety, food, and water. He grew up an orphan. His father died before his birth. His mother died when he was six, returning from a journey to Madinah. His grandfather 'Abd al-Muttalib adopted him. This man was the Qurayshi chief and a prince of Makkah. Old and blind, he sat near the Ka'ba every day, surrounded by his sons and the tribal elders.

When Muttalib died, Muhammad came under the protection of a successor, the Hashimite clan chief Abu Talib. This man was Muhammad's father's brother. He took the boy at age fifteen on a caravan trip to Syria. Thereafter Muhammad became a trader.

In his early twenties he served as agent to a prosperous widow, a distant cousin named Khadijah, who entrusted him with her Syrian caravan. A few years later, at her suggestion, they were married. Fifteen years his senior, she was already the mother of several sons. The couple lived in a house with a peristyle, on the eastern side of the shrine, in upper Makkah. Three of their sons died in infancy. Four daughters lived.

In his thirty-fifth year fire and flood weakened the Ka'ba masonry, and the structure was rebuilt by the Qurayshi. Four groups of workers went into the hills and carried back stones on their shoulders. Each group resolved to build one wall. When a fight broke out for the honor of resetting the black stone, oaths were taken and hands dipped into blood. At the last moment it was agreed that the next man to enter the shrine should act as arbitrator. The man was Muhammad. At his suggestion a delegate from each faction held the stone between them in a cloth. Muhammad raised the stone and placed it.

In the year 610, at forty years of age, Muhammad began to receive the revelations that make up the Qur'an. Makkah did not find his monotheism appealing. A city that housed all the gods of the Middle East and earned its revenues from pilgrim visits saw no profit in a man who declared that God is one and that he is everywhere. Makkah was a small, urbane republic, subtly run by plutocrats. Their powers, however, were checked by tribal networks. No one attached to a clan chief went unprotected, even when his thinking posed a threat.

When his uncle died Muhammad's teaching came under attack. Even his own tribe opposed him. Factions of merchants, who stood to lose the most, persecuted his followers. A few were stoned to death in public. After three years of hardship all the city's Muslims were banished. Ta'if and the nearby towns refused them asylum.

In the end an agreement was reached with more distant Madinah. Muhammad had relatives there, on his mother's side, and the town, torn by strife between pagans and Jews, was in desperate need of an arbitrator. Makkah was now unsafe for Muslims. They slipped out of town after dark in twos and threes. Muhammad stayed behind to see them off.

Near the end of this period Muhammad learned of a plot to take his life. Ten men, each from a different tribe, were sent one night to stab him, but before they reached his bedroom, he was gone. Muhammad escaped into the desert with his father-in-law, Abu Bakr. The Makkans pursued and lost his trail. Riding day and night, he reached Madinah ten days later. He did not return to Makkah for eight years.

We flew up to Madinah on a Thursday. Only Mardini did not go along. His glasses had been crushed on his final trip to the *jamarat,* the prescription was complex, and he stayed behind to fix them. The rest of the delegation, including a few too ill to talk, boarded a bus and rode to the Jidda airport.

The road ran to dunes on either side of the highway. We were deep into upland desert in half an hour. Wherever a few tufts of reeds topped a rock-strewn field, herds of goats, then camels, munched the stubble. We descended through passes of magma, down violent mountains topping the Red Sea. Dust devils swirled beside the road. A burning wind slapped the windows. Whenever I saw this desert, I knew again why the early Muslims had considered it a blessing to wash often. We flashed by Babrah, a large granite oasis ringed in brush. A junkyard of smashed cars lay on the outskirts. Jidda was only an hour's ride away, but country and town in the Hejaz were opposite elements, strong in their absoluteness and divided.

Up in the air it seemed clear which side was winning. Volcanoes ruled here—more than I could count—strewing the sand with black basalt extrusions: bulbous stacks of metamorphic rock humped up in baking piles like giant flapjacks; sawn-off buttes; red, freestanding sandstone spires planed and isolated by the winds. History dropped like a pea in a bowl in this region—Aelius Gallus's Roman legions, Tetrarch of Egypt, Saladin—the echoes of great movements faded fast here. North of Madinah the twisted tracks of a Turkish railway, blown up in World War I by T. E. Lawrence, jutted rusting from the sand. Nasser pointed them out as we came in for a landing.

Makkah and Madinah, so close together on a map, are utterly different in character and look. Both lie along the caravan route of an ancient incense trade, but Madinah possesses the advantage of fertile soil. Its air feels benign, softer, with the mysterious chemistry of growing things. It is also as flat as the deck of an ocean liner. The Anglo-Indian writer J. F. Keane likened it to a pearl mosaic set in a border of brilliant green. These days it is a candidate for the cleanest of Arab cities, with low white buildings, palms all around, and six-lane roads with gardened traffic islands. At night wisps of Day-Glo neon light shop windows.

We did not have long in Madinah. The sheikhs moved quickly. That night we walked to the mosque for evening prayers and filed into a niche on its western side. The mosque, not nearly so large as the one at Makkah, was a collection of interlinking porticoes and pillars, laid out around a central yard. The exterior walls were a uniform soft, pink granite. Seen from Mount Uhud some miles away, the mosque was meant to resemble a huge rose.

The principal colors inside the building are dark red, deep orange, bright gold, and a range of greens. Terra-cotta columns wear boots of gilded paint around their feet. Up in the vaults the decoration ranges from geometric fields to simple landscapes—the most representational mosque art I had seen. If the Makkan *haram* affected absoluteness, the rose-pink

Prophet's mosque belonged to man. Overlaid in changing styles by caliphs from Baghdad to Cairo, it displayed more obvious historical texture. Certain gates were Damascene. One minaret looked Saracen. The effect in this part of the building was Ottoman.

When the prayer was done, we stayed seated on carpets, meditating, reading, or reciting the Qur'an. Most of my companions had large parts of the Arabic by heart. As I watched and listened, I envied the range of their learning. By now I had memorized four short passages. I alternated these for half an hour.

When the mosque had emptied out and the gates were closed, Nasser led us through a hundred yards of pillars. Over centuries the mosque has been transformed, by many extensions, to a building the size of a small village. But size is not why so many pilgrims come here. In the transept, facing south toward Makkah, lies the heart of the temple—a modest enclosure where Muhammad preached and lived.

The dimensions of this area are impressive for their smallness. The steps where he preached stand a few dozen yards from the mud-brick house where he ate and slept. In place of the house there is now a baldachin, a brass-gated mausoleum that protects three tombs. Inside rest Muhammad; his close friend, the first caliph Abu Bakr; and 'Umar, the second caliph. These three men, together with 'Ali and 'Uthman, buried elsewhere, are considered the founding figures of Islam. Their biographies have filled many books, and Muslims around the world know their stories. The three lie behind a grille, in descending order, with Abu Bakr's head at Muhammad's feet.

A few carpets worth of floor divides the tomb from the oratory. This patch of ground is called the Prophet's garden. It is one of Islam's most revered sites. When Fayez reached the spot, he performed two *rak'ah*s as a greeting. Coming behind him, the rest of the delegation did the same. Nobody faced the tomb, however. As always, we bowed in the direction of the Ka'ba. No one here would think of praying to a human figure, even a teacher of Muhammad's stature. You did not seek his blessing, either. Instead, you prayed for him, as for a friend.

Most mausoleums bore me. I felt electrified to be in the garden. At a time when palm trees grew here, this modest space of fifty yards had served as the tiny headquarters of an empire. Here Muhammad forged a government in exile. Here he maintained his household and raised children. Across the way, on a wall near the tomb, lay a spot where he received new revelations. Fazeel, who revered great writing, dubbed that part of the mosque "the Prophet's study."

The next day I walked to Friday prayers with Ahmad. Crossing a road to the mosque on its southern side, we passed al-Baqi cemetery. This must be Islam's most famous graveyard. Today it resembled an empty parking lot. A thin line of hadjis stood at the front wall, peering into a field of black clinkers. I went over and joined them. Among the cinders unmarked stones poked up. Nothing distinguished the grave of the third caliph, 'Uthman ibn 'Affan, from those of Abu Bakr's daughter 'A'ishah or Muhammad's uncle al-'Abbas. Half the Prophet's companions lay buried here, but you had to know it. Once there had been signs, but these were gone—destroyed in the 1920s to discourage saint worship. Nobody at the white wall seemed to mind this. An old man stood with some near relations, pointing and assigning names to the grave sites. Flocks of white doves pecked among the cinders. Boys in the crowd were hawking bags of birdseed.

There was more to the mosque than I had seen last night. An extensive system of porticoes runs away from the main roof for many blocks. The outer walls are a uniform rose hue. As we continued down the west side of the building, I was suddenly struck by a total absence of women. In Makkah the sexes circulated freely. Here the mosque was divided in two parts, the eastern side reserved for women, the western side for men. Dinosaur cranes loomed up at the rear of the buildings, where building crews were adding on.

I wanted to inspect this building further. Its early lines had been the model for every subsequent mosque from Spain to China. Today the place was packed. There were no views. We sat wedged tight as rows of teeth. The congregation performed the prayer as a joint maneuver. When we rose, we rose together. We bowed, then knelt down in a unit, as naturally as waves hitting a beach. With acres of pilgrims the murmurs ran like water.

I enjoyed keeping in step with the congregation. It was part of the secret of the hadj—that the more chaotic events became, the less control you had to exert to get through them. The trick was to pay attention to the rites. The perfect aim one needed at the *jamarat*, for instance, saved a lot of people from being crushed. Here the precision of the prayers dissolved claustrophobia.

Saturday we made a tour of the city. My principal partners on this trip were Mohamed Fayez, Rafeeq Manifa, and a mystical Bolivian named Abd al-Mumin. Each one saw Madinah differently.

Our bus made a slow circuit of the town. The verdant oasis came as a pleasant shock after Makkah. With the date harvest approaching, swaths of sky were filled with hanging clusters. Next to Zamzam water, Madinan dates were the best gift to bring home. The guidebooks mentioned 170 varieties. The air smelled faintly of caramel as they ripened.

Tribes of Semitic traders had been living on this spot since ancient times. In 1266 B.C.E. their lives were improved when an earthquake shifted the course of several rivers toward town. Since then one has only had to dig a few yards down to find fresh water. This was the secret of Madinah's groves. Their fruits had been famous long before Muhammad. His mosque and home were built on the site of a date barn.

Fayez took real delight in facts like these. He often repeated the popular view that Muhammad was a "Muslim at his best" and that one should never stop trying to know him better. As we drove from site to site, he consulted a guidebook.

In this way I learned that the Battle of Badr had taken place in the second year of Muhammad's flight, when the Makkans sent a thousand men against him. The community at Madinah was still small. Muhammad managed to raise a counterforce of three hundred men, including some teenagers, and marched out to meet the invaders. It rained that day, a distinct hometown advantage, and Allah was with the underdogs. As the Qur'an notes, "He helped you at Badr, when you were a contemptible little army."

*   *   *

The next year the Makkans returned in triple force, taking revenge at the Battle of Uhud. I strolled around these more impressive grounds with Rafeeq, the Libyan economist. The field lay tucked into foothills north of the city.

It puzzled me that the Makkans would ride so far to fight a few exiles. Rafeeq said they were angry with Muhammad, for raiding their caravans. I asked what had been the purpose of these raids. He explained that once the Muslims quit Makkah, local merchants had moved into their homes and shipped their goods for sale to Damascus.

"One thing you have to remember," Rafeeq said. "Muhammad didn't start out as a prophet. He began as a trader. He lived like a monk, but he understood commerce and money. His own great-grandfather Hasheem had forged Makkah's trade agreements with the Roman Empire. Muhammad knew the trade routes forward and backward. He knew when the caravans traveled and where they camped. He also had hundreds of disenfranchised exiles to care for, men and women and children in need of food. The Makkans understood all this. It terrified them. They rode up to Uhud to finish him quickly."

They nearly succeeded. Muhammad fielded an army of seven hundred men. Fifty archers were told to guard his back. When the clash began, however, as the Makkans were retreating, these men broke ranks, running downhill for the spoils. Within minutes the Makkan cavalry broke through. Seventy Muslims were killed and forty wounded. Muhammad was struck by an arrow and lost four teeth. The grave of his slaughtered uncle, Hamza, lay below us.

Rafeeq went down to pay his respects at the grave site. I continued on around the hill. We were four miles from town, on a sandy height with views of orange groves. The battlefield looked windy, bare. I have never been much at calling up the hoofbeats of legendary horsemen. Where the path met a fence, I turned and was starting down when somebody called me. Abd al-Mumin stood waving from the ridge.

Abd al-Mumin was a guide from La Paz, Bolivia. I assumed he was born Catholic. He had a cheerful, weathered face and knew Morocco. He had turned to Islam in his twenties, in Fez, during the *'id* celebration. He had subsequently traveled to the desert and lived two years there. He had married a Moroccan woman, too, from the oasis of Zagora. Ultimately they had returned to La Paz together. There he established that city's first Islamic center—in his house.

Abd al-Mumin had a real gift for not becoming sidetracked by minor complications. Unlike a lot of the delegation, he was lighthearted. He told me the first joke I heard in Makkah: "Cross an atheist with a Jehovah's Witness, what do you get? A stranger banging on your door for no reason." Abd al-Mumin did not take an interest in battles and guidebooks. For him there was historical religion on the one hand and spiritual transmissions on the other, and only the more transcendent questions mattered. He was respectful, but he had no head for dates.

He *was* good at interpreting dreams. So good, in fact, that riding here from Badr on the bus, I had told him a dream of mine from the previous evening. The part of it that stumped me involved a jar of miniature salmon swimming around inside my refrigerator. The jar was made of clear, green glass. The fish had adult proportions. I could not fathom the image. Nor was it clear why, later in the dream, I had cooked and was feeding pound-size fish steaks to a group of hungry children in my kitchen.

Abd al-Mumin had said he would think it over.

I went up the path to ask about it now. He was not forthcoming. Either he had come up with something he did not want to tell, or he was puzzled. He chewed his lip. He wished his wife were here. "She's like a book when it comes to these things," he said and glanced across the plain as if looking for her.

"The fish," he said at last, "were they from the ocean?"

"Yes, they were salmon."

Abd al-Mumin wore a green and white *kaffiyeh*. The wind sent it flapping. His face lit up. "I'm not sure about the kids. But the fish are your future. Fish are signs of bounty, like the sea."

"Bounty?"

"Well, some people say that a fish in a dream means money. My wife says they're spiritual nourishment, like blessings.

"*Baraka.*"

"Exactly."

I waited.

"Did the kids have a mother?"

"Yes. She was neglecting them. That's why I fed them."

"I'll think it over."

We went down the hill together. We were standing by the bus when he touched my elbow. "I just remembered! I had a dream myself last night. I'd forgotten all about it. I was in the Prophet's mosque here in Madinah. I found a door I'd never seen before, and I walked into this room with a king-size bed. It was beautifully designed. I was amazed. I did not know that such a room existed."

As the bus started up, I asked what else had happened.

"Nothing," he said. "I saw the room. That's all."

We continued along a ring road to al-Khandaq and pulled into a verdant parking lot. Thanks to Fayez, I was soon made aware that here, on a plain near Mount Sil'a in 626 C.E., the Makkans, with nine thousand soldiers, had laid siege to Madinah for a month. A freak winter hurricane drove them home and saved the Muslims from starvation. The Khandaq siege was Makkah's last aggression against the city.

The name Madinat al-Nabi, "the City of the Prophet," dates from Muhammad's arrival in the town. Before that it had always been Yathrib. *Medinta,* an Aramaic word, denotes an area of jurisdiction. According to Rafeeq, numerous Aramaean Jewish tribes had settled in the Hejaz in talmudic times. At Yathrib they preceded the city's Yemeni Arabs, who learned the arts of cultivation from them. They probably also changed the city's name. They were certainly well represented when Muhammad arrived here. One tribe had its center in the palm groves at al-Kaybar, on the city's outskirts. We pulled up there beside a ruined fort as the sun was setting.

We strolled down a trail of lava clinkers into a date grove, where remnants of rock wall crisscrossed a clearing. The settlement's outlines were well marked. Most of the delegation hiked their *thobe*s and climbed the ruins. I took a few snapshots, then sat down on a boulder with Rafeeq. He filled me in on where the Jews had gone.

Apparently during the Khandaq siege the tribe at al-Kaybar had colluded with the Makkans against Muhammad. When the siege broke up, he drove them out. He also changed the direction of prayer, from Jerusalem to Makkah, and walled up the north-facing niches in the mosques. "As a war, al-Khandaq meant nothing," Rafeeq said. "Just two armies encamped for a battle that never happened. But it did serve a purpose. It brought Muhammad's foes into the open. Until Khandaq, he wooed them. After, he cut them off."

As the sun went down, a full moon topped the peaks across the road, rising like the light end of a seesaw. I sat thinking of Arabs and Jews for some minutes, then shook my head and strolled into the groves.

A short way down the path Abd al-Mumin leaned on a crumbled wall, staring up through the leaves at a cluster of fruit. I tried to get him to talk. He became distracted.

"Allah, I wish those dates were ripe right now!"

He scaled the broken wall and disappeared. A minute later he was back. "I wanted a date. And I got one!" He twirled the pit in his mouth and spat it out.

Out on the road the bus was starting. As we walked along, I asked about my dream. "The mother represents your past," he said, fixing me with a look I still remember. "I've thought about it now, and I'm pretty sure."

"My past?"

"The hard parts. What was done to you, I mean. All those terrible things that scarred your heart so much you couldn't accept them."

I must have looked dumbstruck.

"You think I'm joking?"

"Of course not." I shook my head.

"But now that's all over. Things have changed. You're going to get the good part. It may be money or something more . . . direct. Others are going to benefit, too. You're going to nourish them. Wait and see. It's a good dream. And you had it in the Prophet's city. That's why we call him a mercy to the people."

"Thank you, Abd al-Mumin."

"God be praised." He reached into the pocket of his *thobe*, produced a second date, and held it up. "Do you want this other one?"

* * *

When Muhammad first approached Madinah in 622, he stopped to rest on the outskirts, at a settlement named Qubah. His followers, who hastened out to meet him, found him lost in thought under a palm tree. Although he left for Madinah in the morning, Qubah became the site of the world's first mosque. This place held special meaning for Muhammad, and throughout his exile he made it a practice to visit every Saturday. A certain grace is still attached to this activity.

Going up the stairway to the mosque, a group of pilgrims surrounding Nasser praised him for his usual good timing. He had not only managed to give them the Prophet's garden. He'd delivered up Qubah on the proper day.

We washed off the dust of the battlefield in a building lined with spigots and stone troughs. The evening *adhan* began ringing from the tower. Inside, the mosque looked modest and perfectly proportioned, the size of a village library in the States. In the prayer hall the plaster ceilings were sky blue. The walls looked paler, the decorations spare. The effect was an open feeling, congenial, with nothing monumental to distract. Light filtered down through casements near the ceiling. The carpets were enormous and handloomed.

After the prayer people strolled the building or lounged and talked. I was impressed with what I had learned about Muhammad. For anyone raised in the West, it was startling to find how much was known. Jesus, we *suppose*, spoke Aramaic. The life of Muhammad brims with history. Every day for several decades he made the decisions that forged a religion. His words, his deeds, his moods, his facial expressions were noted on the way. Direct quotes abound—thousands of judgments, parables, aphorisms:

- Silence adorns the learned and veils the ignorant.
- Avoid anything that requires an excuse.
- Removing an obstacle from someone else's path is charity.
- Nothing is easy except what you make easy.
- Reducing pride is a seventy-year labor.
- Gluttony hardens the heart.

• You won't have real faith until you want for your brother what you want for yourself.

In terms of social vision, the Western philosophers who most nearly mirrored Muhammad's precepts were the English empiricist John Locke and the French Romantic Jean-Jacques Rousseau. Among poets I thought first of John Keats, who said in a famous letter, "Call the world if you please the vale of soul making." I was also reminded again of Wallace Stevens, who wrote in "Asides on the Oboe" about

> *The impossible possible philosopher's man,*
> *The man who has had the time to think enough,*
> *The central man, the human globe, responsive*
> *As a mirror with a voice, the man of glass,*
> *Who in a million diamonds sums us up.*

A peace of sorts was reached with the Makkans after the Khandaq siege. When the Makkans broke the treaty, Muhammad marched against them. The Makkans gave up without resistance. In return they were granted a general amnesty. It was January 630. The hegira, the decade of exile, was over. Inside the Ka'ba, Muhammad spared the likeness of Jesus and Mary, covering the figure with his hands. Otherwise the shrine was cleansed completely.

He did not remain in his birthplace. Muhammad returned to Madinah, the town that had taken him in when no one would have him. He likened the Madinah mosque to the cradle that had saved Moses on the Nile. There he continued to live simply and to receive the final parts of the Qur'an. When one man asked him, "How is the Qur'an revealed to you?" he replied, "I remember the inspiration. I grasp what is inspired." He was the sort of prophet predicted by John: "He shall not speak of himself; but of whatsoever he shall hear, that shall he speak." He continued to insist that except for this, he had worked no miracles.

✧   ✧   ✧   ✧

*O*n Sunday morning Ahmad and I went shopping in a souk near the Prophet's mosque. As we strolled past painted carts of dates, its green dome came and went between low buildings. The dates lay neatly divided by size and color, their prices chalked on squares of wood. I wanted to take a five-pound box back to Mostopha and his family. Ahmad knew all the varieties. He warned me not to buy from the first two vendors.

As we walked along, sunlight glanced off the windows of second-story flats above the road. It was in this district that Burckhardt found a room in 1816. He had come up from Makkah in perfect health, given away all his quinine to Muhammad 'Ali's son, and then was stricken with malaria. He had languished all winter immobilized, prepared, he wrote, to die. The returning warmth of spring put an end to the illness, but his isolation had been horrible. Burckhardt, whose texts Thomas Carlyle and Washington Irving drew on later, had only one book to read in this period, a pocket edition of Milton's *Paradise Lost*. His seclusion was occasionally broken by the landlady, an old Egyptian woman who appeared at a trapdoor in the ceiling and spoke with him sometimes for half an hour.

We found a bookstore up the street and browsed the shelves. Madinah has always been famous for its libraries. These days official translations of the Qur'an were printed in huge editions outside town. (The million copies that King Fahd had recently shipped by jet to Russia came from Madinah.) On the shelves I counted fifty-four separate editions in every imaginable size and binding. There were also significant caches of *hadith* and scholarly commentary. I bought a volume each for Brahim and Sharif and a map of the Gulf region for myself. I was looking at the map when Ahmad came over.

"My sister's wedding will take place here," he said. He laid a little finger on the city of Kuwait, spread his hand, and touched Madinah with his thumb. "Do you want to come with me?"

A few days before, I'd arranged a flight in the opposite direction, with stops in Algiers, Morocco, and New York. I thought I would look up Hamza Kropf's friends, at the al-'Alawi center in Algeria, and I wanted to see Mostopha in Marrakesh. My family in California was starting to miss me. In retrospect, it was lucky, I suppose. Three weeks later Iraq overran Kuwait with tanks and soldiers and occupied the capital for months.

We worked our way into a pleasant street of well-lit, modern shops bulging with clothes. I found mohair hats from Tbilisi, kaftans from Korea, sandals marked with Arabian tribal patterns, made in China. There were prayer rugs and wall hangings, too, and stores that sold nothing but audio tapes of Quranic recitations. I struck up a conversation with one of the vendors and soon was receiving a crash course in muezzins and the mosques they made famous from here to Malaysia. One of the best of these callers was twelve years old.

We were crossing a dusty parking lot near the hotel when Fayez came running down the path, calling my name. He had been in the Prophet's mosque since early morning. Walking back, he had stopped to chat with three Baghdadi pilgrims, men who had never been out of Iraq and were full of questions. "You only know what they tell you there," Fayez explained. One topic of world news had led to another—Beirut, Israel, Afghanistan, the collapse of Soviet Russia. When Washington came up, he'd mentioned me.

"They want to meet you."

"Why?"

Fayez looked sheepish. "One of them thinks you're CIA."

"I'm a hadji, for God's sake."

"I told them."

"Where are they?"

Ahmad didn't want to go. "Some of these people don't like me. They think I drank their oil."

"Well?" Fayez said.

Ahmad said. "The emir drank it."

"Yes. I'm sorry."

Fayez and I turned back to find the men, but the streets leading to the mosque were choked with pilgrims.

"Don't let this upset you," Fayez said. "It's the same all over the region. Most Iranians believe the CIA installed Khomeini! The fact that Nixon backed the shah means nothing to them." As Fayez went on, I began to see humor in the Iraqis' accusation: Agent Wolfe performs the hadj to improve his cover. Mostopha, with his taste for espionage, would have loved it. It was probably better that we did not meet the men from Baghdad. Being mistaken for one's flag brings out the worst in everyone, even a pilgrim. Ahmad had wisely returned to the hotel.

*   *   *

We flew back to Makkah Sunday evening, aboard a stripped-down Saudi air force C-130. The airplane, lightened for transport, had no walls or insulation. Electrical wires and vacuum hoses snaked down the fuselage like open veins. The engine noise was blinding. The seats rocked on their bolts. Even the round moon framed in the porthole shook like a jellyfish. Adnan, a pious professor from Ann Arbor, sat praying storms of *bismillah*s beside me. Half the delegation appeared bilious.

Strapped to a window seat, I tried unsuccessfully to lose myself in the sights and moonlight. Except for volcanism, the Hejaz is a poor diversion from the air. It has never been settled, really, for the simple reason that no one has known what to do with it. Occasionally I admired its jagged serenity, its composure, but that was probably caused by sudden drops in altitude. The flight did have one constant. All the way back to Jidda, the pump on a fuel-booster reservoir filled my ears with a whine like a dentist's drill bit. The unit was mounted two feet behind me. I could still hear it hissing the next day.

✧   ✧   ✧   ✧

*M*akkah looked just as packed as when we had left it. In the morning I worked my way down to the *haram*. The hollow still stood at maximum capacity. Where the road met the square, the cement lay thick with blocks of pilgrims. Entering the mosque from the street was impossible. In the end I managed to slip through a sublevel gate near the barber shops, but the first-floor carpets were filled to overflowing. Normally a man can perform *salat* on a spot the size of *Life* magazine. No such space was available indoors. I retraced my steps into the courtyard. The yard was lined with rice farmers from Java, a thousand families planted in neat rows. I decided to try the roof and was still wading through when the call to prayer began and the farmers stood, adapting to my height like a tide to a piling. I never made it to the escalator.

*   *   *

By two o'clock the mosque had emptied out enough to enter. This time I made for a wedge of rugs facing the well and stayed until nightfall. In my shoulder bag were paper, pens, a few books, and a small pink prayer rug. From where I sat, I could watch a constant troop of pilgrims descend the well. People went down exhausted. They came back cool, hair slick, refreshed. To the left of the stair old pilgrims, men and women, soaked their winding sheets in buckets, then spread them on the marble in the sun. Farther down the floor the counterclockwise bands of the *tawaf* circled the shrine. Water bearers and cleanup crews pushing wide brooms moved through the building.

As my stay wound down in Makkah, I spent more time here, marking my notebooks, meditating, reading. I strolled, performed my circuits, sat and watched. At meal times I ducked out of the mosque to eat from wooden stalls in the jewelry market.

I had come back from Madinah with an overview of the hadj different from the hadj I had imagined, and I wanted to fix it while my thoughts were fresh. I began to fill a notebook with summations. From California, I had viewed the hadj as a journey to a physical destination. In fact, the hadj was protean, all process. It surprised me now to see how off I'd been. In the West the notion of pilgrimage centered on going, on reaching, on arrival. Nailing this moribund image to the hadj was a mistake, like claiming that "going home to dinner" began with getting off work and ended when you reached the porch—omitting any mention of the meal.

Reaching Makkah was only a beginning. The goal of the hadj was to perform it well. The rites were hard, sometimes unfathomable—like living. Yet they provided a counterweight to the usual view of life as a dog-and-cat fight. Elsewhere, except at the best of times, every person looked out for himself. During the hadj people looked out for each other. The hadj is a shared rite of passage. I saw it through the eyes of others as much as through my own. In that way it was like an act of love.

At night the streets around the mosque were lined with vendors. Many more people were out selling goods now than before. Besides the established local shops, jammed with imported gifts for the homeward bound, there were itinerant African market women, too. They sat at the curb with their wares spread on carpets, earning coins to buy a passage home. I liked to stop and joke with them and hear their bright patois, which refreshed me. Uphill along a wall stood wooden stalls selling nothing but prayer beads. Electronics shops overflowed with Japanese equipment. There were toy stores, too, in which I searched for Nishwa's giant robot.

On Tuesday the Hotel al-Waha began to empty out. I returned from the mosque that evening to a lobby stacked with luggage. Two vans bound for Jidda sat outside. The delegation was breaking up. Abd al-Mumin was leaving. So were Rafeeq, Fayez, and Dr. 'Ali. Our good-byes were swift, in the Arab manner: a light embrace, a wave of the hand, and *pffft.* The next night John Muhammad and Abd al-Qadir were going. I returned to the hotel early, to see them off.

I found them on a white couch by the window. John Muhammad, heading back to Georgia, would be picking up his work with disabled children. Abd al-Qadir would return to his prison programs. Both men had families and full lives in the States. They seemed glad to be going. As people of color they were returning to a nation that has always been deeply racist, but coping with that was a permanent fact of their landscape. They managed in spite of it, and they had Islam.

I suppose we were on the subject. In my notebook for that day I find these lines, ascribed to Abd al-Qadir: "People tell you racism is natural—a part of human nature. Let me tell you about nature. Nature *adapts.*"

On a couch across the way three men sat snoring. Their heads were thrown back on pillows. One came from Pakistan. One came from Djakarta. The third was Russian. Abd al-Qadir laughed. "It reminds me of something Malcolm said: 'Everybody snores in the same language.' "

Malcolm X was a popular figure in Makkah. Indeed, it says something about the hadj that of the three Americans whose names one heard over and over, all were blacks. Muhammad 'Ali, the first of them, had everyone's respect, because of his talent and because he had embraced Islam at a time when it was not popular to do so. He had brought the religion new prestige and educated Americans, many of whom believed the word Muslim meant a type of cloth. 'Ali had performed the hadj in the 1970s. Now he devoted his time to charity.

The second famous American was Malcolm X, better known here as Al-Hadj Malik al-Shabazz. Malcolm had begun to take an interest in Islam at the end of a youthful career in crime marked by self-destructive behavior and random violence. Abd al-Qadir called him a "beacon to the street kids" because if Malcolm could turn his life around after all he had suffered, then a fifteen-year-old could walk away from crack. Most literate pilgrims I met had read his autobiography.

Alex Haley, the third in the trio, had coauthored Malcolm's book. Haley was less popular, however. His second book, *Roots,* received harsh reviews from many hadjis. Some I spoke with called it pure fiction. Abd al-Qadir felt it was not possible to know half the things Haley claimed about his family. John Muhammad said the South was full of people who after reading *Roots* had thrown away time and money seeking their ancestors, only to run up against the usual dockets lumping boatloads of slaves under one landowner's name. If you were a Smith or a Good or a Haley and you traced your family back too many years, you met a cotton farmer and his chattel. Haley had pressed his investigations far beyond this. Some readers were jealous. Others felt misled.

One hadji, a man from the Gambia, disliked *Roots* for more personal reasons. He had moved to the al-Waha with his family during the *'id.* His name was Kaorama. A businessman living in London, he came here twice a year. He spoke a lilting African version of British English, and he had quite a story. Kaorama Kinteh, educated, in his early sixties, was a very near living relation of Kunta Kinte, Haley's original ancestor in *Roots.* Being a Kinteh scion, Kaorama was disturbed by Haley's book because it so terribly jumbled his family story. Kaorama claimed that while in the Gambia for research, Haley had met a minor family relation, Simon Kinteh, and had been told a degraded version of the tale.

"Degraded?" I asked. "In what way?"

According to Kaorama, Simon's lineage went back to a Kinteh princess who had married a blacksmith. This union constituted the only break in an otherwise more distinguished family line. Haley never heard the real story.

"How could he hear it?" Kaorama asked. "Haley went to Banjul by the sea and then to Juffure. He did not speak with the principal family members. Their villages were too far upriver."

Twenty years before this I had spent some pleasant weeks on the Gambia River. When Abd al-Qadir and John were gone, Kaorama asked me to his room. We talked until midnight.

❖   ❖   ❖   ❖

*M*ardini woke me in the morning. His lids drooped weakly behind new glasses. His legs became unsteady on the stairs. Three weeks of assisting novice pilgrims had taken their toll on him. The days between pairs of glasses had produced a splitting headache. Now he felt feverish again. At breakfast I gave him the last of my antibiotics. We left the hotel and taxied to Al-Aziziyah.

We found Saleem in the dining room, conversing with his right-hand man, Hameed. Shafeeq sat across the table, leafing through a Qur'an. The topic was oil, which exercised Saleem. Two days before, Iraq and Kuwait had convened their Jidda meeting. According to the BBC, Kuwait had agreed to abide by OPEC's production quotas. They would, in effect, stop helping to undercut the price of oil. Iraq, with its weak-kneed dinar, was delighted. In response to the announcement petroleum spot prices rose two dollars a barrel overnight. Then in the morning Kuwait tacked on a stipulation—that it might reverse its decision in October. This implicit aside to big oil buyers, to wait a few months before placing orders, incensed Iraq. Sadaam had already replied with a radio tirade.

I asked what it meant.

Saleem said, "It's not a small matter." Taking up a pad, he scratched out the border between the two countries, then drew a banana through it. The banana stood on end, running north to south. "That's the Rumaila oil field. Ninety percent of the oil lies in Iraq. Its reserves are three times larger than your Alaskan Prudhoe Bay. For about ten years most of the pumping here has been done by Kuwaitis. I would say it looks bad for Kuwaitis."

Shafeeq closed the Qur'an. He had heard enough. "It's just a squabble over who will pay," he said. "Iraq owes them billions in loans from the war with Iran. Kuwait owes Iraq for the oil it has stolen. This is over oil, over money."

Shafeeq was leaving for Florida in the morning. He had other ways to spend his final day here, and they did not include political speculation. He excused himself and drove off to the mosque.

Discussion turned from oil to other business. Saleem wanted to move quickly on the car deal. This puzzled me. He had always seemed patient when it came to business. Now as we talked, he busily scratched out figures and made projections. I supposed he was simply rounding off the deal before I left town. As we talked, I began to sense a different motive.

Saleem was not merely "attuned" to Middle Eastern politics. He was Lebanese. That is, he put even less faith than others in dictators and emirs. He viewed their governments the way Franz Kafka viewed the castle, as a giant, looming presence brooding over all men say and do. He had no more notion than anyone that war lay on his doorstep, but he was sensitive to the temper of the Gulf, and he knew that war was never good for traders. It ruined communications. It spoiled transportation. It drove the price of imports through the ceiling.

This time his intuitions were right on target. On July 17, Sadaam threatened military reprisals against any Gulf state flouting oil quotas. On July 21, Iraqi troops began massing near the border. A week later they numbered one hundred thousand soldiers. Kuwait was occupied on August 2, in about twelve hours. Within three months an enormous allied airlift had landed a force of a half million soldiers in Saudi Arabia. Twenty-eight nations, led by the United States, took part. By December two of the world's largest armies stood nose to nose across a patch of desert. On January 16, a six-week air war started. Iraq's defeat was televised worldwide. A UN report called the round-the-clock bombing "near-apocalyptic." Several hundred thousand Iraqis died.

The northeastern corner of Saudi Arabia became the staging ground for the allied activities. Neither King Fahd himself nor Saleem nor anyone else I met in Makkah that summer had the slightest inkling of what lay ahead. But Saleem sensed something. To hurry our deal, he now proposed to visit California. Mardini's marriage in the States had been set for September. Saleem would fly to Detroit, attend the wedding, then meet me in LA and buy the cars. He seemed delighted by the prospect. I looked forward to showing him my country. Of course, the war of the big banana wrecked our plans.

*   *   *

I rounded out the gift list for my Marrakeshi friends with an afternoon visit to the market. The curbs were already jammed with departing buses. On the sidewalks footmen hoisted luggage onto vans. I found a gorgeous sari for Qadisha, a clock that rang the prayers hours for Mostopha, and a yellow party dress with bows for Nishwa. I combed the toy shops for a giant robot, but the robot had not reached Makkah yet.

On my last night in town I went down to the mosque at twilight to perform a final ritual. A farewell *tawaf* is obligatory for every pilgrim leaving Makkah. As Nasser put it, "Go down and say good-bye to the Ka'ba." This was not a collective rite performed to a schedule. You went when you felt your time was almost up. Throughout my travels I had mostly steered clear of venerable architecture. The Ka'ba was different. I liked the idea of saying good-bye to this building. Our first night in town Sheikh Ibrahim had called it sacred, but "not so sacred as the people who surround it." The band of circuiting pilgrims looked smaller this evening. The city was emptying.

Banks of spotlights bathed the marble floor as I entered the circle on its northeast corner. As we went around, the prayer hour drew near, and the outer edge of the floor began filling with pilgrims. They spread their one-man carpets and sat down cross-legged in rows. When the *adhan* began, the air rippled. People rose to greet the mosque.

The *tawaf* continued until the prayers began. In the horseshoe arc jutting off the Ka'ba, as we came around for a final time, I saw a dozen tight-packed rows of men in *thobes*. This wedge of floor was a favorite spot to meditate. It enclosed the grave of Hagar, Ishmail's mother. For a faith that stressed equality before God, its emblem of racial equity seemed perfect. At the core of the House of Friendship lay the grave of a slave woman.

The imam announced the prayer. The *tawaf* wound down and turned to standing rows. Bodies fell into line like chips in a kaleidoscope. Having finished my circuits, I surfaced in a crowd of hadjis ten yards from the shrine. We were near enough to count the gold threads in the *kiswa;* I could see palm sweat gleaming on the brick. Then the mosque grew quiet. The only discernible sound I heard was an undertow hum of half a million people waiting, breathing.

After the prayers the dead were borne in on their boards again. This time they came from behind me and passed quite near. I had grown used to observing death from a rooftop rail, a stately pageant witnessed at a distance—the bearers in red head wraps, the shiny satin shrouds. Closer up it was not so easy. The corpses passed a few yards away. The bumpy gait of the bearers made limbs quiver. Heads lolled. I could smell the perfumed shrouds. "For a person with no imagination death is simple," wrote Céline. "With it, it's awful." Then the bearers set down the boards and people prayed.

Two weeks later I recalled this scene. I was back in Morocco, preparing to fly home, when the bad news caught up with me. My mother had died July 9, in Cincinnati. The news hit me strongly. The lag time made it worse, and I was glad to have new resources to draw on. In particular, I remembered this Janaza prayer.

The hadj had been hard to pin down from day to day, and yet it stayed with you. In a span of four weeks I'd perceived it first as a city, then as a building, then as a group of ambulating rites, a desert retreat, a rehearsal for death, a League of Nations. Not only did it appear in these ways to everyone who performed it, but it went on working after you were gone.

Mardini was not only better in the morning. He had been up for hours, he had been to Saleem's house, he had come back with a car to take me shopping. Muhammad said helping a friend is like walking downhill. I told Mardini that this time he'd gone too far. He waved me off, laughing. "I must shop, too. We can't go home without Zamzam water."

Two empty gallon jugs sat on the car seat. I set them on the floor and Mardini drove. On the way downtown I asked about Saleem. I said he'd seemed nervous the other day, about the car deal.

"Yes. He still plans to come to California."

"What do you think?"

Mardini smiled. "I'm coming to California, too. For my honey-moon."

I said, "Terrific!"

"Saleem's a good trader. He knows how to do the paperwork, and he knows how to sell cars. If it can be done, he'll do it. If not . . ." He shrugged. "Have you heard the joke about the two bedouins?"

"No."

"A bedouin is standing under a mountain on the desert. This man is so poor he can't afford a head wrap. He calls out, 'Allah, give me money or take my soul.' Another bedouin standing above him overhears. He throws a pebble down the cliff and hits the man on the head. 'Allah!' the injured one cries. 'How slow you are to grant my wish. How quick you are to try me.' "

We inched downhill beeping the horn and drew up in front of a one-story brick building. Outside I bought six scarves from a sidewalk vendor. Meanwhile Mardini carried the jugs inside. He brought them out a few minutes later, dripping at the brim with Zamzam water. We were twelve blocks from the well. To discourage crowds, the water was piped to dispensaries like this one all over the city. Otherwise the mosque would have been mobbed, so great is the demand for holy water.

We drove the jugs uphill to the hotel. As we entered the lobby, tall Ahmad came downstairs, loaded with luggage. A van of Kuwaiti hadjis was waiting outside for him. I wished him a safe trip and we shook hands. That was the last I saw or heard of Ahmad. He took off that day for his sister's wedding and flew into an invasion, then a war. I tried to track him down later, with letters and phone calls.

Mardini and I went upstairs and ate a light breakfast. Although a lot had passed between us, there were no prolonged good-byes. People at Makkah were by nature informal about leave-takings. Besides, we planned to meet in a few weeks.

Mardini did come to visit me on his honeymoon that fall. As for Saleem, when the war began, he canceled his trip to California. He called one day in September to say that our deal was off. Overnight the Red Sea had filled up with gunboats. Importing cars was not possible that year.

That afternoon I was sitting near the window, talking with Nasser and Abd ar-Rahman. Abd ar-Rahman owned a bookstore in Chicago. I had promised Nasser my copy of *Lord Jim*, then given it to Ghafel at Muzdalifah. Now

I was hoping Abd ar-Rahman would send Nasser a copy. When the cab pulled up outside, I hardly noticed. When the driver came into the lobby and called, "Algiers!" I glanced around. No one else in the delegation was going there. I rose and shook hands with Abd ar-Rahman and a few of the others. Then Nasser picked up my bags and walked me out. Thus, without any fanfare, as simply as stepping on the gas, I passed from the most extraordinary city in the world.

Whereas the hadj is a culmination for most pilgrims, it felt more like a starting point to me. I had been traveling through a religion as much as through a landscape. Now I was leaving my physical goal behind. The hadj at its best is a vivifying factor. Later I hoped to internalize its meanings. Today as we left the hotel, the cabbie took a final swing around the *mas'a* bridge. For just a minute I could look down again into the old *medina,* with its arcades of lace, its matchbox stalls, its Quranic cassettes and back-alley bookstores. Then the town slipped away, and we were climbing.

BIBLIOGRAPHY

Ahmad, Jalal al-e. *Lost in the Crowd*. Translated by John Green. Washington, D.C.: Three Continents Press, 1985.

'Alawi, Ahmad Ben Mustapha al-. *Extraits du diwan*. Paris: Éditions les Amis d'Islam, 1984.

Asad, Muhammad. *The Message of the Qur'an, Translated and Explained*. Gibraltar: Dar al-Andalus, 1984.

———. *The Road to Mecca*. London: Max Reinhardt, 1954.

bin Baz, 'Abd al-'Aziz bin Abdullah. *A Guide to Hajj, Umrah, and Visiting the Prophet's Mosque*. Riyadh: Ifta and Propagation, 1410/1990.

Borges, Jorge Luis. *Labyrinths: Selected Stories and Other Writings*. Edited by Donald A. Yates and James E. Irby, preface by André Maurois. Translated. New York: New Directions Books, 1964.

Bowles, Paul. *Their Heads Are Green and Their Hands Are Blue.* New York: Ecco Press, 1984.

Bukhari, Sahih al-. *The Translation of the Meanings of Sahih al-Bukhari.* Translated by Muhammad Muhsin Khan. Beirut: Dar al-Arabia, n.d.

Bunyan, John. *The Pilgrim's Progress.*

Burckhardt, John Lewis. *Travels in Arabia.* London: Frank Cass, 1968.

Burckhardt, Titus. *Sacred Art in East and West,* Middlesex, England: Perennial Books, 1986.

Burton, Sir Richard F. *Personal Narrative of a Pilgrimage to Al-Madinah and Meccah.* 2 vols. New York: Dover, 1964.

Canetti, Elias. *Crowds and Power.* Translated by Carol Stewart. New York: Viking Press, 1963.

————. *The Voices of Marrakesh.* Translated by J. A. Underwood. New York: Seabury Press, 1978.

Conrad, Joseph. *Lord Jim.*

Crapanzano, Vincent. *The Hamadsha: A Study in Moroccan Ethnopsychiatry.* Berkeley: University of California Press, 1973.

Dermenghem, Emile. *Muhammad and the Islamic Tradition.* Translated by Jean M. Watt. New York: Harper and Brothers, 1958.

Doughty, Charles M. *Passages from Arabia Deserta.* Selected by Edward Garnett. Middlesex, England: Penguin, 1984.

Dunn, Ross E. *The Adventures of Ibn Battuta.* Berkeley: University of California Press, 1989.

Eaton, Charles Le Gai. *Islam and the Destiny of Man.* Albany: State University of New York Press, 1985.

Eickelman, Dale F., and James Piscatori, *Muslim Travellers.* Berkeley: University of California, 1990.

Esin, Emel. *Mecca the Blessed, Madinah the Radiant.* Photographs by Haluk Doganbey. New York: Crown, 1983.

Evans-Pritchard, E. E. *The Sanusi of Cyrenaica.* Oxford: Clarendon Press, 1968.

Gellner, Ernest. *Saints of the Atlas.* Chicago: University of Chicago Press, 1969.

Gellouz, Ezzedine. *Mecca, The Muslim Pilgrimage.* New York and London: Paddington Press, 1979.

Gibb, H.A.R., and J. H. Kramers, *Shorter Encyclopaedia of Islam.* London: Luzac, 1953.

Haley, Alex. *Roots.* New York: Doubleday, 1976.

Hertzberg, Arthur. "What Future for the Jews?" In *New York Review of Books,* November 23, 1989, pp. 26–29.

Hitti, Philip K. *Islam: A Way of Life.* Minneapolis: University of Minnesota Press, 1970.

Hobson, Sarah. *Through Iran in Disguise.* Chicago: Academy Chicago, 1982.

Hourani, Albert. *A History of the Arab Peoples.* Cambridge, Mass.: Harvard University Press, 1991.

Ibn al-'Arabi, Muhyiddin. *Sufis of Andalusia.* Translated, with introduction and notes, by R.W.J. Austin. Berkeley: University of California Press, 1971.

Ibn Battuta. *The Travels of Ibn Battuta.* 2 vols. Translated by H.A.R. Gibb. The Hakluyt Society, Second Series, no. CX. Cambridge, England: Cambridge University Press, 1956.

Iqbal, Sir Allama Muhammad. *The Reconstruction of Religious Thought in Islam.* Lahore: Sh. Muhammad Ashraf, 1982.

Irving, Washington. *Life of Mohammad.* Introduction by Raphael Patai. Ipswich, Mass.: Ipswich Press, 1989.

Kaidi, Hamza [Tidjani Bammate]. *Mecca and Medinah Today.* Paris: Les Éditions J.A., 1980.

Kamal, Ahmad. *The Sacred Journey.* New York: Duell, Sloan Pearce, 1961.

Khalifa, Saida Miller. *The Fifth Pillar.* Hicksville, N.Y.: Exposition Press, 1977.

Khan, Z.-I. and Y. Zaki, eds. *Hajj in Focus.* London: Open Press, 1986.

Kirashima, Hussein Yoshio. *The Road to Holy Mecca.* Tokyo: Kodansha International, 1972.

Knappert, Jan. *Islamic Legends.* Leiden: E. J. Brill, 1985.

Lings, Martin. *Muhammad: His Life Based on the Earliest Sources.* Rochester, Vt.: Inner Traditions International, 1983.

————. *A Sufi Saint of the Twentieth Century.* Berkeley: University of California Press, 1973.

Long, David Edwin. *The Hajj Today.* Albany: State University of New York Press, 1979.

Makky, Ghazy Abdul Wahed. *Mecca: The Pilgrimage City.* London: Croom Helm, 1978.

Mansfield, Peter. *The Arabs.* Middlesex, England: Penguin, 1987.

Marsh, Clifton E. *From Blacks to Black Muslims: The Transition from Separatism to Islam, 1930–1980.* Metuchen, N.J.: Scarecrow Press, 1984.

Melville, Herman. *Journals.* Edited by Howard Horsford and Lynn Horth. Evanston and Chicago: Northwestern University Press and Newberry Library, 1989.

Moorehead, Alan. *The Blue Nile.* New York: Harper and Row, 1962.

Muslim, ibn al-Hajjah. *Sahih Muslim: Traditions of the Prophet.* 4 vols. Translated by Abdul Hamid Saddiqi. Beirut: Dar al-Arabia, n.d.

Nurbakhsh, Javad. *Sufi Women.* New York: Khaniqahi-Nimatullahi, 1983.

————. *Traditions of the Prophet.* New York: Khaniqahi-Nimatullahi, 1981.

Peters, F. E. *Jerusalem and Mecca.* New York: New York University Press, 1986.

Philby, Harry St. John B. *A Pilgrim in Arabia.* London: Robert Hale, 1946.

Porch, Douglas. *The Conquest of Morocco.* New York: Knopf, 1982.

Al-Qur'an: A Contemporary Translation. Translated by Ahmed Ali. Princeton, N.J.: Princeton University Press, 1988.

Rogerson, Barnaby. *Morocco.* Chester, Ct.: Cadogan Guides, Globe Pequot Press, 1989.

Rosa, Rodrigo Rey. *Dust on Her Tongue*. Translated by Paul Bowles. San Francisco: City Lights, 1992.

Rutter, Eldon. *The Holy Cities of Arabia*. 2 vols. New York: G. P. Putnam's Sons, 1928.

Sabini, John. *Armies in the Sand*. London: Thames and Hudson, 1981.

Sardar, Ziauddin, and M. A. Zaki Badawi. *Hajj Studies*. Vol. 1. London: Croom Helm, 1977.

Schimmel, Anne Marie. *Mystical Dimensions of Islam*. Chapel Hill: University of North Carolina Press, 1975.

Shariati, Ali. *Hajj*. Translated by Ali Behzadnia and Najla Denny. Houston: Free Islamic Literatures, 1980.

Siddiqui, Muhammad Abdul Aleem. *Elementary Teachings of Islam*. Chicago, Kazi Publications, n.d.

Smith, Jean Edward. *George Bush's War*. New York: Henry Holt, 1992.

Stark, Freya. *A Winter in Arabia*. London: J. Murray, 1940.

Stewart, Desmond. *Mecca*. Photographs by Mohamed Amin. New York: Newsweek, 1980

Theroux, Peter. *Sandstorms: Days and Nights in Arabia*. New York: W. W. Norton, 1990.

Twain, Mark. *The Innocents Abroad, Or The New Pilgrims Progress*.

Westermark, Edward. *Wit and Wisdom in Morocco*. London: Routledge and Sons, 1930.

Woodward, Bob. *The Commanders*. New York: Pocket Books, Simon and Schuster, 1991.

Malcolm X. *The Autobiography of Malcolm X*. With the assistance of Alex Haley. New York: Grove Press, 1966.

APPENDIX

*A Partial Text of the Sermon at Arafat**
1990

You have come all these miles to Arafat, but that is nothing unless you arrive at the teachings of Islam. Gather together and support God's words. Live by them and be worthy of what you are. Take hold of the rope of God's oneness and haul yourselves forward. Be generous. Be the nation of Islam. . . .

War, torture, oppression are the tools of the lost, loosed on the world by those who want to keep you from your faith. Believe in the

---

*"The Hadj sermon consists chiefly of instruction in the rites of pilgrimage, together with very frequent repetitions of the *talbiya* and supplications to God to protect and strengthen of the Muslims" (Eldon Rutter, *The Holy Cities of Arabia*).

way of simplicity, not in the false information they spread out like a trap
to discourage you. They fight you by taking over your wisdom and your
theology. They invade your homes and make you forget the pleasure of
your lives. Don't let them interfere or control your lives. Control your
own lives. If you have your independence, you can live happily. Forget
about sects and groups and the poor division of your countries by
colonialists who came and now have gone. These forces were set into
motion to weaken you. Are these the people who can help you
now? . . .

Our leaders have a duty to think clearly and to use the media to
clarify our lives. We have to be aware of what we teach and what we
learn. Islam is a religion of education and of ethics. It is up to us to
make ourselves good people and to encourage others to act well in this
life. All the world's countries have the same duty before them. Let the
nation of Islam be the first to take a step in this direction. It is the
business of our leaders to help the people, to correct mistakes and
permit us to live happily, with a sense of justice. Don't let anyone
pollute what you believe. . . .

By becoming a pilgrim once in your life, you are fulfilling your
covenant with God. For people of different countries, different colors,
different climates, different tongues, the hadj is a chance to gather
together in one hall. It is a proof and a reminder that all Muslims are
brothers and sisters. We meet here to get the benefit of each other and
to convey experience. This visit to a sacred house is a perfect means to
bring people together and help them understand.

You came here today to a sacred place. It is safe and secure, and
everything is available. It will do you no good to have come all this way
if you don't leave with something worth taking back to the others.
When you leave, don't forget. Be as you are now, standing here on
the Plain of Arafat: remember God before everything else, the
Enabler. . . .

The Prophet said in his farewell speech, "Listen to me, people, for
I don't know if we will meet this way next year." The Prophet stood
right here beside this column. He explained the requirements of Islam
and of the hadj. He said, Do not spill each other's blood; do not steal

from each other. He reminded men again of the rights of women. He gathered the people inside this precinct, and he fulfilled his duty and performed his hadj. He rode here and he rode away. He did not fast during this period. Follow what the Prophet said: "To make the Hadj is to stand at Arafat."

GLOSSARY OF TERMS

adhan the vocalized Muslim call to prayer.

al-ʿAlawi name denoting the spiritual followers of the Sufi teacher Ahmad al-ʿAlawi (d. 1932).

Allah God; used by all Muslims and Arabic-speaking Christians.

Arafat the valley plain fifteen miles east of Mecca where hadjis perform the "standing" rite of *wukuf* (q.v.).

ʿasr the third, "afternoon," prayer of the Muslim day.

ayat a verse of the Qur'an; also "a sign."

al-Baqarah Chapter 2 of the Qur'an, the longest chapter; often memorized in its entirety by Muslims.

baraka "spiritual power, blessedness"; a miraculous force that emanates from certain people and places.

bedouin the traditional desert people of Saudi Arabia.

belra in Morocco, a backless leather slipper.

bidʿa religious innovation; diverging from the established way to the point of heresy, although not to the point of actual unbelief; the opposite of *sunna* (q.v.).

bismillah the first word of the first line of the Qur'an; probably the word most often heard in a Muslim country. It is spoken before almost any action, from eating and drinking to entering a house.

burnoose a long, loose-fitting hooded cloak of wool.

chipati Indian flat bread.

Dar al-Islam the "realm" or "region" of Islam; composed of all those areas in the world with Muslim majorities.

dirham in Morocco, the common monetary unit, currently worth about 11 U.S. cents.

djellaba a hooded, ankle-length outer garment popular throughout Morocco.

djema in Morocco, an open public square.

fajr the first, predawn, prayer of the Muslim day.

Fatihah the opening verses of the Qur'an, and the most frequently recited Muslim prayer.

fitna creating turmoil where there should be peace. Muhammad's advice "Let there be no difficulty in religion" is often quoted in this context.

al-fitra in Islamic theology, a human being's innate disposition toward virtue; the opposite of the concept of Original (unforgiven) Sin.

foqra (singular, *fqir*) members of a Sufi order; adepts.

ganbri a three-stringed African instrument, the centerpiece of the Genowa (q.v.) ensemble.

gandoura in Morocco, a loose-fitting sleeveless cotton outer robe worn by men indoors or in warm weather.

Genowa one of Morocco's many, loosely organized religious cults. The Genowa tradition of music and healing dates back to sixteenth-century West African Guinea and Mali.

guirsh a coin representing the smallest division of the Moroccan dirham (q.v.), currently worth about 1/100 of eleven U.S. cents.

hadith any reliable report of what the prophet Muhammad said or did. Collectively these represent a vast and active literature for Muslims.

al-Hamdulillah literally, "May God send peace and blessings"; a general expression of thanks for good fortune. In Morocco, it is sometimes colloquially shortened to *Hamdullah*.

haram a sacred precinct; the area of a mosque. In Mecca, it includes the entire city.

Haram al-Sharif popular name for the mosque complex at Mecca; literally, "noble sanctuary."

harira a vegetable-and-lamb-based soup that Moroccans widely prefer as the best food with which to break a fast.

hayeek in Morocco among certain tribes, a length of towel that serves as an outer, upper garment worn by women.

'Id al-Fitr feast that celebrates the end of the Ramadan fast; in Morocco, also called Aeid es-Seghir.

ihram two lengths of seamless terry cloth worn by male pilgrims during the hadj and *'umrah* (q.v.) rites at Mecca.

imam the leader of the prayer in a mosque.

insha' Allah "God willing." Among Muslims, the phrase follows any conditional statement concerning the future.

'isha' the fourth prayer hour of the Muslim day, falling around sunset.

Jabal al-Rahmah a hill on the Plain of Arafat (q.v.) where a sermon is delivered during the hadj; literally, "Mount Mercy."

jamarat a group of three pillars that pilgrims stone during the hadj; also the place they are located; also the rite and the pebbles thrown.

Janaza the Muslim prayers for the dead.

jihad "struggle." The word may be applied to any great effort in the name of God, a fight in defense of Islam, or the battle against one's ego.

Jilala in Morocco, the name for an order of religious followers of the Sufi sheikh Abd al-Qadir al-Jilani (d. 1166), founder of the Qadiriya order.

jum'a the congregational Muslim Friday prayer.

Ka'ba the stone shrine at the center of the mosque at Mecca, toward which Muslims look when they pray and around which they circle as pilgrims. The English word *cube* derives from this.

kaffiyeh the head scarf worn by Arab men in various fashions throughout the Middle East.

kafir originally, "one who conceals God's blessings"; thus, "ungrateful"; commonly used by Muslims to refer to unbelievers. The term was first applied to Meccans who did not believe in Mohammad's mission.

kaftan a woman's ankle-length robe or shift of silk or cotton.

kiswa the cloth covering of the Ka'ba (q.v.).

laila "night." Among the Sufis, it refers specifically to a night of prayer and chanting; among the Genowa (q.v.), it specifies an all-night healing ceremony.

maghrib the fifth prayer hour of the Muslim day, falling around dusk.

majlis a public sitting room for guests in a Saudi Arabian house; similar to the Moroccan *sala* (q.v.).

mas'a the course along which the rite *sa'y* (q.v.) is performed.

matarba in Morocco, a popular form of couch or banquette.

medersa a Muslim theological school. The spelling here is a colloquial Moroccan version of the Arabic *madrasa*.

medina "city"; in Morocco, the part enclosed within ramparts; hence, the old city, the traditional part of town.

Mina a village and valley four miles east of Mecca, where the hadj convenes on its way to and from Arafat (q.v.).

muezzin the mosque crier who calls Muslims to prayer from the minaret; accepted English spelling of *mu'adhdhin*.

mujahid a Muslim freedom frighter.

Mutawwif a pilgrim's guide at Mecca.

nafrah the stage of the hadj when pilgrims leave Arafat (q.v.) for the night vigil at Muzdalifah; literally, "the rush."

niya "intention"; the statement of purpose preceding any ritual action.

qibla the direction of the Ka'ba in Mecca (q.v.), from wherever one is standing; therefore, the direction of prayer. In a mosque, the *qibla* is marked by a niche, or *mihrab*.

qurra in Morocco, professional reciters of the Qur'an.

raita in Morocco, a double-reed wind instrument related to the oboe.

rak'ah a unit of prayer, composed of four alternating postures—(1) standing, (2) bending, (3) kneeling, (4) bowing—accompanied by the appropriate verses at each point. The five daily prayers are composed of two (pre-dawn), four (near noon), four (afternoon), three (near sunset), and four (near dusk) *rak'ahs*.

Ramadan the annual month-long daylight Muslim fast.

ramal the quickened pace of the first three circuits around the Ka'ba (q.v.) in *tawaf* (q.v.).

riyal the Saudi Arabian monetary unit, roughly one quarter of a dollar.

sala the living room of a Moroccan home.

Salaam aleikoum universal greeting throughout the Islamic world; "peace be upon you."

salat prayer, as an act of piety; an expression of humility; the attitude to the deity most befitting human beings. It is not an entreaty or supplication.

sa'y ritual walk between two hills; a rite of the hadj.

serwal in Morocco, a pair of knee-length pants, often worn in warm weather beneath a *gandoura* (q.v.).

sharif (plural, *shorfa*) in Morocco, a descendant of the prophet Muhammad; therefore, one who has inherited spiritual power *(baraka)*.

Shaytan Satan; Iblis.

sheikh a person of knowledge and understanding; in Sufi circles, a guide and teacher; in modern Middle Eastern society, a polite form of address, like Monsieur or Mr.

souk a market area, sometimes with covered lanes.

sunna the practice and example of Muhammad, of which the *hadith* (q.v.) are illustrations; prophetic traditions.

sura a chapter division of the Qur'an.

tajine a popular Moroccan stew of meat and vegetables.

talbiya a prayer frequently chanted by pilgrims; an answer to a divine summons; literally, "acquiescence."

tariqa literally, "way"; used especially to refer to the mystical paths of the Sufis; by extension, an order of those who follow one.

tawaf a pilgrim rite comprising seven circuits of the Ka'ba (q.v.); literally, "turning or circumambulation."

thobe one-piece long sleeved, ankle-length cotton or silk robe favored in the Gulf region; anglicized spelling of *thawb*.

'umrah a pilgrimage to Mecca of a more individual nature than the hadj; it may be carried out at any time.

wudu' the ritual ablution establishing a state of purity required before Muslim prayer.

wukuf the hadj rite of standing at Arafat (q.v.).

Zamzam the sacred well inside the mosque at Mecca.

zuhr the second prayer hour of the Muslim day, usually falling between noon and one in the afternoon.